From the Pen of Pastor Paul

1–2 Thessalonians

Daniel R. Hyde

EP

EP BOOKS
1st Floor Venture House, 6 Silver Court, Watchmead, Welwyn Garden City, UK, AL7 1TS
web: www.epbooks.org
e-mail: sales@epbooks.org

EP books are distributed in the USA by:
JPL Fulfillment
3741 Linden Avenue Southeast,
Grand Rapids, MI 49548
orders@jplfulfillment.com
Tel: 877.683.6935

First published 2015

British Library Cataloguing in Publication Data available

ISBN: 978–1–78397–142–8

Scripture quotations marked (KJV) are from The Holy Bible, King James Version.

All citations of the Westminster Confession of Faith and Larger and Shorter Catechisms are from *Westminster Confession of Faith* (1958, reprinted; Glasgow, Scotland: Free Presbyterian Publications, 2009).

All citations of the Heidelberg Catechism are from *Reformed Confessions of the 16th and 17th Centuries in English Translation: Volume 2, 1552–1566*, ed. James T. Dennison, Jr. (Grand Rapids, Mich.: Reformation Heritage Books, 2010).

All citations of the Belgic Confession and Canons of Dort are from *Psalter Hymnal* (Grand Rapids, Mich.: CRC Publications, 1987, 1988).

Danny Hyde unpacks the teaching of Paul's letters to the Thessalonians with a keen eye on the text, a sure grip on the witness of the scriptures as a whole, an awareness of the history of interpretation in the church, and above all with a pastoral heart for people. I warmly commend this stimulating exposition.

—Dr. Lee Gatiss, ***Director of the Church Society, Cambridge, U.K.***

The Reverend Danny Hyde has given us what should be expected from him: attention to the text of Scripture with attention to the church and world to which the gospel is addressed. This volume offers a welcome addition to books on 1 & 2 Thessalonians for its care to be true to Scripture, its regard to lean on exegetical masters, and its devotion to apply the Word of God to a needy and hurting pew. It also stirs up many useful ideas for teaching and preaching these materials. Pastors will especially want this volume on their shelf to assist them in preaching and teaching these two letters of Paul.

—Dr. J. Mark Beach, ***Professor of Ministerial and Doctrinal Studies, Mid-America Reformed Seminary, Dyer, IN***

Danny Hyde's new book on Paul's letters to the Thessalonians strikes a unique balance. It has depth so as to assist the pastor as he prepares to preach but is also accessible to any Christian seeking to understand and apply God's Word to their daily lives. *From the Pen of Pastor Paul* will be a great blessing to all who read it!

—Dr. Tim Witmer, Professor of Practical Theology, Westminster Theological Seminary, Philadelphia, PA

The best commentaries on New Testament Epistles are often those that were born the same way as the Epistles themselves: out of the womb of real pastoral concern and ministry. That is what you find in this highly readable book on 1 and 2 Thessalonians. It has an aroma of authenticity about it. Read it and you will sense the heart of the apostle Paul for the 1st century church brought with fresh power into the 21st century.

—Dr. Conrad Mbewe, Pastor of Kabwata Baptist Church and Chancellor of the African Christian University, Lusaka, Zambia

To Karajean

Ubi duo, ibi et ipse; ubi et ipse, ibi et malus non est

"Where the two, there also He;
Where also He, there also the evil one is not."

Tertullian, *To My Wife*, 2.8.8

Contents

2 Thessalonians

Abbreviations

Aquinas, *Thessalonians*—Thomas Aquinas, *Commentary on Saint Paul's First Letter to the Thessalonians and the Letter to the Philippians*, trans. F. R. Larcher and Michael Duffy, Aquinas Scripture Series 3 (Albany, NY: Magi Books, 1969).

Bruce, *1 & 2 Thessalonians*—F. F. Bruce, *1 & 2 Thessalonians*, Word Biblical Commentary 45 (Waco, TX: Word Books, 1982).

Calvin, *Thessalonians*—John Calvin, *The Epistles of Paul the Apostle to the Romans and to the Thessalonians*, trans. Ross Mackenzie, Calvin's Commentaries, Volume 8 (Grand Rapids, MI: Eerdmans, 1961).

CD—Canons of Dort (1618–1619)

Fergusson, *Thessalonians*—James Fergusson and David Dickson, *Galatians, Ephesians, Philippians, Colossians, Thessalonians & Hebrews*, Geneva Series Commentary (1841, reprinted; Edinburgh, Scotland: Banner of Truth, 1978).

HC—Heidelberg Catechism (1563)

Morris, *1–2 Thessalonians*—Leon Morris, *The First and Second Epistles to the Thessalonians*, The New International Commentary on the New Testament (1959; reprinted, Grand Rapids, MI: Wm. B. Eerdmans Publishing Co., 1984).

Stott, *1 & 2 Thessalonians*—John R. W. Stott, *The Message of 1 & 2 Thessalonians*, The Bible Speaks Today (Downers Grove: Inter-Varsity Press, 1991).

WCF—Westminster Confession of Faith (1647)

WLC—Westminster Larger Catechism (1647)

WSC—Westminster Shorter Catechism (1647)

Acknowledgements

I am so thankful for my brothers and sisters at the Oceanside United Reformed Church, who listened to the original sermons from which this book was developed. You have always encouraged me to be a pastor whose duty and delight is to "preach the Word" (2 Timothy 4:2).

I thank my wife, Karajean, who continues to be my most honest and helpful sermon critic, telling me what I need to hear not what I want to hear. I also thank my boys—Cyprian, Caiden, and Daxton—and my little girl—Sadie—who, without their knowing it, have made me a better preacher.

Preface

The substance of this book came from a preaching series through 1 and then 2 Thessalonians in the Lord's Day morning service of the Oceanside United Reformed Church (OURC) from September 26, 2010 through July 31, 2011. The context in which I preached those sermons is important to understanding the exposition in this book. I add this by way of preface because preaching is a dynamic enterprise. After all the requisite training to prepare for the ministry and after all the reading, writing, and meditating throughout a week, preaching has to be practiced. And it's not practiced in the vacuum of the preacher's mind; it is practiced among real living and breathing people. As a preacher, then, the people before whom I stand, all the ups and downs we experienced together in the ministry, and my own emotions play a vital part in what I do. So if I were to preach through 1–2 Thessalonians again, either in another congregation in another context or even at OURC, I would not and could not just re-preach the same notes and what developed into a book here.

Before September 2010 I had previously preached through Genesis and Exodus and was making my way through Leviticus. Then I received a call to serve another congregation after a decade of serving OURC. When I declined that call because I was convinced God's call was that I continue serving the OURC, I wrapped up that Leviticus series as soon as I could. I had originally intended to finish the entire Pentateuch, moving into Numbers and then Deuteronomy. But I believe God had other plans for me and for us as a congregation. After much prayer, Bible reading, and meditation, I decided upon 1 Thessalonians. Why? I believe in 1 Thessalonians Paul opens his pastoral heart more than to any other congregation to which he wrote. As the Anglican preacher and commentator, John Stott (1921–2011), said, Paul's Thessalonian correspondence "reveal the authentic Paul. ... We hear his heart-beat and see his tears."[1] And since I had just declined a call and recommitted myself to my current call, I believed it was important to express my pastoral heart to my people like never before.

Those sermons were, therefore, more personal than any other sermons I had ever preached. Those sermons were, therefore, more earnest than any other sermons I had ever preached. Those sermons were, therefore, more applicatory than any other sermons I had ever preached. If that was a fault of those sermons, at least I have John Calvin (1509–1564) on my side: "The greater part of this Epistle consists of exhortations."[2]

Let me also say a word about commentaries. I do not presume my method of using commentaries is normal nor do I insist my pastoral interns should follow it. With all my expository preaching, I have an eclectic approach to commentaries. I have not read every modern exegetical commentary. What I do, though, is follow a reading plan in which I read something from the ancient fathers, something from the medieval period [if possible], something from the Reformation, something from the Puritans, and then something from the modern exegetical commentaries. With Thessalonians, my main reading conversation partners were the ancient preacher St. John Chrysostom (349–407), the medieval theologian St. Thomas Aquinas (1225–1274), the reformer John Calvin, the Scottish Presbyterian James Fergusson (1621–1667), and the modern commentators F. F. Bruce (1910–1990) and John Stott.

I pray the substance and the spirit of this exposition moves you to receive the inspired apostles' words afresh, "not as the word of men but as what it really is, the word of God" (1 Thessalonians 2:13).

Daniel R. Hyde
Oceanside, California
August 2015

I

From the Pen of Pastor Paul

1 Thessalonians 1:1

First and Second Thessalonians are two of the least known of the New Testament letters of the apostle Paul. Yet it is quite possible that 1 Thessalonians was his first letter, written after his labors in Thessalonica in AD 49–50.[1] This lesser known letter to a church planted by Paul has many parallels to what those involved in the ministry of church planting and missions have known and experienced.

The church in Thessalonica was planted by Paul, along with his ministry partners Silas (given his Latin name here, Silvanus) and Timothy (1:1).[2] This occurred during what we call Paul's second missionary journey, as we read in Acts 17:1–15. As was Paul's custom, he found the local synagogue and "on three Sabbath days he reasoned with them from the Scriptures, explaining and proving that it was necessary for the Christ to suffer and to rise from the dead, and saying, 'This Jesus, whom I proclaim to you, is the Christ'" (Acts 17:2–3). The core group of this church plant (to use our modern terminology) began with "some" of those from the synagogue, some "devout Greeks," and many "leading women" from Thessalonica (Acts 17:4). This caused the Jews to form a mob and storm the house of Jameson (Acts 17:5). When Paul and Silas were not found, they hauled Jameson and some believers before the *politarchas*, the five to six magistrates of the city.[3] When they did so they uttered some of the most famous words to describe the church: "These men who have turned the world upside down have come here also" (Acts 17:6). Christianity was an unwelcome intrusion to the *status quo* of Thessalonica. The Thessalonian Jews' description echoed that of the Emperor Claudius (AD 41–54), who in the year AD 41 described the spread of the gospel as "a general plague which infests the whole world."[4]

Like those new believers in first century Thessalonica, what we know today is this: Jesus has utterly revolutionized our lives. To the world, we turn everything upside down. To the believer, God is making everything right side up. The world has fallen and it is God who is picking it up. The world is like a shattered vase and it is God who is restoring it. The world is like a filthy mirror and it is God who is renovating its luster.

This charge of "turn[ing] the world upside down" caused the ears of the city rulers to perk up: "They are all acting against the decrees of Caesar, saying there is another king, Jesus" (Acts 17:7). The church, then, sent Paul and Silas "away by night to Berea" (Acts 17:10). The Jews, though, followed them there, causing Paul to flee even further into Athens while Silas and Timothy stayed behind (Acts 17:14–15).

As a persecuted pastor himself, Paul's great pastoral desire in his first letter back to the persecuted Thessalonian Christians was that they would persevere in their faith, hope, and love. He said in his second letter to them, "do not grow weary in doing good" (2 Thessalonians 3:13), but he wanted them to rekindle their zeal (cf. Hebrews 12:1). 1 Thessalonians is a book that challenges us today. As with Paul, a pastor's desire for his people is that they would continually rekindle their passion for the gospel of our Lord Jesus Christ. Because the Thessalonian congregation began and continued to exist under such duress, Paul wrote to spur them on to continue persevering. You notice this in what is really the occasion for his writing as well as the theme for his exhortation: "Remembering before our God and Father your work of faith and labor of love and steadfastness of hope in our Lord Jesus Christ" (1:3).

1 Thessalonians is also a book that challenges us as pastors. Paul writes about his ministry in such personal and passionate ways that the Holy Spirit should break us down as we meditate upon it. I've always been told that to be a successful pastor I need to have the thick skin of a rhino to encase my heart within. I do not see this in Paul. We should be changed men after reading Paul's message. And members of local congregations should pray for their pastor to be transformed into a "shepherd [...] after [God's] own heart" (Jeremiah 3:15). In the words of Robert Murray M'Cheyne, "My people's greatest need is my personal holiness."[5] The apostle Paul wrote elsewhere to young pastor Timothy, that he was to "keep a close watch on [himself] and on the teaching ... for by so doing you will save both yourself and your hearers" (1 Timothy 4:16).[6] Pray that you would not only hear more of Jesus through your pastor but that you would see more of Jesus in him.

1 Thessalonians exhorts a new congregation to be steadfast in faith,

hope, and love in a very pastoral and personal way and it exhorts pastors concerning the duties of the pastoral ministry.

Ministering for Progress

It is not only the duty of a minister, like Paul, to labor in the planting of a church but to continue to labor in the cultivating of that church over time. Whereas in Corinth, Paul planted but it was Apollos who watered (1 Corinthians 3:6), here Paul says the same minister may be called to do both in a local church. After initially planting the church (Acts 17:1–9), he was forced to leave because, as he goes on to say, he, Silvanus, and Timothy "were torn away from you" (2:17). This is why he also writes, "we sent Timothy … to establish and exhort you in your faith" (3:1). Through this inspired letter Paul is now checking in on his spiritual children's progress.

What kind of progress should we be seeking to cultivate? In 1 Thessalonians Paul has the particular theme of his people's steadfastness in the faith. He praises them for their "steadfastness of hope" (1:3) and that they were "standing fast in the Lord" (3:8). What does Paul mean by "steadfastness?" One great illustration is at the very end of *The Pilgrim's Progress*. Just before Christiana and her companions were about to cross the river and enter through the beautiful gate we read these great lines: "Then there came forth a summons for Mr. Standfast. This Mr. Standfast was he whom the rest of the pilgrims found upon his knees in the Enchanted Ground."[7] This character stood up to all the temptations of the Christian's three enemies: the world, the flesh, and the devil (HC, Q&A 127). And having stood up to them, he resisted them. At the end of his life he entered into the celestial city. The minister is to labor that his people would stand fast against everything all the enemies of Christ throw at them for the sake of the Lord. As John Calvin said, as a minister, Paul's purpose here was "not so much to commend them as to encourage them to perseverance."[8]

Paul consistently exhorts the Thessalonians to progress in their Christian walk by being steadfast. He remembers that they received the preached Word of God in much affliction (1:6). Paul says he and his cohorts suffered for what he preached (2:2). He says he, Silvanus, and Timothy suffered as examples to the people (2:14). Paul and Silvanus sent Timothy to exhort them to stand fast in the midst of their many afflictions (3:2–4). Finally, Paul exhorted the Thessalonians to persevere in godliness even as they were already doing (4:1, 10). But why does Paul spend so much time exhorting the Thessalonians to progress in their life of sanctification? Because, as one ancient writer said, "God is pleased if we are growing in Christ."[9] The new believer is one in whom the Lord himself has planted the imperishable seed of the gospel (1 Peter 1:23, 25). That seed is now growing upward and outward to the point where we have the fruits of good works sprouting from us.

This perpetual progress is not only hard work for the believer, but it is even harder work for the minister as he seeks through prayer, preaching, and pastoral care of every soul entrusted to him that they progress in their walk with the Lord. Although it is hard, it is the minister's calling. Although it is hard, the Lord blesses this labor. The Lord gives the minister his Spirit and all the means necessary to bring progress to his people: prayer, the Word, the sacraments, visitation, and hospitality, just to name a few. This is one of the reasons why I have always favored a long pastorate and have not understood the typical method in so many evangelical, Bible-believing churches for a minister to take a call elsewhere every five years. When I was in seminary, one thing that struck me about this was a comment to me after I commented on how many pastors a local church had, as evidenced by the ministers' pictures in the Council room. The comment was: "After five years we've heard everything he has to say." How can a pastor actually see any fruit in just five years?

Why should we minister with the expectation that our people will progress in the steadfastness of their faith? Our people must become practically what they are theologically. What do I mean? Look at the opening greeting Paul writes: To the church of the Thessalonians in God the Father and the Lord Jesus Christ: Grace to you and peace (1:1). The Thessalonian church was in this particular locality, but it was also in the Father and the Son. Paul typically speaks of being "in Christ" but here as in Colossians 3:3 he speaks of being in God. While being in Thessalonica meant being in a local place, for example, Judea (2:14), being in God and his Son speaks of having a vital relationship with them.[10] As Jesus said, we are branches that are in him as the vine (John 15). As Paul said, we are members that are united to the body (Romans 12; 1 Corinthians 12). And this relationship with the vine as its branches, and with the body as its members is vital and life giving. So we are, as Christians, livingly, organically, spiritually, and vitally connected to the Triune God; that's our theological identity. Practically, then, we need to reflect that truth as we progress in faith, hope, and love in the context God places us.

Ministering in Person

This ministry to see progress in our people must be done in person, personally. No doubt you have heard the pastoral adage that people do not care how much you know until they know how much you care. For many who enter the ministry at a young age, they are clearly captivated and taken up with studying the Word, reading lots of theology, and even learning church history. But oftentimes their words—even as true as they are—go in one ear and out the other of their people. What people clearly need to feel is a pastor's heart before they will listen to his words.

Why mention this? Notice again the opening word of this epistle. It is very simple: Paul (1:1). What is so striking about the way he addresses the Thessalonians? He humbly calls himself merely Paul here without any other titles.[11] To see the significance of this, survey with me the opening greetings in Paul's other New Testament letters.

- In Romans he is "Paul, a servant of Christ Jesus, called to be an apostle" (Romans 1:1).
- In 1 Corinthians he is "Paul, called by the will of God to be an apostle of Christ Jesus" (1 Corinthians 1:1).
- In 2 Corinthians—when Paul's apostleship was being questioned—he was "Paul, an apostle of Christ Jesus by the will of God" (2 Corinthians 1:1).
- In Galatians he is "Paul, an apostle—not from men nor through man, but through Jesus Christ and God the Father" (Galatians 1:1).
- In Ephesians, Colossians, and 2 Timothy he is "Paul, an apostle of Christ Jesus by the will of God" (Ephesians 1:1; Colossians 1:1; 2 Timothy 1:1).
- In Philippians he and Timothy are "Paul and Timothy servants of Christ Jesus" (Philippians 1:1).
- In 1 Timothy he is "Paul, an apostle of Christ Jesus by command of God our Savior and of Christ Jesus our hope" (1 Timothy 1:1).

- In Titus he is "Paul, a servant of God and an apostle of Jesus Christ" (Titus 1:1).

- In Philemon he is "Paul, a prisoner for Christ Jesus" (Philemon 1).

So why did Paul merely use his first name here? We can infer one reason being that there was no controversy about his apostolic authority in Thessalonica.[12] They respected him and received the message he brought. Therefore Paul had no need of asserting his titles. It is not titles that matter, it is the man.[13] John Owen (1616–1683) once spoke of common ecclesiastical titles such as "reverend" and "doctor" by saying, "I have very little valued it." He went on to quote Martin Luther (1483–1546), who said, "Religion is never put in danger except amongst the most reverend."[14] We should not be so fast to assert our titles and authority. It's the person people want to know.

We learn, then, that Paul ministered as an apostle very personally among the Thessalonians. As the Scottish divine, James Fergusson said, "The Spirit of the Lord in Christ's Ministers makes them of such an humble condescending temper … as they will not stand to stoop somewhat below what they are, and to make use of all lawful means and helps, which may serve to procure respect unto their message among the people."[15] While it does show respect for the office of the pastor when a believer calls him "reverend" or "pastor," and while this is extremely beneficial to teach children within the church a healthy lesson in respect, it is not the title, but the man behind the title that matters.

We see this personalness of Paul later in this letter, as he could very easily have asserted his office with them to demand their attention. As he says, "we could have made demands as apostles of Christ" (2:6). Instead, he speaks throughout 1 Thessalonians of the ordinariness of his ministry among them, which is an example to those of us who minister. What kind of an example do ministers give to the world when they do hospital visitations and use the front row, "clergy parking?" As the minister walks into the front door, there is a man in a wheelchair waiting for his ride. What does it communicate to people when "you" are only in front of them on a screen or if you just pop in the assembly right before the sermon, as if the people whom you are speaking with are so privileged to have you? We need to be personal and ordinary, not a privileged class.[16]

We see Paul modeling a different kind of life before the world. He says, "you know what kind of men we proved to be" (1:5). What kind of men were he and his helpers? They were not seekers of glory from men nor greedy for money (2:5–6). Instead, they were "gentle among you, like a nursing mother taking care of her own children" (2:7). They were "affectionately desirous" and willing to "share … our own selves" (2:8). They were "like a father with his children" (2:11).

What a picture Paul is of a personal pastoral ministry. He was available, he was open, and he lived his life as an open book before his people. That's what the church in our time needs today. It does not need the superstar, who is distant and has nothing to do with the average believer. It does not need the pastor shielded behind layers and layers of associates and ministry helpers so that he can do the "real" work of the ministry. The church does not need icons, but persons. It does not need its ministers living behind a fortress but living in the fishbowl of public life.

Ministering by Pouring Out

To accomplish this it is the duty of a minister to pour himself out for his people that they might receive the grace and peace of the Triune God.

As Paul writes to the Thessalonians of his brief past ministry among them and of his present concern for them from a distance, he exemplifies to us that the minister is to pour himself out for his people's good from beginning to end. Fergusson, again, said, that ministers "would endeavour to have their own hearts readily affected with enlarged desires after the people's good."[17] The pastor's heart towards his people leads to the pastor's labors for his people.

Listen to how Paul expressed his heart, which led to pouring out his life for the Thessalonians: "So, being affectionately desirous of you, we were ready to share with you not only the gospel of God but also our own selves, because you had become very dear to us" (2:8). This word "share" (*metadounai*) is used of something that belongs to a person that they take of their own initiative and give to others, whether their money for the needy (Ephesians 4:28) or God's gifts to his people (Romans 12:8). As God has shared his word with Paul, Paul wanted to share it with the Thessalonians. Even more, as God had shared himself with Paul, in giving his Son for him, so Paul wanted to share himself with the Thessalonians. This is what he told the Corinthians, when he said, "I will most gladly spend and be spent for your souls" (2 Corinthians 12:15).

What a call this is to all of us as believers as well. As ministers are to follow the example of Paul, God's people are then to follow their pastors. "Remember your leaders, those who spoke to you the word of God. Consider the outcome of their way of life, and imitate their faith" (Hebrews 13:7). What a shuddering thought! Ministers are to share their lives with their people. Then the people are to share their lives with each other. By such love, broken hearts will be mended, sorrowing hearts will be cheered, and weak hearts will be strengthened. We need this; the world needs this.

What a high calling this is to pastors. As John Owen once wrote:

"he will have little benefit by his own ministry who endeavours not in the first place an experience in his own heart of the power of the truths which he doth teach unto others."[18] How can a pastor call upon his people to strive for holiness if he is not striving himself? How can a pastor call upon his people to serve if he is not serving himself? May God lead all God's people to pour themselves out for the good of the church and salvation of the world.

Conclusion

What kind of bar does Paul set for the life and duty of the minister in his pastoral letter to the Thessalonians? He calls upon the pastor to minister for the godly progress of his people's souls. He calls upon the pastor to minister in a very personal way, so that his people would truly know that he cares for them. He calls upon the pastor to minister by pouring himself out for his people's spiritual good. What a high bar this is. This should cause pastors to cry out, "Who is sufficient for these things?" (2 Corinthians 2:16) This should also cause us to rejoice:

> Not that we are sufficient in ourselves to claim anything as coming from us, but our sufficiency is from God, who has made us sufficient to be ministers of a new covenant, not of the letter but of the Spirit. For the letter kills, but the Spirit gives life. (2 Corinthians 3:5–6)

This is why the ministry is ultimately Christ's heavenly ministry through the means of sinful, earthly men (2 Corinthians 4:7). Why must pastors strive for their people's progress? Because Jesus is holy and has given his Spirit to lead us. Why must pastors know their people personally? Because Jesus knows our names and cares for us individually. Why must pastors pour themselves out for their people? Because Jesus did. He "loved us and gave himself up for us, a fragrant offering and sacrifice to God" (Ephesians 5:2). When you pray for your pastor, pray particularly that he would grow in love, holiness, service, and concern for you, not for his own personal benefit, but that you might experience Jesus more until he comes again.

2

Pastor Paul's Prayer

1 Thessalonians 1:2–3

One of the means by which we rekindle our zeal for the Lord and press on in our race as Christians is prayer. We need to be challenged as people and churches to become more a people of prayer than we already are. Church history shows that the "success" of the church is directly linked to the prayer of the church. When God's people pray, especially as they gather for prayer, God pours out his Spirit and blessing.

And what is true of God's people as a whole is especially true of the church's pastors. The passage before us details Paul's prayer for the church in Thessalonica. In fact, all of chapters 1–3 are one long prayer. Notice that as Paul opens in prayer here, saying, We give thanks to God (1:2), he continues his prayer in the next chapter, saying, "We also thank God" (2:13), and then he concludes this lengthy prayer, saying, "As we pray most earnestly night and day" (3:10). His prayer climaxes in 3:11–13 with a beautiful benediction for the Thessalonians. All this shows us that Paul was a praying pastor. The opening of this long prayer teaches us about the relationship of a pastor to his people in prayer.

Men of Prayer

Paul's example—which is also the example of Silvanus and Timothy—sets before us that the pastor is to be a man of prayer. As we hear him praying, especially as we saw above (1:2, 2:13, 3:9–10), behind these words is the realization that Paul was devoted to prayer: We give thanks to God always for all of you, constantly mentioning you in our prayers, remembering before our God and Father your work (1:2–3). Paul uses present tense verbs here when he says, give thanks … constantly mentioning … remembering. The translators of the English Standard Version recognize Paul's language here speaks of a pattern, a habit of prayer when it translates Paul's literal construction, "making mention," as constantly mentioning, since this is a present tense verb that speaks not of Paul's present prayer for them only when he wrote it, but of his pattern of prayer for them in an ongoing way.

Paul fleshes out what he means by giving thanks to God always and mentioning the Thessalonians to God constantly a little later, when he says he, Silvanus, and Timothy prayed for them "night and day" (3:10). While it is true that this is a literary way of saying what Paul says elsewhere, "pray without ceasing" (5:17), it is also true that Paul reflects here an Old Testament pattern of prayer from the daily morning and evening burning of incense in the tabernacle (Exodus 30:7–8). One of the practical and outward ways he expressed his praying "always" and "constantly" was to pray every morning and every evening for them. This is a beautiful pattern for pastors—and all of God's people for that matter—to pray, opening and closing their days in devotion to God.

It goes without saying, then, that Paul prayed a lot. The ever-present temptation for pastors and those preparing for the ministry is to think, "Well, I'm off the hook. After all, Paul was an apostle." But let me remind you that when a man is called to the office of minister of the Word he is also called to a ministry of prayer:

> Now in these days when the disciples were increasing in number, a complaint by the Hellenists arose against the Hebrews because their widows were being neglected in the daily distribution. And the twelve summoned the full number of the disciples and said, "It is not right that we should give up preaching the word of God to serve tables. Therefore, brothers, pick out from among you seven men of good repute, full of the Spirit and of wisdom, whom we will appoint to this duty. But we will *devote ourselves to prayer* and to the ministry of the word." And what they said pleased the whole gathering, and they chose Stephen, a man full of faith and of the Holy Spirit, and Philip, and Prochorus, and Nicanor, and Timon, and Parmenas, and Nicolaus, a proselyte of Antioch. These they set before the apostles, and they prayed and laid their hands on them. And the word of God continued to increase. (Acts 6:1–7; emphasis added)

The apostles' devotion as ministers was just as much to prayer as it was to preaching. A minister of the Gospel in the New Covenant, then, fulfills his calling in two ways. First, he is a spokesman of God to his people in preaching God's Word to them. Second, he is a spokesman of the people to God in his prayers on their behalf. This is why one of the fathers of English Puritanism, William Perkins (1558–1602), described the pastoral ministry as "the art of prophesying."[1]

He said this because just as prophets in the Old Covenant both preached and prayed, so in the New Covenant the ministers have this prophetic anointing to preach and to pray. In fact, in the Dutch Reformed tradition this was codified in the various church government documents of its particular reformation in the synods of Middelburg (1581), The Hague (1586), and finally culminating in the Church Order of the Synod of Dort (1618–19). The Church Order that I operate under continues this tradition, saying, "The office of ministers is to continue in prayers and the ministry of the Word."[2] What we go on to read in the book of Acts is that when the ministers of God's Word devote themselves—and when their people allow them sufficient time to do this—the ministry of the Word spreads and increases (Acts 6:7) in the conversion of lost sinners and the edification of the church.

Perpetual in Prayer

Pastor Paul's prayer is also illustrative of the Christian life. All Christians, like their pastors, are called to be perpetual in prayer. Yes, *we* all, as God's people, are to be devoted to prayer. While it is Paul, Silvanus, and Timothy who are praying for the Thessalonians here always and constantly mentioning them in their prayers (1:2), Paul goes on to remind them that "you became imitators of us" (1:6). Therefore Paul goes on to exhort them later in this same letter to "pray without ceasing" (5:17). Why? Because this was "the will of God in Christ Jesus" (5:18). God's will for your life is that you pray perpetually. Why does God call the church's members to be devoted to perpetual prayer? Let me give you two basic reasons.

First, there is so much to be thankful for. Thank God for his goodness to you in the beauty of his creation, which is the theater of his glory. For some of us who struggle with depression, feeling depressed, and having a melancholic personality, it is so important to remember this and to enjoy God's good creation. Thank God for his mercy to you in his providence. Those of you who have much, rejoice, and be a blessing to those who have little. Those who have little, rejoice that God is still providing for you in amazing ways—even through the hands of those who have much. Thank God for his grace to you in his beloved Son. Where your sins abound, his grace superabounds (Romans 5:20). When your sins make you feel dried up, his grace is poured upon you. When you feel spiritually empty in your sins, his grace is lavished upon you in his Son. All of this is so wonderfully expressed in the *Book of Common Prayer's* "General Thanksgiving," which begins like this:

> Almighty God, Father of all mercies, we thine unworthy servants do give thee most humble and hearty thanks for all thy goodness and loving-kindness to us, and to all men; We bless thee for our creation, preservation, and all the blessings of this life; but above all, for thine inestimable love in the redemption of the world by our Lord Jesus Christ; for the means of grace, and for the hope of glory.[3]

This idea that at its root prayer is grateful thanksgiving is so important to remember. Prayer is not an attempt to earn anything from God. Prayer is not an attempt to repay God for anything he has given to us. Prayer is our response of gratitude for the blessings of God. The Heidelberg Catechism captures this so beautifully, when it says,

> Q. 116. Why is prayer necessary for Christians?
>
> A. Because it is *the chief part of thankfulness* which God requires of us, and because God will give His grace and Holy Spirit only to those who earnestly and without ceasing ask them of Him, and render thanks unto Him for them. (emphasis added)

Prayer is the chief, or most important part, of our thankful response to God. The Westminster Larger Catechism also has a wonderful question and answer on the topic of prayer, which gets to the heart of why we are grateful in the first place:

> Q. 180. What is it to pray in the name of Christ?
>
> A. To pray in the name of Christ is, in obedience to his command, and in confidence on his promises, to ask mercy for his sake; not by bare mentioning of his name, but by *drawing our encouragement to pray*, and *our boldness, strength, and hope of acceptance* in prayer, *from Christ and his mediation*. (emphasis added)

Do you see that? As the Lord perpetually prays for you (Hebrews 7:25), you are to be encouraged, emboldened, strengthened, and assured to respond in prayer perpetually to him.

The second reason we are called to perpetual prayer is because there is so much to be on guard for. As Paul goes on to say later in this letter, "keep awake and be sober" (5:6). Why? Our own sinful nature rises within us perpetually. Pray perpetually for strength to resist perpetually. The world in which we live is relentless. Pray perpetually for protection perpetually. The devil is ever-prowling (1 Peter 5:8). Pray perpetually for confidence to stand with the armor of God perpetually (Ephesians 6:10–17). We have to fight our entire life against our sins. There is a spiritual battle at hand. Engage it. But isn't it interesting how after Paul exhorts us to stand and fight against the devil, he says this, "praying at all times in the Spirit, with all prayer and supplication?" (Ephesians 6:18) We pray because we need to fight in the strength that God alone can supply.

Persevering by Prayer

We also learn in Pastor Paul's prayer that we are called to persevere by prayer. In prayer, Paul and his companions brought before the Lord the remembrance of the Thessalonians' work of faith and labor of love and steadfastness of hope in our Lord Jesus Christ (1:3). His prayer was not a sentimental remembrance of a bygone time with them. His prayer was that they would continue in these spiritual gifts and graces. Paul wanted to enliven them to persevere. We are to persevere in prayer that we might persevere by prayer. One practical thing we learn here is that in prayer we meditate upon God's grace to us in Christ as well as in us by the Holy Spirit. And as we remember his work in us we are aided to persevere.

We need to persevere in three areas, according to Paul's prayer: faith, hope, and love. These three "cardinal virtues" are frequently mentioned in the New Testament by Paul (1 Corinthians 13:13; Galatians 5:5–6; Colossians 1:4–5) and by Peter (1 Peter 1:3–8), and even later in this very letter (5:8). They are so important that John Calvin called them "a brief definition of true Christianity."[4]

First, we need to persevere in the work of faith by means of prayer. The Thessalonians' faith in Christ in the midst of great opposition was hard. But that's what made it faith. In the same way pray that your faith will persevere and that it will be focused outside yourself and rest in Christ's past work and become productive.[5]

Second, we need to persevere in the labor of love by means of prayer. The Thessalonians' love for each other was in the midst of great opposition from their very neighbors, whom they were called to love. As well, their love for building the body of Christ was laborious, but it was a building that had lasting value. Paul's term here labor is not the same as that for work above. The word for labor speaks of the exertion associated with work.[6] Paul is saying that these believers needed to pray so that their love, which was exhausting, would not grow cold. They needed to persevere in love that was focused outward towards others.

Third, we need to persevere in the steadfastness of hope by means of prayer. The Thessalonians had a resolve that all they were doing was of lasting value, because it would be brought to its culmination at the coming of our Lord Jesus Christ. They didn't see this before their eyes in the present, but they persevered in its hope for the future. As Paul says to the Romans, "Now hope that is seen is not hope. For who hopes for what he sees? But if we hope for what we do not see, we wait for it with patience" (Romans 8:24–25). In the same way pray that your hope of heaven will persevere and that it will be focused outward and cling to the promise of Christ's future coming.[7]

In saying that we need to pray for our faith, hope, and love, no doubt you noticed that they are described in arduous terms: work, labor, and steadfastness? As St. Chrysostom said, "Merely to love is no labor at all. But to love genuinely is great labor."[8] Why is it that things of lasting value take so much effort? One reason is because life itself is hard. As the Scottish preacher, James Fergusson said, "The life of a Christian is not a life of idleness, not a life of ease, nor yet a life mutually prosperous and free from the cross. His faith must have work, his love must have labour, and his hope must be attended with patience under the cross."[9] Prayer is a necessary means of bringing our faith, hope, and love to a stronger place. This is why we can call prayer a means of grace (WLC, Q&A 154). It is not a sacrament, as that requires an outward sign, but it is a means of growing in the grace and knowledge of our Lord Jesus Christ. The means of grace are chiefly and primarily the means that God uses to communicate his grace to us: preaching and sacraments. In response to this, prayer is a means by which we cleave to and continue in that grace, by which we persevere, by which we long for more.

Conclusion

Therefore God calls us to be praying individuals, but especially to be a praying people, a praying church. Prayer is not flashy, showy, or a matter of our ingenuity. As E. M. Bounds, a nineteenth-century Methodist minister, once wrote in his little book, *Power Through Prayer*,

> We are constantly straining to devise new methods, new plans, new organizations to advance the Church and secure enlargement and efficiency for the gospel. This trend of the day has a tendency to lose sight of the man or sink the man in the plan or organization. God's plan is to make much of the man, far more of him than of anything else. Men are God's method. The Church is looking for better methods; God is looking for better men.[10]

Will you be one of those men, women, young adults, and children? Will you devote yourself to pray unceasingly for yourself, your brothers and sisters, and for the ministry of the church and its gospel message to the world? Let us be grateful for Christ's prayers for us by being a praying church to him.

3

Pastor Paul's Preaching

1 Thessalonians 1:4–5

What is preaching? I want you to pause for a moment and think about your answer. What are you thinking about? Maybe you're thinking, "It's the pastor's time to give his opinions about what he wants the church to be like." Or, "I don't really know what it is, but I do know that I need to hear stories." Or, "I like it to be quick and uplifting." We all have our personal opinions and preferences about what we like in preaching from our point of view—what we want, how long it should be, and the kinds of passages to be preached from. But the problem is that today too many Christians do not know what preaching is from God's point of view.

The passage before us leads us to meditate upon preaching and come to some confidence about it. Paul thanks God for the graces of the Holy Spirit in the lives of the Thessalonian believers (1:2–3) and then goes on to thank God for electing them (1:4). What is so fascinating is how Paul says he knows that God chose them: it is because the Holy Spirit was at work among them through the preaching of the gospel (1:5). Preaching must be something special if it can be an evidence of eternal election. These believers were "in God the Father and the Lord Jesus Christ" and now he says they are loved by God who has chosen you. What a gospel promise! And that promise of eternal life is related to the temporal and outward means of preaching.

As we focus in upon Paul's words here in 1 Thessalonians 1:4–5 we learn about *Pastor Paul's Preaching*. And we note well that Paul describes preaching as a two-sided coin. He speaks of preaching, on the one side, in terms of what the preacher does, and then on the other side, in terms of what God does. This is why our forefathers said there were two preachers in the ministry of the Word. There is the external minister and there is the internal minister. The external minister is the man who uses words while the internal minister is the Holy Spirit who effects by his omnipotent power all the Word promises. As Calvin said, "The external minister administers the vocal word … But the internal minister, who is the Holy Spirit, freely works internally, while by his secret virtue he effects in the hearts of whomsoever he will their union with Christ through one faith. This union is a thing internal, heavenly and indestructible."[1] So what is preaching?

A Ministry of Man

What is preaching? In the first place, Paul's words teach us that the preaching of the Word is *a ministry of man*. Let me explain by breaking this down into several parts.

In Human Words

Preaching is a ministry of man because it comes in human words. This should be an obvious point. It is Paul, Silvanus, and Timothy who write in verse 1; who thank God in prayer in verse 2; and who preached, even calling what was preached, our gospel (1:5), as it was something they too embraced.[2] As a ministry of man, preaching comes in human words. Paul thanks God because these believers received *the Word* (1:6). And while this word is "the word of the *Lord*" (1:8) and "the word of *God*" (2:13), it came through the means of men's words: because our gospel came to you *not only in word* (1:5). While it was not only in words, it was still in words.[3]

Let me give an application of this that we need to stress today in our culture. We live in such a visual age that as we are constantly bombarded with images we need to be constantly reminded that God primarily communicates to us through words. For example, our English word sermon comes from a Latin word, *sermo*, that means a speech, a discourse, or a word.[4] And God's Word in preaching is not communicated by skits; it is not conveyed through art; it is not taught to us through music; it is not expressed through deeds; but in words. What an opportunity we have as Word-centered churches to be a counter-cultural people that cling to words in a visual age.

In the Power of the Gospel

So how are the minister's mere words going to communicate in such a culture? Paul also rejoices that the Word came to the Thessalonians in power and in the Holy Spirit (1:5). It is important to recognize that Paul uses the singular noun, power (*dunamei*), and not the plural "powers" (*dunameis*). This is significant because if he wanted to say the preached word was accompanied with the miracles, signs, and wonders of the Holy Spirit he could have used the common term for that, the plural "powers." What he is saying, then, is that the word of the gospel came to them in the power of the Holy Spirit. "When the gospel is preached God is there and God is working. The gospel *is* power."[5] As he says elsewhere, the gospel is the power of God (Romans 1:16).

And this is the great irony, isn't it? The power of God is communicated through the weakness of words. In other words, the Word and Spirit are united. The reason is that it is the Holy Spirit who makes this preaching powerful.[6] As Paul says elsewhere,

> For the word of the cross is folly to those who are perishing, but to us who are being saved it is the power of God … For Jews demand signs and Greeks seek wisdom, but we preach Christ crucified, a stumbling block to Jews and folly to Gentiles, but to those who are called, both Jews and Greeks, Christ the power of God and the wisdom of God. For the foolishness of God is wiser than men, and the weakness of God is stronger than men. (1 Corinthians 1:18, 22–25)

To illustrate this, think of what we parents oftentimes tell our children: "Sticks and stones may break my bones, but words will never hurt me." We teach them this because when someone says something mean to them, we do not want them to be sad. Yet mean words do make our children sad. No matter what we might say to ourselves or to our children to make us feel better, words are powerful. And most of the time they are more powerful than physical actions. In the same way God does not need to shoot a lightning bolt at someone or do a powerful miracle because he has his words that are powerful to save.

This is so vital in our time. We live in an age that the apostle predicted: "For the time is coming when people will not endure sound teaching, but having itching ears they will accumulate for themselves teachers to suit their own passions" (2 Timothy 4:3). God wants you to hear and he wants preachers to speak not words that tickle your itching ears, but words that fill your ears with truth—regardless of how you feel about it. God wants preachers to preach like Paul, "not in plausible words of wisdom, but in demonstration of the Spirit and of power" (1 Corinthians 2:4). Why? "That your faith might not rest in the wisdom of men but in the power of God" (1 Corinthians 2:5).

In Total Confidence

The preaching of the Word, then, is a ministry of man in human words and in the power of the gospel. As well, Paul says his words of the gospel came in total confidence, with full conviction or assurance (1:5). This is not the conviction of the hearers, though, but of the preacher.[7] He says our gospel came in three ways: powerfully, Holy Spirit-ually, and confidently (1:5).

This came home to me early in my ministry. A young man in the congregation who seemed to have it all together took his own life, tragically. Before that he renounced his once firm faith in Christ. When I sat with him in the living room of his apartment I pled with him about the reality of God, the need for satisfaction for our sins, and the proof of everything being the resurrection of Christ. At the end of our conversation, he said to me, "I wish I had your confidence."

Sadly, the preachers' confidence does not always persuade. Nevertheless, the preacher must have total confidence, total conviction, and total assurance of his message. In the words of C. H. Spurgeon (1834–1892), "If ministers are not absolutely certain of what they preach, they are not likely to convince others."[8] If preachers do not have total confidence in the gospel, the people might as well stay home. Why should the minister be so confident? He should be because he is totally gripped by the fact that God exists, that he exists as a gracious God to miserable sinners, and that he has chosen to bring that salvation through fellow sinners. If I can put it like this with all reverence: the preacher needs to be confident because as far as he is concerned, the balance of heaven and hell is in his hands. The weight of what the preacher does necessitates total conviction without hesitation. This is why the old adage is true for those who aspire to the ministry: if you can do anything else on the face of this earth, do it.[9]

The Scottish preacher James Fergusson said it like this: "The more a Minister be persuaded and above all doubt of the truth of that he preaches, the more he believe and doth therefore speak, and the more he speaks as one who believes and hath ventured his soul upon the truth which he preaches, his preaching will prove the more powerful, and apt to work effectually upon the hearts of hearers."[10]

In the Evidence of Godliness

Now, one final thing needs to be said about preaching being a ministry of man. With all Paul says about the necessity of words, the pastor's words cannot communicate, "Do as I say, not as I do." He cannot fake zeal, passion, and confidence only to have his life not back his word up. The ministry of the Word must also be joined with the evidence of godliness: You know what kind of men we proved to be among you for your sake (1:5). As another great Scottish preacher, Robert Murray M'Cheyne (1813–1843), once said, "It is not great talents that God blesses so much as likeness to Jesus. A holy minister is an awful weapon in the hand of God."[11]

What does this mean? It means the minister of the Word must live among you (1:5), knowing his people. As Leon Morris commented on this passage, "No preacher can expect a hearing for his gospel unless it is bearing fruit in his own life."[12] The minister's life must be an open and honest book before his people. That's a dangerous thing. But it is what God commands of the pastor. John Owen once wrote, "If a man teach uprightly and walk crookedly, more will fall down in the night of his life than he built in the day of his doctrine."[13] Do you want to know what you can do for your pastor and his family, should the Lord bless him with one? Pray for him and them. Pray that he is godly. Pray that he loves his wife. Pray that he loves his kids and raises them in a godly way. Pray that he spends necessary time with them. Pray that he does not neglect them. In John Owen's famous treatise, "Of the Mortification of Sin," he speaks of one of the evils of sin being that it takes away the minister's usefulness to his generation:

> If he be a preacher, God commonly blows upon his ministry, that he shall labour in the fire, and not be honoured with any success or doing any work for God; and the like may be spoken of other conditions. The world is at this day full of poor withering professors. How few are there that walk in any beauty or glory! how barren, how useless are they, for the most part! Amongst the many reasons that may be assigned of this sad estate, it may justly be feared that this is none of the least effectual,—many men harbour spirit-devouring lusts in their bosoms, that lie as worms at the root of their obedience, and corrode and weaken it day by day.[14]

It also means the minister of the Word must live for your sake (1:5). His life is a labor of love for others. As Paul told Timothy, "Keep a close watch on yourself and on the teaching. Persist in this, for by so doing you will save both yourself and your hearers" (1 Timothy 4:16). The minister does not live for his own sake, but he lives for the Lord and then for his people. Paul taught this to the Corinthians when he said he—and by extension the minister—is "always carrying in the body the death of Jesus, so that the life of Jesus may also be manifested in our bodies. For we who live are always being given over to death for Jesus' sake, so that the life of Jesus also may be manifested in our mortal flesh. So death is at work in us, but life in you" (2 Corinthians 4:10–12).

Because preaching the Word of God is a ministry of man, pray for your minister and for all Christ's ministers everywhere.

A Ministry of God

But this is where our second point is so necessary. Paul teaches us that the preaching of the Word is *a ministry of God*. The English Puritan, Thomas Watson (1620–1686), once said, "Ministers knock at the door of men's hearts, the Spirit comes with a key and opens the door."[15] When he speaks of his preaching coming to the Thessalonians, Paul says it came not only in words, but also in power and in the Holy Spirit (v. 5). In fact, the power Paul speaks of is the Holy Spirit. The way Paul writes here equates the power (*kai en dunamei*) with the Holy Spirit (*kai en pneumati hagiō*).[16]

What Paul is saying is that while the Word is clothed in the frail words of frail men, the ministry of the Word is the ministry of the Holy Spirit. As Paul even said, "For they say, 'His letters are weighty and strong, but his bodily presence is weak, and his speech of no account'" (2 Corinthians 10:10 cf. 11:6). While the minister may speak way too fast for some or way too monotone for others, while he may stutter from time to time over words or mess up tenses of words from time to time in the passion of the preaching moment, the Word is the means *by which* God executes his power. While sinners are the ones speaking the gospel, it is still the work of the Spirit. As John Kershaw (1792–1870), a nineteenth-century Baptist preacher, once said, "God saves all kinds of people, even ministers."[17] Although the message of the gospel is weakness, humanly speaking (1 Corinthians 1:18–31), it is the power of God.

What this means for the preacher is that he should be confident in God's work through his ministry. He should not base the results of his preaching upon anything but the promise of God to bless his own Word. This means the preacher must also preach in reliance upon the Holy Spirit. As John Owen wrote in his masterful treatise, *On Communion with God*, believers have an intimate and personal relationship with the Holy Spirit. Applied to the minister, this means he must know the Spirit's Word and be able to say in his preaching, "Let him who has ears, hear what the Spirit says to the church."

This also means that the congregation must hear and experience the Word in reliance upon the Holy Spirit. As one commentator said, the Thessalonians "did not need to be taught the doctrine of the Holy Spirit as part of a program of theological education; his person and power were matters of living experience to them."[18] Come to worship ready and willing to hear the Word for your souls. God is speaking; listen up!

Conclusion

Let me conclude by asking you again, what is preaching? Paul's answer is that it is God's means of communicating to us and bringing us into a saving relationship with him. To do this he enlists weak men to speak on his behalf the truth of the gospel with full confidence and in the convincing power of godliness. And while he is doing this, the power of the Holy Spirit is accomplishing everything he promises to do through the means of his own Word. May God provide such preaching in our age! May God bless such preaching in the ages to come!

4

Fruits of Gospel Ministry

1 Thessalonians 1:6–8

All of us are working hard to leave some sort of legacy behind. For those of us in the United States, we speak of the typical, "American dream." A part of that dream is to give to your kids more than you yourself have. What they didn't tell us in the American dream manual was how you are supposed to do that while not spoiling your kids. We want to give them a better life than we had ourselves. For some of us, this legacy of passing down means having something tangible to give to our kids. Maybe it means to honor your family name. Maybe it means something like continuing on in some career path that is in your family. Many in the military follow in a great family tradition by serving. Maybe it means just to work hard and to be known as a good hard worker, a good citizen, and a good person.

But for us believers in Christ, there is something greater, of course, than passing down just money, an inheritance, a name, a house, or something else. For those who are the first believers in their families, the prayer is that God would continue to work through them to bring children and grandchildren into the kingdom of God. For all of us we should work dutifully for this as Christians, as citizens of a lasting kingdom. We should desire to leave behind in our children as well as in our church something of lasting eternal value—the Gospel; faith in Christ; holiness; dedication, zeal, and passion for Christ and for his church.

It is the same with ministers. We see Paul here as a minister praying for these Thessalonian believers in Christ. He thanks God the Father for them, for all the fruit of the Holy Spirit in their lives—faith, hope and love. Then he continues to give thanks here because they believed the Gospel, which came to them in great power in the Holy Spirit with great confidence. And then he prays that because of that Gospel these believers became imitators of us (v. 6; cf. 1 Corinthians 4:6; 11:1), their pastors, and imitators of the Lord. What was there to imitate, to mimic? (*mimētai*) As we saw in verse 5, "You know what kind of men we proved to be among you for your sake" (1:5). The minister of the gospel, then, must be able to be imitated. Paul was not the kind of minister that says, "Do as I say and not as I do." Instead he lived among his people "like a nursing mother taking care of her own children" (2:7). He did not just pop in to preach a message and then leave them to live on their own the rest of the week. He lived among them as a nursing mother. He goes on to describe himself "like a father with his children." As the book of Hebrews says, "Remember your leaders, those who spoke to you the Word of God. Consider the outcome of their way of life, and imitate their faith" (Hebrews 13:17).

The Thessalonians in turn became an example (v. 7). They became a type (*tupon*), literally, of faith to others, types of hope to others, and types of love to others especially in Macedonia and in Achaia (v. 7). Notice Paul's double use of a past tense verb became (vv. 6, 7) as he writes about their conversion and imitation of the apostle and how that in turn made them imitable to the church universal.

It is a part of the high calling of the minister of the gospel of Christ to labor among the vineyard of the Lord to produce fruit. But not merely fruit that lasts for a moment, but fruit that is cultivated and pruned to last beyond his own life and ministry among his people. Paul was only among the Thessalonians for a short time. According to Acts 17 he preached in the Jewish synagogue on three consecutive Sabbaths. This would mean he was there for as short as the week before and after, so five weeks, or for just a few months, based on his description in 1 Thessalonians 2:7–9 of working hard while among them. Despite the short length he had fruit of lasting value.[1] Paul describes for us in this passage the calling of all true conscientious ministers of the gospel. In Colossians he says that the true minister's goal is to present everyone mature in Christ; not a sapling, but a mature lasting fruit: "that we may present everyone mature in Christ. For this I toil, struggling with all his energy that he powerfully works within me" (Colossians 1:28–29). Paul describes the gospel legacy of a minister not in terms of the size of his congregation, not the beauty of the building in which he preached, and certainly not himself. But the true fruit of the gospel is found in the people and the quality of their lives that he leaves behind.

A Love of the Word

The first fruit of the gospel ministry that Paul says was produced in these Thessalonians was *a love of the word*. We see that because he says the gospel not only came to them "in word, but also in power and in the Holy Spirit and with full conviction" (v. 5). They believed the truthfulness of the apostle's preaching with full confidence. And he goes on to say that they received that very same word (v. 6). This word was also the word of the Lord (v. 8), "the gospel of God" (2:2, 9), and "the word of God" (2:13).

They received that word in love because Paul was exemplifying to them a passion for and a love of that word. He brought it in "full conviction" (v. 5). It was not their conviction believing it but it was his conviction in preaching it. And he shows them the truthfulness of the gospel even in how he preaches it. They could see in his reading of it, in his preaching of it, in his thinking about it, in his counseling with it, and in his teaching of it that he loved this word. He says later on, for example, "For you yourselves know how you ought to imitate us, because we were not idle when we were with you, nor did we eat anyone's bread without paying for it, but with toil and labor we worked night and day, that we might not be a burden to any of you" (2 Thessalonians 3:7–8). Paul was to be imitated in his diligence, his hard work, his toil, his pain, and his anguish. And how much more should he have been imitated for his love, his passion, and his devotion for the Word of God?

He goes on to qualify that love for the Word in two ways: first, they received the word in much affliction, and second, they received the word with the joy of the Holy Spirit (v. 6).

In Affliction

They received the Word in the midst of affliction. In the account of the planting of the Thessalonian congregation in Acts 17, you can hear what Paul meant by receiving the Word in much affliction. After preaching the gospel on three Sabbath days, we are told that there was jealousy and the gathering of a rabble of wicked men who formed a mob and set the city in an uproar, attacking the house of Jameson (Acts 17:5). But when the mob could not find Paul, Silvanus, and Timothy "they dragged Jameson and some of the brothers before the city authorities, shouting, 'These men who have turned the world upside down have come here also'" (Acts 17:6).

The Thessalonians experienced the power of the Word of God like Paul had in the midst of many afflictions. In all of his imprisonments, in all of his countless beatings, in all of his shipwrecks, in all of his floating at sea, in all his danger from rivers, in all his danger from robbers, in all his danger from his own people, in all his danger from Gentiles, in all his danger in the city, in all his danger in the wilderness, in all his danger at sea, in all his danger from false brothers, in all his toil and hardship, in all his sleepless nights, in all his hunger and thirst, in all his cold and exposure (2 Corinthians 11:23–27) he received the Word of God. And the Thessalonians knew this themselves. They loved the Word in the midst of struggle, anguish, toil, and persecution.

But do not think this was a random thing that just happened to them once or might just happen to us once in a while, as a strange or random act. The Lord Jesus Christ says to us, "In the world you will have tribulation. But take heart; I have overcome the world" (John 16:33). In the same way Paul calls us to be imitators of him, of the Lord, and of the minister of the gospel who loves the Word of God in the midst of affliction. As Thomas Aquinas commented, "You imitated me not in my human failings, but in those points in which I have imitated Christ by patience in the midst of suffering."[2] We know that the world assaults us. We know the world tempts us. We know the world as it seeks to bring affliction upon us for the sake of the gospel. And we should love the Word despite this. We should know by experience the travail, the anguish, and the tribulation of the world. We may not know of the persecution of having to run out of town in the middle of the night but the world works in other insidious ways in our time and place. The world works especially to young women, saying to you constantly how you should dress, how you should act, how you should look, and what you should be. The world has a model, it has an image of what the ideal woman is to be like but it's not what the Scripture says. The Scripture calls us to love the Word despite what the world says. You are called to love what God says a godly woman is to be like despite the world. Love him and his word in the midst of such struggles, afflictions, and pressures. There is another way that we most often experience the affliction of the world right here where we live. We struggle as we are pressured to work on the Lord's Day. We are assaulted with the necessity of working on the Sabbath, of giving up what God calls us to do very clearly in his word. Many of you may have had to struggle with this very thing; yet many of you may have overcome this assault of the world. You have trusted in God himself, not knowing exactly how your ends would be met if you did not work on the Lord's Day. As the psalmist says,

> Put false ways far from me
> and graciously teach me your law!
> I have chosen the way of faithfulness;
> I set your rules before me.
> I cling to your testimonies, O LORD;
> let me not be put to shame! (Psalm 119:29–31)

We know that when we love the Lord and his word that has come to us, that the Lord will uphold us in affliction and not put us to shame.

In Joy

There is a beautiful contrast here. He says that they received the Word in much affliction; yet, with the joy of the Holy Spirit (v. 6), one of the fruits of the Holy Spirit (Galatians 5:22). There was affliction, but there was joy. While there was the world's tribulation, there was the Holy Spirit. He is the key to Paul's contrast. Chrysostom said it like this: "The affliction is in things bodily, and the joy in things spiritual."[3] While they were having struggles, while they were having persecutions, there was "the joy of the Lord" for their strength (Nehemiah 8:10). As the Psalmist again says, "In the way of your testimonies I delight as much as in all riches" (Psalm 119:14). The epistle to James says, "Count it all joy, my brothers, when you meet trials of various kinds" (James 1:2).

As regenerated children of God, God has given us new hearts and new affections like he gave to these Thessalonians. We have new hearts in the midst of the world, in the midst of our dysfunctional families, and in the midst of our co-workers and neighbors. He changes us to say that we love the Lord's Word more than all riches. That's the joy of the Holy Spirit. We have it because when the gospel came to us it came in the power of the Holy Spirit. And when the Spirit of God creates this new heart in us he creates the fruit of the Holy Spirit of joy. That joy is a deep, true, lasting, complete satisfaction; it's a total contentment in enjoying God and him alone. As we confess, we exist "to glorify God, and to enjoy him forever" (WSC, Q&A 1). We won't have that completely in this life; yet that is what God begins to put in our hearts so that you can say, "I have the joy of the Spirit." You can say, "I rest my life in the Spirit and in the Word of God." You can say, "I receive the word as it is, in truth, the very word of the Lord Himself to my soul." In the words of Calvin, "The Gospel cannot be truly or genuinely received without a glad heart."[4]

This connection between the Word and joy is described in the book of Acts. We read in Acts 8 that as Saul was persecuting the church very violently and causing the church to scatter, eventually some disciples made their way to the city of Samaria. And it says when they preached the Word, those who received it did so with much joy (Acts 8:4–8). Despite Saul's violent persecutions there was great joy.

Why? Because the Holy Spirit creates joy through the Word of God. When Philip proclaimed the meaning of the prophecy of Isaiah to the Ethiopian eunuch, the Ethiopian rejoiced and glorified the Word of the Lord (Acts 8:29). When the gospel continued to spread they rejoiced despite great persecution (Acts 15:32). Why? Because of the Word. The Word implants deeply into our hearts and minds beyond joints and marrow, flesh and body and bone (Hebrews 4:15). That means that to be severed from the Word is to be severed from true joy. Not to be totally sold out to the Word of God is to lack that joy, that fruitfulness. Not to give yourself to it more than all riches is to lack, is to struggle, is to trip, and is to stumble along in our Christian life. The Thessalonians received that Word in imitation of their Lord himself, "who for the joy that was set before him endured the cross, despising the shame, and is seated at the right hand of the throne of God" (Hebrews 12:2).

What a love for the Word. The first fruit of the preaching of the gospel; the great fruit that I desire above all else for you, brothers and sisters and friends, is to love the Word. "Lord, to whom shall we go?" Peter said to Jesus. Five thousand disciples all scattered, and a mere twelve were left, and one of them was a devil, Judas. And Jesus asks Peter, "Do you want to go away as well?" Peter says, "Lord, to whom shall we go? You have the words of eternal life" (John 6:68). We must cling to the Word more than all riches.

A Love of the World

And that love of the Word leads to action. It leads to a second fruit of gospel ministry: *a love of the world.* What do I mean by that? Certainly not loving the world as we are forbidden from doing. What I mean is that as the gospel is preached to us and we receive it in full conviction, and we come to love that Word, how can we not be filled with passion and purpose to share and to spread that Word among the world? And as they imitated their Lord and their ministers in loving the Word in the midst of affliction, they became examples to the world, examples to others in far off lands in sharing the Word (vv. 7–8).

Jesus teaches us like little children that the Word of God is like a seed (Matthew 13). Preachers are called to spread it by preaching (1 Peter 1:23–25). When they preach it is like spreading seeds in the dirt. Some of the seeds take root and they grow. Some of the seeds do not. And God has put a seed into our hearts when we trust in Jesus Christ. God begins to water the seed so that it begins to grow roots, a trunk, and branches with all kinds of fruits on it. And we should want to share those fruits with others.

God calls us to share the Word with our lips and with our lives as we love and as we serve. Even as God himself "so loved the world that he gave his only begotten Son" (John 3:16), so we are to love the lost world around us. These Thessalonians loved the world and evidenced it, as Paul says, the word of the Lord sounded forth from you in Macedonia and Achaia, but your faith in God has gone forth everywhere (v. 8). This is why Paul can say elsewhere that we are like perfume to the world: "But thanks be to God, who … through us spreads the fragrance of the knowledge of him everywhere" (2 Corinthians 2:14). Remember that Paul was there for only three consecutive Sabbath days and perhaps a short while after among Christians. Yet in that brief time his love for them was so great that they were set on fire to love the world as the Word sounded forth from them to the world. This verb is only used here in the New Testament and carries the idea of trumpeting out (*exēchētai*) a sound. And their love was so great, that Paul says we need not say anything (v. 8).

We are called by these Christians to have an evangelistic passion. But this is not just in caustic or awkward conversations with people. Notice that it all begins with a passionate life for Christ that is noticeable by the world. As Paul says to the Corinthians, their lives were on display as living epistles of what God can do with sinners; living epistles walking around with the Word of God written upon them (2 Corinthians 3:1–3). One of my favorite Puritans, Thomas Manton (1620–1677), once wrote that we are to exhibit the gospel. He said this, "As artists hang up their masterpieces in their shop to draw customers, so God sets forth these instances to show what He will do for poor returning sinners."[5] When people saw the Thessalonians, they saw love, zeal, and gospel. When the world sees you, what do they see? Do they see arrogance? Do they see you being stuck up? Do they see you as too good for them? Does the world see you projecting a "holier than thou," "I'm better than you," attitude? Or, are you an example of a sinner saved by grace? Do they see you as a jar of clay that has been broken into a thousand pieces that God himself is putting back together; and even as he puts you back together those cracks are still visible? Our evangelistic zeal must be shown in our lives living amongst the world; in truthfulness of who we were; in honesty about what we are; in hope of what we will become. Like a masterpiece of art shown in a window, show the world what God can do.

The Thessalonians' zeal was also shown on their lips, of course, as the gospel sounded forth from them. This does not mean that every single believer is a minister or that every single believer is an evangelist. There is nothing of the sort here. Paul of course says there are those who are set apart for special office: pastors, teachers, evangelists, apostles, and prophets (Ephesians 4:11). But every believer must be ready to give an answer for their hope (1 Peter 3:15), and that means using words. You must be prepared to give an answer to those who would ask of the hope that lies within you with gentleness and self-control. What's your hope? Why do you have it? Where does it come from? Why do you believe? Why do you do what you do? Why do you not do what you don't do? Why do you go to church on the Lord's Day? Why do you give your money? Why do you give your time? Why do you care about these things? Give an answer. Sound it forth; spread seeds, knowing the power of growth belongs to the Holy Spirit. The Spirit saves. The Spirit regenerates; not the minister and not the members. The believer is empowered by the gospel to serve and to give evidence to the gospel by lips and lives, knowing that it is the Holy Spirit who does this. That shouldn't lessen our zeal; that should increase our zeal to know that all we must do is spread seed and live a life of godliness and let God do the work. Luther once told his congregation that as he sat around drinking Wittenberg beer with his friends, it was the Word that accomplished the work of reformation.[6] Not that I want us all to sit around drinking beer; but the point is the gospel is the power of God. You spread seeds; we spread seeds; together we live lives of godliness and let God figure it out. Let him give the increase. "I planted, Apollos watered," Paul said, "but God gave the growth" (1 Corinthians 3:7).

The Thessalonians' passion was guided by an evangelistic purpose. Why did they sound forth the Word, so that even Macedonia and Achaia heard of Thessalonian Christians? The purpose was this: that sinners need to be made righteous; that the lost must be found; that those in darkness need light; those who are sick need to be healed. We need to capture that purpose, that zeal, and that passion of the early church. As the church fathers described, even when the Roman Empire brought great persecution, the blood of the martyrs became the seed of the church. In the words of Exodus: "the more they were oppressed, the more they multiplied" (Exodus 1:12). That love for the Word leaves a love for the world that causes us to capture a purposeful zeal for the gospel as new creatures in Christ. God had destined us that we should be here in this place at this time. You're here; God has put you here for a purpose. Now be zealous.

Conclusion

What is that legacy that we will leave behind? Know that God has put you in your place for this time for a reason. There is work to do, then, and Paul knew this. That is why he says in Colossians 1: "Him we proclaim, warning everyone and teaching everyone with all wisdom, that we may present everyone mature in Christ. For this I toil, struggling with all his energy that he powerfully works within me" (Colossians 1:28–29). There was work for these Thessalonians to do. They knew it so they sounded forth the Word. There were others who had yet to hear it. There's work for us to do in the vineyard of the Lord brothers and sisters. God has called us to be the workers. I pray that you will join in it. May we be faithful; may God cause us to be fruitful. May the gospel ministry produce in us, our children, and our children's children until the Lord returns, the fruits of love for his Word; total devotion to it and love for the world that is still lost and still desperate. Who is sufficient for these things? May God help us.

5

Our New Life in Christ

1 Thessalonians 1:9–10

We all have a reputation that precedes us. The question is, of course, whether our reputation is one that is positive or one that is negative. Our reputation is created by the things that we say with our mouths as well as by the things that we do with our hands and feet. But more than that are the ways in which our reputation is formed and fashioned by how others perceive us, how they interpret the things that we say, and how they understand the things that we do.

According to Paul, the Thessalonians' reputation was not so much based on what they were saying—"the word of the Lord sounded forth from you" (v. 8)—or what they were doing—"you received the word in much affliction" (v. 6). Instead, it was more how the Macedonians and Achaians perceived, understood, and grasped what was happening among them.

And what a reputation they had! It went forth, it preceded them, it was heard about, and it was seen in living color. It was summed up in Paul's words, "we need not say anything" (v. 8). The Thessalonians did not need the apostles to go before them doing market research on how they could best infiltrate the culture and then trumpet their name. Nothing the apostles could have said would have improved their reputation. When it came down to it, their reputation was that they were known for living a new life in Christ. The world of Macedonia and Achaia knew these people (v. 8). Their neighbors saw them in action. They worked alongside them. They conversed with them. They saw them in the marketplaces. And they saw a drastic difference between their lives before Christ and after Christ.

Notice the three main verbs that describe their new life in Christ in our passage: turn, serve, and wait. Those three main verbs described their reputation that preceded them. But notice something else about those verbs: they come in two different tenses. The first verb, turned, is in the past tense, which led to present action: to serve God and to wait the coming of our Lord. And this last verb, wait, had a future orientation to it.

That new life is also for us. Not only did the Thessalonians imitate Paul, Silvanus, and Timothy as well as the Lord, they themselves were being imitated. And since Paul writes under the inspiration of the Holy Spirit, this was a letter that eventually was read in churches throughout the entire region. Paul writes about *our* new life in Christ.

A Change of Direction

Our new life in Christ is characterized by *a change of direction*: you turned to God from idols (v. 9). This means that they were living a life in another way. They had been facing idols and had their backs to the true and living God. But when the gospel came to them in words but especially in power and in the Holy Spirit, with full conviction, the Spirit of God changed the direction of their hearts, minds, and lives. They were changed and turned around to the living and true God. They once awaited nothing, living with the philosophy: "Let us eat and drink, for tomorrow we die!" (1 Corinthians 15:32) But now they awaited something greater—the coming of Jesus Christ.

This change of direction that Paul describes here with the verb turn is describing what we call "conversion." There is so much misunderstanding in our time as it is understood to be the result of some activity, some choice, or something that we have done in the exercise of our will. But notice several things about what Paul says here in terms of turning from idols to serve God.

Conversion is a Complete Change of Direction

Conversion is a complete change of direction, a total break from how you were living before to how God now calls you to live for Christ. It is the conversion of our whole lives that he is speaking of and not merely repentance. Repentance is one part of conversion. The New Testament ordinarily uses a different verb to describe repentance (*metanoeō*), which is a change of mind. For example, Paul says a true minister of the gospel must be patient and must teach opponents praying that God would grant to his hearers repentance. He describes that as God granting repentance "leading to a knowledge of the truth, and they may come to their senses" (2 Timothy 2:26–27).

But Paul doesn't use that verb here. He uses a verb that is more than just a change of mind. A change of mind is an inward, internal thing that only you know, that may not necessarily manifest itself in an outward way. You can change your mind and no one would ever know. Paul uses a verb here that oftentimes is used in the New Testament to describe not a change of mind, but a complete and a whole change of life. It is a real, true conversion. They turned (*epestrepsate*) to God from idols. This was a radical reorientation. Paul uses this same verb to describe turning to the Lord from the dead letter of the Old Covenant law (2 Corinthians 3:16). He also uses it negatively of those who "turn back again to the weak and worthless elementary principles of the world" (Galatians 4:9). So Paul was saying that this was a change not only in mind but also in will and affection. This was a complete one hundred and eighty degree turn. In Acts 14:15 Paul and Barnabas exhorted the Lystrans to "turn from these vain things to a living God." As their backs were once to God so now they were turned to him with their backs to those idols. This is what we call "evangelical repentance." What Paul says elsewhere of unbelievers was once true of us, that they "exchanged the glory of the immortal God for images resembling mortal man and birds and animals and creeping things" (Romans 1:23) and "they exchanged the truth about God for a lie and worshiped and served the creature rather than the Creator, who is blessed forever! Amen" (Romans 1:25).

To become a Christian you must turn. To be a Christian you have been turned. Your face must be towards God and your back must be towards the devil. Your eyes must be lifted to heaven and off the earth. You must be turned from yourselves to the living and true God. We learn here that while the idols are not the same in all times in all people, that everyone "is in bondage to idolatry, and immersed in blindness and insanity."[1] You cannot have one foot in the church and one foot in the world. As Jesus said, "No one can serve two masters, for either he will hate the one and love the other, or he will be devoted to the one and despise the other. You cannot serve God and money" (Matthew 6:24). "Whoever is not with me is against me, and whoever does not gather with me scatters" (Matthew 12:30). So conversion is a complete change of direction.

Conversion is a Public Change of Direction

Conversion is also a public change of direction. They turned to God from idols and this was more than just an inward thing. Unlike Nicodemus, who came to Jesus at night for fear of the Pharisees (John 3), the Thessalonians came to Jesus publicly. It was not merely in the night, but in the day. Conversion must not be in private but it must be in public. As Paul says later, as believers we must live a converted life out in the open: "For you are all children of light, children of the day. We are not of the night or of the darkness" (1 Thessalonians 5:5).

Recall the story of Paul and Barnabas as they were in the city of Lystra. After Paul had just preached and healed a man the Lystrans called Paul "Hermes," the god of eloquence, and Barnabas "Zeus," the great god of the Pantheon. Even the high priest of Zeus came out of the temple with bowls to sacrifice and with garlands to put upon their heads. Paul and Barnabas tore their robes, and they proclaimed to the Lystrans, "We bring you good news, that you should turn from these vain things to a living God who made heaven and the earth, and the sea, and all that is in them" (Acts 14:15). What happened next? They were stoned. They were run out of town. Later as they began to preach in the city of Ephesus, there was a coppersmith who was making idols to Artemis, also known as Diana. This caused a riot because idolaters were turning to Christ and no longer going to the marketplace to buy their copper and silver gods. Calvin described conversion like this: "only those who renounce the worthlessness of their own instincts and embrace and receive the pure worship of God truly believe in Him."[2]

Conversion was so complete, so public that it even affected them in terms of how they spent their money, whether it was on idols or not. Conversion cut into the world's business and the devil's profits. Of course there are internal idols, covetousness being the worst. As

Paul says, "Covetousness … is idolatry" (Colossians 3:5). Idols can be statues but also things that we might conceive in our minds, things we might worship, serve, devote ourselves to (HC, Q&A 95). Idols can be money, prestige in the eyes of the world, fame, power over people, our jobs, and ourselves. To be converted is to turn your back on a former way of life, which has public consequences. Many of us who have come to Christ after a lengthy time in the world should know by experience the consequences of conversion. The consequences of turning to Christ are being mocked by so-called friends, being shunned by your very own family members, being slammed by enemies, and being held to a ridiculous standard which no-one can meet. That is the price, but it is worth it. Paul paid the price of not being able to return to Thessalonica. Instead, he had to send Timothy back there to get a report. It was worth it though, for those ancient Christians, and it should be for us, to turn our backs on everything for the sake of Christ. As Psalm 84 describes the joy and worth of belonging to Christ: "for a day in your courts is better than a thousand elsewhere. I would rather be a doorkeeper in the house of my God, than dwell in the tents of wickedness" (Psalm 84:10).

Like Moses, we need to make a public change. Moses is described as having turned his back upon Pharaoh, Egypt, and all its riches: "like Moses who chose rather to be mistreated with the people of God than to enjoy the fleeting pleasures of sin, He considered the reproach of Christ greater wealth than the treasures of Egypt" (Hebrews 11:25–26). Why? "For he was looking for a reward." All the wealth of the world, all its power, all its prestige, all its fame, and all that it could offer to us, is as Paul says, "rubbish" (Philippians 3:8). It is filth, it is trash, and the greater riches are those that are to come. For us, in Jesus Christ, an inheritance that is in heaven awaiting us, unspoiled, unspotted, immutable, preserved for us, and kept by the power of God.

Conversion is a Divine Change of Direction

But recognize something else that we don't necessarily get here because Paul says to us that you turned to God from idols (v. 9). The question is always asked, "Whose work is conversion, then?" Or, "Where does the ability and power to turn come from?" Paul says that they turned, but the question is how?

The Scriptures make it abundantly clear to us that conversion is a part of the graciousness of salvation. In conversion we undergo a divine change of direction. God himself turns and bends the will to convert us. God himself opens up the eyes of the blind like the apostle Paul on the Damascus Road (Acts 9). God himself converts and humbles to bring us to our knees. We see this in the Old Testament in terms of the prayers that the church has prayed for millennia. They prayed, "Turn us again, O God, and cause Thy face to shine, and we shall be saved" (Psalm 80:3). It is God who turns us. It is God whose face shines upon us, and therefore who saves us—"we shall be saved."

The prophet Jeremiah says this in two places: "Turn Thou me, and I shall be turned" (Jeremiah 31:18) and, "Turn Thou unto us, O Lord, and we shall be turned" (Lamentations 5:21). They prayed as sinners that God himself would do the turning so that they would be turned towards God. Then they could repent of their sins and embrace the gospel—even as these Thessalonians. Their whole entire life was transformed. As we read in Acts 17, these men were "turning the world upside-down," because they had been turned. This prayer is even cited in the Canons of Dort in response to the Arminian doctrines of repentance and conversion being "only an act of man." Instead, recognizing that "God does infuse or pour into our hearts the new qualities of faith, obedience, and the experiencing of his love," we follow the continuous practice of the Church, which prays with the prophet: *Convert me, Lord, and I shall be converted* (CD, 3/4, Rejection of Errors 6).

They were converted, and so they turned to God; they were changed by God, and so they turned to him with a changed lifestyle; they were restored by God unto him from idols, so they could be described as having turned from idols to the Lord.

A Change in Affection

This change in direction led to *a change in affection*. Because of what God did to turn them they began to serve the living and true God, and to wait for his Son from heaven (vv. 9–10). The implication is that before they served the living God they served a dead god. Before they served this true and genuine God, they served not false gods, as though there is one among many, but they served unreal, imagined gods. And so they were changed, they were turned and as the result of this change and turning from the greatest idol of all, which is self, they had come to serve God, and to wait for his Son from heaven.

It was not just the mind that was changed, not just the will, in which we are able then to choose, and to do, and to follow a path and a course of life; but the affections were changed. This is the deep-rooted aspect of our being. They are the things that we long for most, that we admire the most, and that we love the most. They are not really emotions, as that is one aspect—but it is that quality of our humanity that loves, and that longs and desires for something. This has been changed as well. Christ has healed our wills, our minds, but also our affections. And having done this we even more and more constantly pray that Christ would turn us even more in our day-to-day lives towards these things, to serve and to wait.

Recall the story of Jesus' temptation in the wilderness. Our Lord's final temptation was that the devil brought him up to a high point to show him all the kingdoms of the earth in all their glory. The devil then says, "These all I shall give you if you will only serve, bow down and worship me" (Matthew 4:9). Our Lord Jesus Christ, amazingly being God in the flesh, cries out and rebukes the devil with the words of the book of Deuteronomy: "You shall worship the Lord your God, and Him only shall you serve" (Matthew 4:10 cf. Deuteronomy 6:13). Throughout Deuteronomy there is another verb that is added on to that service of the one true God: "cleave" or "cling." We are to cling to this one true God, to serve this living God, to cleave to this true God, who has revealed Himself to us in Christ. We were saved that we might serve.[3]

But how do I know if I am serving him? It goes back to the Word. They received the Word in a context of much affliction yet with the joy of the Holy Spirit. We need to love the Word, brothers and sisters. We need to receive it as the Word of God without any qualifications, any hesitation, and with no qualms about it. As his Word, it is God's communication to us. Receive it and love it.

But when do I serve this living and true God? You serve him at all times, even as the Thessalonians did in times of great blessing and times of great persecution. We serve the Lord at all times. We cannot live our lives as schizophrenic "Sunday Christians." We love and we serve him, and him alone, at all times.

But where do I serve him? These new Christians used to serve their gods in temples. Where do we serve our God now? We've turned our back on these idols and temples, they say, but now, where do we serve him? "Neither on this mountain nor in Jerusalem," Jesus said to the Samaritan woman, "But the hour is coming, and is now here, when the true worshipers will worship the Father in spirit and truth" (John 4:21, 23).

And with what shall I serve this living God? With bodies, and souls, with mind and with might, with lives and with lips. Our whole person is to serve him. Not one part of us is reserved for ourselves. Not one aspect of our thought life can we keep to ourselves and indulge that favorite idol. Not one part of our actions that we can somehow keep sealed off from God, and his lordship over us.

Why do we serve this God? Why do we serve him as a living and true God, and why do we turn our back upon idols? It is because we are servants. The verb here used "to serve" is the same root as the noun that is used throughout the New Testament to mean that we are bondservants of God, and slaves of Christ, as Paul says in Romans 6. We want to give our lives to serve ourselves, and whatever thing we give ourselves to, we become its servant, its slave. But now we have given ourselves, having been delivered by the Lord of self, Jesus Christ, we give ourselves to the Lord, we lay our lives down as living sacrifices, as bondservants of Christ. We find our true freedom in serving him. We find our true liberation by being given to him, and to him alone. Serve him, brothers and sisters. Give your life to him. Give yourself to him. Do not hold back. Serve this living and true God.

What is so interesting here is that he says our purpose now is to serve (*douleuein*) God, but also to wait (*anamenein*) for his Son from heaven. Paul here juxtaposes two verbs, one that is very active—to serve—but also one that seems to have something of passiveness—to wait. Our affections are changed not only in how we love the Lord, which causes us to actively serve him, but also in terms of how we even await the Lord. We are called to work, but we are also called to rest. We are called to be active but also to be passive. We are called to be in the world but also not of the world, to serve God while we are here on earth but yet to long for him who is described literally as "the Deliverer" (*ton rhuomenon*) who will take us back with him to heaven.[4]

We serve him in every way possible in this life, but at the same time we are doing so, awaiting. We are doing so, longingly. In his treatise, "On the Mortification of Sin," John Owen described one result and one response to our sin that we need to have. We have a constant longing and breathing after deliverance from our sins.[5] A longing and a breathing after, meaning, that our lives should be characterized by this longing aspect, this waiting aspect, for Jesus Christ from heaven. We need to be more and more a heavenly-minded people. We need to be aware of our blessed hope, the coming of our Lord and Savior from heaven. More and more we should live our lives in the light of eternity, with all the afflictions around us, with all the world's temptations, with all of the things that we do, our jobs, and our relationships. In all of this we must long. As Calvin said, "Unless, therefore, we learn to look to Christ, our hearts will fail us at every moment."[6] We must have our affections more and more transformed by eschatology, what we believe about the coming of our Lord Jesus Christ. Paul goes on to say that they themselves knew of his coming, that they were awaiting his coming, and that his coming would be a great and climactic and a triumphant victory (1 Thessalonians 4).

That coming should impact how we live our lives now. The one whom God raised from the dead is coming to deliver[…] us from the wrath to come (v. 10). He is coming for us, to rescue us, literally. He is not coming to us. To come for us, is for him to come in grace and mercy—to rescue and to deliver us from the wrath to come. He is not merely coming to us in wrath, and judgment, and flaming fire, as he goes on to say in 2 Thessalonians 1. His coming to us is not a thing that we should want. His coming for us is what we should long for.

Is he coming for you, or is he coming to you? If you long for him and his word; if you serve him and wait for him; if you've been turned by him, then know that he is coming for you in grace and in mercy.

The coming of Christ should not be a fear to us, but it should be something that we long for and love. Not to make us afraid but to cause us to cry out even more, "Maranatha," come quickly, our Lord!

Conclusion

Wouldn't it be amazing for our churches to be like the church in Thessalonica? Wouldn't it be amazing for us as individuals, but especially as churches, if our reputation preceded us in these things? What if we were known for having been turned by God dramatically? What if we were known for serving God night and day with heart and mouth and mind? What if we were known for longing for his coming and loving that coming? Is that our reputation? May God by his Spirit make it so!

6

The Motivation of Gospel Ministry

1 Thessalonians 2:1–6

For all of us, there is something that gets us out of bed. What is it for you? You can be motivated by fear of failure. You can be motivated by the hope of success. For us as believers, we should also be motivated by the reality that God has redirected our lives so that we can live according to our original calling: "to glorify God, and fully to enjoy him forever" (WLC, Q&A 1).

In 1 Thessalonians 2:1–6, the apostle Paul speaks of *the motivation of gospel ministry*. We see in this larger section of verses 1–16, as the heading in your Bible may say, that Paul is reflecting on his ministry among them. And as we look at verses 1–6 keep in mind what Paul said previously in 1:9–10. Paul spoke there about our new life in Christ, which means we have a new direction and we have new affections.

Affections are the deep-rooted longings and desires in our hearts. Note in 2:1–6 how Paul's affections have changed. John Stott said one of the abiding lessons we learn from 1 Thessalonians 2–3 "is the insight it gives us into Paul's pastoral heart … more perhaps than anywhere else in his letter, he discloses his mind, expresses his emotions and bares his soul."[1] He gives three false motives for ministry in verse 3, but then goes on to clearly distinguish his motives from them.

First, he says one motive may be error: For our appeal does not spring from error (v. 3). Instead of error he says he speaks the gospel of God (v. 2). Second, he says another motive may be impurity, meaning, impure motives for greed: For our appeal does not spring from … impurity (v. 3). In verses 5–6 he goes on to refute that he was greedy and in verse 8 he says he actually shared his life with them, and not the other way around. This is why he says he preached not to please man, but to please God (v. 4). Third, a final false motive may be deception: For our appeal does not spring from … any attempt to deceive (v. 3). Deception is doing one thing over here, but then doing a totally different thing over there. It is hypocrisy in action. Instead, he says he had been approved by God … who tests our hearts (v. 4).[2] His ministry was not conducted in hypocrisy but simplicity.[3] He goes on to say in verse 10 that he and his cohorts were open in their godly conduct among the Thessalonians. So what does Paul say about the true motivation of gospel ministry?

The Need of Humanity

The first motivation for gospel ministry is *the need of humanity*. He says his, Silas', and Timothy's coming to the Thessalonians was not in vain (v. 1). Quite possibly this can mean that his ministry was not fruitless, as they were his fruit. Better yet, what he is saying is that they as ministers came not empty (*kenē*), that is, not with empty hands so that they needed to receive from the Thessalonians.[4] Instead, they came with full hands and hearts to give to them. Paul is saying that like our Lord, he "came not to be served but to serve" (Mark 10:45).

So what was their need and what did he have in his hands to give? Their need, as verse 9 says, was to be turned away from idols and to be turned to the living and true God that they might be saved. The need of humanity is salvation.

The world needs salvation because it is born into sin. I recently listened to a conversation between one of my pastoral interns and a well-meaning young man at a coffee shop. The young man talked about how we're all born with a clean slate and depending on what we do we go up or down with God. Whether the world realizes it or not, all of us were born sinners because every one of us is a son or daughter of our first father, Adam (Romans 5:12–19). And because we were born sinners we were born guilty before God (Ephesians 2:1–3).

The world needs salvation because it continues to sin actually. Do you love your Creator more than yourself? Do you love your neighbor as you love yourself?

The world needs salvation because it cannot save itself. Like a prisoner on death row, there is no escape. Like a person stuck in the middle of quick sand, you will slowly and surely be pulled down and down to your death.

This was the great need of humanity, including the Thessalonians, and Paul was motivated by it. As he says in Romans 10, his "heart's desire and prayer to God" for his own people was "that they may be saved" (Romans 10:1). And notice that he was so motivated by their need that despite the great risk of persecution and violence, he opened his heart and mouth to give them what they needed—the gospel. As he says, he was willing to bring this message despite persecution: though we had already suffered and been shamefully treated at Philippi, as you know, we had boldness in our God to declare to you the gospel of God in the midst of much conflict (v. 2). Nonetheless, their need was so great that no obstacle could stand in Paul's way to be bold to preach the gospel. The ancient preacher known as Ambrosiaster (4th c.), said of this text: "it is a sign of a devout and faithful preacher not to be afraid to preach the Word of God under pressure, indicating thereby that whoever is afraid to preach because of current fears is useless."[5]

So what does this mean for us today as a church? Don't be trapped into thinking, "This is for you, Pastor, but not for me." Remember, Paul says he was an example to them and they emulated him. Peter speaks of shepherds being examples to their flocks, as well (1 Peter 5). You can profit from this text in two ways. First, join in your pastor's ministry by praying for the lost and that he would be motivated to see them saved. Second, follow your pastor's lead in seeking to clearly articulate the gospel to those who need to be turned from idols to the living and true God. Remember, like we learned from the Thessalonians in 1:8, we need to have a love of the world.

The Approval of God

And it is this living and true God who also motivates Paul. The second motivation for gospel ministry is *the approval of God*: we have been approved by God to be entrusted with the gospel (v. 4). This is a motivator because it made Paul—as it should make any true minister—stand in sheer wonder and say "God has set his approval on me of all men!" Paul was a persecutor, now he's a preacher. Paul sought righteousness in the law, now he sought it in Christ. Paul was an enemy, now he was a friend. Oh, this is why Paul sat back and reveled in the gospel, saying, "The saying is trustworthy and deserving of full acceptance, that Christ Jesus came into the world to save sinners, of whom *I* am foremost" (1 Timothy 1:15).

Those of you who are preparing for the ministry don't ever forget who you were. Don't ever forget where you came from. Don't ever forget how rebellious you were. Don't ever forget how wicked you were. Don't ever forget where you were going—hell. But don't ever forget how you were snatched from a one-way ticket to perdition (Jude 23). And stand in wonder and amazement at what God has done.

Brothers and sisters, this is such a motivator to a true gospel minister. And I want you to learn from it. I often think of the verses in the New Testament that call you to follow your leaders (Hebrews 13:17). And one of the things I am always thinking of is why does God call whom he calls into the ministry? Why did God call me of all men? I once had a best friend across the street who was such a good kid, who went to church, and who seemed so pious. When I reconnected with him after I graduated from Seminary—and I've never told my mom and wife this—he came to my graduation and we spent time together afterward. I was left with a sense of why? Why did God call me? Why didn't God call this brother who was pious, who never knew a day apart from God's grace? The reason is that God wants to show the surpassing power of his grace in men who know the depths of their hatred towards God, so that you can see a living example of grace (1 Timothy 1:16). It's what Paul said at the end of Galatians 1, when he recounted his conversion and call to the ministry: "And I was still unknown in person to the churches of Judea that are in Christ. They only were hearing it said, 'He who used to persecute us is now preaching the faith he once tried to destroy.' And they glorified God *because of me*" (Galatians 1:22–24).

And it was because Paul was approved by God that he was entrusted with the gospel (v. 4). This really is amazing! He whose hands once were bloody with preachers of the gospel is now considered trustworthy to hold that very gospel! What a picture of God's amazing grace! To be entrusted with the gospel is to be given responsibility over the family fortune while the owner is gone. We call this stewardship. This is another way of saying what Paul said in 1 Corinthians 4:1: "This is how one should regard us, as servants of Christ and stewards of the mysteries of God." Servants and stewards. In other words, a minister is a custodian, a conserver of something that is not his. In my opinion, two of the best ways this has been communicated in historic Christian worship is the preaching robe and the pulpit. The robe covers me up so you can hear Christ. The robe says I have been trained as a servant of the Word. The robe says I have been examined. The robe says I have been called. The robe says I have been ordained and set apart to serve. In other words, it's not about me. Also, the pulpit says to you that it's not about me. I stand behind it because on it the Word sits. The Word is before you, I am behind it. The Word does its work, I am only a voice. In the end, Paul is saying that, "God approves of those whom He has formed for Himself according to His own good pleasure."[6]

And Paul is an example of how to be a steward of the gifts God has given. In fact, Peter speaks in the same way of all believers in 1 Peter 4:10: "As each has received a gift, use it to serve one another, as good stewards of God's varied grace." Stand in awe, brothers and sisters, that no matter our gift, God has approved us and called us to be stewards of it.

The Glory of God

The third motivation for gospel ministry is *the glory of God*. As those who came not with empty hands to receive, but with full hands to give; and as those who were called to be servants of the divine Word, the gospel minister is one who serves for the glory of God. As he says, so we speak, not to please man, but to please God who tests our hearts (v. 4).

This is a necessary mark of a true gospel minister. Listen to what Paul says in Galatians 1:10: "For am I now seeking the approval of man, or of God? Or am I trying to please man? If I were still trying to please man, I would not be a servant of Christ." To please man is not to be a servant of Christ; to please God is to be a servant of Christ.

"But I want a little more entertainment." No, you need the gospel. "But I want a little more humor." No, you need the gospel. "But I want a few more stories." No, you need the gospel. Shall I continue? It's not about what *you* want, it's about what you need. Thank God he doesn't give us what we want, but what we truly need.

This is also the necessary goal of true gospel ministry. Calvin said "true ministers of the Gospel should make it their purpose to do their utmost for God, and to do it from the heart, not with any outward regard for the world."[7] As the ministry of the Word seeks to bring glory to God, this should lead you to give him glory. My prayer is that after each and every sermon my people can go away praising God for his Word, praising God for his grace, and praising God for who God is. If they leave remembering an illustration or the color of my tie or how my hair looked or how I made them feel, I have failed. As a pastor and preacher, I am to lead people to the "throne of grace, that [they] may receive mercy and find grace to help in time of need" (Hebrews 4:16), and having found it, to give unceasing glory to God.

Conclusion

Brothers and sisters, what should motivate your minister? What should motivate us as a people who sit under the ministry of the Word? We need to be motivated by the great need of the world around us for what we have here. What is that? What Martin Luther said in his ninety-five theses: "The true treasure of the church is the most holy gospel of the glory and the grace of God."[8] The world needs that.

May the ministry of the Word be approved and entrusted to offer it to the world to the glory of our gracious triune God.

7

An All-Round Ministry

1 Thessalonians 2:7–12

What is "the ministry," as we speak of it? As historic Christian and Protestant churches, we do believe that there is such a thing as the ministry as distinct from the members of the Church of Jesus Christ. For example, Paul says that God himself "has appointed in the church first apostles, second prophets, third teachers" and then he goes on to ask rhetorically, "Are all apostles? Are all prophets? Are all teachers?" (1 Corinthians 11:28, 29) Of course, we know the answer is no. There is such a thing as the ministry of the gospel. There are those who are *set aside* to serve Christ in a particular way. They are *not* set above the church, but they are set apart from the church for the church.

Like everything else in life we all have our opinions, ideas, and ideals. But like everything of necessity and of importance in the church of Jesus Christ, we can thank God that he has not left us to our opinions, but he has given to us his Word to shape our minds and our attitudes as to what the ministry of the gospel really is.

This passage speaks of what C. H. Spurgeon described once as *An All-Round Ministry*, meaning a well-rounded ministry of the gospel.[1] As Paul writes of himself he lays out an ideal for all ministers to attain. His ministry was well-rounded and we, like common rocks you might find out at the beach, must have our edges smoothed according to the Word of God. Like a common rock, there is not much to look at except a bunch of rough edges. But like a rock that is placed in a tumbler that begins to cause its color and its luster to shine and to make those rough edges smooth and appealing, in the same way God has given to the church sinful men to be smoothed out even in our own midst. And we recognize, of course, that some of us need a little more vigorous turning in that tumbler, and a little extra time in it than others, to smooth us out and to cause us to shine as God would want us to.

So what is an all-round ministry? In contrast to what Paul said were false motives for the ministry of the gospel—words of flattery, greed, and self-aggrandizement (vv. 1–6)—he says, but we were gentle among you (v. 7). Beginning with this verse he describes the all-round ministry.

A Gentle Ministry

An all-round ministry is *a gentle ministry*. Paul shows his heart towards the Thessalonians in the words before us and throughout these early chapters of 1 Thessalonians. Speaking on behalf of Silvanus and Timothy, he says that they were affectionately desirous of you (v. 8). A pastor has a longing, a deep desire for his people. This word is used only once in the entire New Testament, and it comes out of the

Greek translation of the Old Testament. There it is used in contexts describing a great desire, even the desire to die as with Job (Job 3:21). Thus Paul is saying that they had a deep-rooted, deep affection, and deep longing for the believers in Thessalonica, because they had become very dear to us (v. 8). Notice how he describes this gentleness and affection by using two metaphors. He speaks of himself as a mother as well as a father.

First, he speaks of himself as a mother: We were gentle among you, like a nursing mother taking care of her own children (v. 7). He was like a nursing mother (*trophos*),[2] looking upon her little baby with nothing but love, care, concern, and affection. As a nursing mother totally gives herself to her little one, to care and give life, and raise and to protect, so, too, was Paul with them. As a mother holds a little baby close to her heart, so, too, the apostle Paul says that he held them dear and near to his heart. Like a nursing mother pours her life into a little baby, in the same way Paul says he poured out his life for them like a nursing mother. As John Calvin said, "a mother … reveals a wonderful and extraordinary love, because she spares no trouble or effort, avoids no care, is not wearied by their coming and going, and gladly even gives her own life blood to be drained."[3] Like a nursing mother "bends down to an infant and speaks to the stammering child, so that the child may learn to speak," in the same way, Paul accommodated himself to the Thessalonians and spoke to them the precious words of truth.[4] What an example Paul gives for the gospel minister to follow.

It is amazing how Paul uses this feminine metaphor and image to describe himself, and to describe the minister in terms of the care and affection towards the church. Notice how he uses this same image, yet in a different way, with the Galatians: "My little children, for whom I am again in the anguish of childbirth until Christ is formed in you! I wish I could be present with you now and change my tone, for I am perplexed about you" (Galatians 4:19–20). In Galatians he had been chastising them: "Who has bewitched you?" (Galatians 3:1) "Having begun by the Spirit, are you now being perfected by the flesh?" (Galatians 3:3) "Does he who supplies the Spirit to you and works miracles among you do so by works of the law, or by hearing with faith?" (Galatians 3:5) In chapter 4, though, he wished to change his tone. He wanted to look in the eyes of these brothers and sisters and be able to communicate face to face. It's like sending emails today. We cannot discern the mood and the facial expressions, the affections from the heart or even the anger that comes through, and instead we assume and impute things. Although the image is used in slightly different ways in these two passages, the same sort of image of a mother and her children is used. Like the mother in anguish, travail, and turmoil brings forth a baby into a new state of life, in the same way Paul describes himself like a mother for his flock to bring them, through anguish, to a new state of affairs, a new state of existence, a new level of understanding and graciousness towards each other.

It is important for us to meditate on this imagery in terms of how we might think of the ministry in our midst. All too often, we might place the minister on a pedestal with a spotlight on him. We speak of the ministry as the highest calling that any man can have, which it is.[5] We speak of preaching as the very voice of Christ to us, his people, which it is. But we romanticize the minister. We think of the minister and the ministry and think it is all positive, all fun and games, and that it must always be like having a direct line to God. Paul says it involved anguish, brothers and sisters. Paul describes it as giving birth. As men we do not know what that feels like, but we know that it involves anguish. Paul says this elsewhere in Second Corinthians as he defends his ministry against so-called "super apostles" (*huperlian apostolōn*):

> ... but as servants of God we commend ourselves in every way: by great endurance, in afflictions, hardships, calamities, beatings, imprisonments, riots, labors, sleepless nights, hunger ... through honor and dishonor, through slander and praise. We are treated as impostors, and yet are true; as unknown, and yet well known; as dying, and behold, we live; as punished, and yet not killed; as sorrowful, yet always rejoicing; as poor, yet making many rich; as having nothing, yet possessing everything. (2 Corinthians 6:4–5, 8-10)

The ministry is a constant dying while the minister lives; the ministry is full of sorrow, yet at the same time full of rejoicing. The ministry is a walking contradiction. We might see with our eyes what looks to be very glamorous and exciting, but what we do not see is the sorrow; what we do not see is the dying; what we do not see is the agonizing. Paul writes as a mother who gave life and who gives of her own self to sustain life. In the same way the minister gives himself for the life of others.

This gentleness in dealing with others is also shown in the high priest of the Old Testament. The high priest wore the ephod, a shoulder apparatus with twelve colorful stones in front, each with the name of an Israelite tribe close to his heart. The people were near to the high priest. On that ephod were also two black onyx stones, with six names upon each. He also bore the weight of his people's sins. He bore their anguish. He bore their burdens. He had to uphold in his own self a congregation upon his shoulders. As a minister, he pointed his people to none other than Jesus, of whom Peter said, "cast[...] all your anxieties on him, because he cares for you" (1 Peter 5:7). The minister of the gospel is an earthly example of this, wasting away, dying yet living, sorrowing yet rejoicing, anguishing to bring life to his people, and bearing their burdens.

Second, Paul also describes this gentleness by speaking of himself as a father: For you know how like a father with his children (v. 11). He was like a father who loves his sons and daughters, who is concerned for them, who is happy for them, and who has great joy to see them grow up. Those of us fathers know what it is to have these feelings that Paul had for the Thessalonians, Paul was very personal in his words toward the Thessalonians. And he was not just personal, he was personal with a passion. The Thessalonians were his spiritual children. They were the ones he loved through hard times and great times. He had been with them; cried for them; prayed with them; rejoiced with them; and he's anguished for them.

Remember how he called himself merely "Paul" (1:1). He did not heap up any titles. He said, "we could have made demands as apostles of Christ" (2:6). But he writes to them just as Paul. They knew him by name and he knew them. He cares for them and they care for him. Describing preaching, C. H. Spurgeon once put it like this: "when we speak as ministers, and not as men; as preachers, instead of penitents; as theologians instead of disciples, we fail."[6] When we do not speak as Paul speaks, personally, sincerely, passionately, and even gently, we fail in our duty as pastors. If the minister distances himself, such as having a "pastor-mobile" like the Pope's "Pope mobile," he is a failure. We must not speak merely as theologians or ministers, but as sinners and disciples; as brothers, or else we fail. This is why we follow Paul's excellent example and as shepherds visit our flocks "from house to house" (Acts 20:20).[7] In the words of John Calvin, "No man will ever be a good pastor, unless he shows himself to be a father to the church entrusted to him."[8]

A Godly Ministry

The ministry is also *a godly ministry*. The ministry is not just the affection and feeling that he has in his heart, but it should lead to tangible expressions of these. Paul, Silvanus, and Timothy worked hard, as he says, that we might not be a burden to any of you (v. 9). They were being an example of hard workers, of toiling and anguishing for them. A good minister "should remove all obstacles in their course as far as they are able."[9] But they were doing more than just working hard; they were striving with all that was in them to be an example of godliness. This is why Paul says to young pastor Timothy elsewhere, "Keep a close watch on yourself and on the teaching. Persist in this, for by so doing you will save both yourself and your hearers" (1 Timothy 4:16). The ministry cannot merely be words, it must also be evidenced in deeds, and the minister must exemplify that to the people of God. Paul goes on to say that they were witnesses, and God also, how holy and righteous and blameless was our conduct toward you believers (v. 10). God help us ministers to be godly and righteous.

Like the high priest who bore his people's names, burdens, and concerns, so the minister of the gospel is to do with the people the Lord has given him. Your minister bears your burdens. Yet the minister often has no one to bear his. He experiences "dying, and behold, we live" and being "sorrowful, yet always rejoicing" (2 Corinthians 6:9, 10). Yet one thing that the people of God can do for their ministers is to bear them up in their prayers. Even as the Israelites would see the high priest going into the Holy of Holies, praying for him not to be struck down, so too it is with Christians today. Although you may not be able to bear your minister's burden, you may be able to bear him up in prayer. One thing in particular to pray for is for your pastor's godliness. Pray that he would be an example, not only in words, but also in deeds. Pray that Paul's words would be true of him: being holy and righteous and blameless (v. 10). "But my Pastor does not sin. He's a perfect husband; he's a perfect dad; he's the best of friends; he's the perfect son." Realize that your minister is a wretched sinner. He is a filthy sinner in thought, word, and deed. Pray for the ministry of the Word across the world to be effective, but pray particularly for *your* minister. Why? Because the point of the minister's godliness is not an end in itself, but is to share it with others. James Fergusson said it like this: "It is not enough that a Minister of Christ abstain from such scandalous sins of flattery, greed and ambition, as time-servers are guilty of; but he must also labor for the exercise of such virtues as may commend his ministry."[10] The minister's greatest fear is that people would say of him, "Do as I say, not as I do." God help us all that that is not true. The minister is to be an example to his people. Paul describes the ministry by saying we were ready to share with you, not only the gospel of God, but also our own selves (v. 8). He literally says, "our own souls" (*tas heautōn psuchas*). The ancient preacher Chrysostom said about this phrase: "For merely to preach is not the same thing as to give the soul. For that indeed is more precious, but the latter, is a matter of more difficulty .... The Gospel we indeed proclaim, because God commanded it; but so much do we love you, that, if it were possible, we would have given even our souls."[11] In the words of Paul to the Corinthians, "I will most gladly spend and be spent for your souls" (2 Corinthians 12:15). A true pastor, then, has "a higher regard for the well-being of the Church than for their own life."[12]

When your minister reads a passage like this about holiness and godliness to you, he is not doing it to commend himself. He does not say it to put himself on a pedestal in front of you, to say that he is "holier than thou" or set above you. Understand that when he reads a passage like this, he feels like a total hypocrite. But this is the Word of God. By faith, we have to see even as God sees, beyond the outward and see the inward. To see the example of the minister for what it is, it is a faint reflection of Christ. But any evidence of godliness that he can exhibit to you is not to commend himself but is to point you to Christ, that you both might decrease, that Christ might increase.

Any ability to speak the gospel is to point us to Christ, our great Prophet and Teacher. Any evidence of being gentle toward you is merely a faint reflection of Jesus, the Great Shepherd of the sheep. Yet Paul does say that he was an example, even as a sinner, and that the Thessalonians followed: "you became imitators of us, and of the Lord" (1:6). That old evangelical adage is true, that people do not care how much you know, until they know how much you care.

A Gospel Ministry

But all the affection of his heart, all the things that he did with his hands, meant nothing apart from the words of the gospel. The ministry, then, ultimately, is *a gospel ministry*. All that gentleness and godliness, all of it was expressed in the best of ways in the words of what he describes so often here as the gospel of God himself (vv. 8, 9). The gospel is God's because he himself has spoken it. He himself has done it in Christ. And all of it came to the Thessalonians through the person of Paul. There was a nineteenth-century Episcopalian preacher by the name of Phillips Brooks (1835–1893) who once defined preaching with three words: "truth through personality."[13] Paul's gentleness and godliness before them was merely the way through which the truth of the gospel could be communicated to them.

Notice the connection between Paul's affection for the Thessalonians and the gospel (v. 8). His longing for them was that he might preach the gospel of God to them. The pastoral heart and concern has a twofold purpose in terms of the gospel. The twofold reason of preaching the gospel is to win sinners to Christ and to prepare saints for a life of godliness. Preaching's purpose is to turn to Christ and then to turn away from sin. He wanted them to flee from idols to God constantly (cf. 1:9–10).

Look also at how Paul speaks to them as a father in such moving verbs: to exhort, to encourage, and to charge (vv. 11, 12). When the

Bible heaps up repetition, we need to listen. This repetition shows how important this is. How did he exhort, encourage, and charge them? To walk in a manner worthy of God (v. 12). Your Christian life, what Paul calls your walk (cf. Romans 16:2; Ephesians 4:1; Philippians 1:27; Colossians 1:10), must be worthy of the new life God has given you. He is calling you into his eternal kingdom and glory so reflect that now. He is calling you into his eternal kingdom and glory so live like that in this life. John Calvin said it like this: "It now remains for us to respond to God's call, i.e., to show ourselves to be such children to Him as He is a Father to us."[14] So Paul wants us to live a Christian life that is worthy of God and that shows thankfulness, gratitude, and amazement that God has saved sinners such as us. We are to live this way because God himself is the one who is calling us into his own kingdom and glory (v. 12).

This is how he speaks elsewhere: "Work out your own salvation with fear and trembling." Why? "For it is God who works in you, both to will and to work for his good pleasure" (Philippians 2:12, 13). Walk in a way that is worthy of God. Show yourself to be of righteousness and holiness and blamelessness in your conduct. Why? Because of the gospel. Because God himself is calling you, knowing full well your sins, and your slavery to the devil's kingdom, and he brings you into his own kingdom. He takes you from sin and shame to glory. How can you do anything less than glorify him? How can you do anything less than lay your life down as a living sacrifice? How can you do anything less than turn to him to serve him (1:9), to serve the living and true God? Not just to pray a prayer to get in, but to serve him, knowing that you'll never repay him. You'll never give him back what he desires or deserves, but yet serve him nonetheless.

Conclusion

"What is the ministry?" I asked you at the beginning. The word ministry means "service." The ministry is just that: a service by a servant, who does not put himself right here in this place because he wants to, or is self-appointed, but because Christ has put him here to serve you. And a minister serves both God and people in proclaiming the Word (2:2, 4, 8, 9, 12) and in loving people (2:7, 8, 11).[15]

All the gentleness, if there be any in us, is to point you to Jesus Christ, the Great Shepherd. It's only a faint reflection, and God help us to be more. All the godliness, again, if there is any, may it only point you to Jesus Christ, and his righteousness. He's the great chief Shepherd and Bishop of our souls—your minister isn't. Any ability to preach the gospel with any bit of clarity whatsoever, is only because it points us to Jesus Christ, the great Prophet of our souls.

The minister merely stammers and stumbles and stutters. But it is Christ that you hear. We don't hear the man, we hear God. We don't see him as he is in truth, not as gentle as he ought to be, but we see Christ. We don't see as he is in reality, a sinner, but we see Jesus Christ. We don't hear merely his words, but we hear Jesus. The ministry brings us to Jesus Christ, to his feet, to his throne, into his glorious kingdom.

8

Hearing the Lord in a World of Noise

1 Thessalonians 2:13

Ever since the serpent assaulted God's Word in the Garden of Eden, God's Word has existed in the midst of a world filled with all sorts of noise. I'm not speaking of the noise that we are accustomed to—the noise of the world around us such as walking on hard floors, clapping hands, or traffic on the roads. What I am talking about is the very real spiritual noise that seeks to drown out what God himself has already said. The devil hid himself in the serpent with Adam and Eve so that he could distract them with the question, "Hath God said?" (Genesis 3:1; KJV). The devil came and tried to drown out God's clear command with his noise, speaking his own version of the gospel—a gospel of self-help and a gospel of your best life now. Not only did Adam and Eve live in a world of noise so did their sons and daughters. For example, Genesis

4 describes the line of Cain as being filled with all sorts of things that they did in a very wonderful way; things that we might describe as common grace. The line of Cain was filled with city-builders, men like Nimrod who challenged the very authority of God, men who herded livestock, played music, and who worked with metal. But we read nothing of the Word of the Lord in their midst. In contrast, we read, as it were, of a huddled little mass in a corner, who in those days "began to call upon the name of the LORD" (Genesis 4:26). The line of Seth existed in a world that had all kinds of distractions, yet they gathered to hear the Word. In the midst of the Promised Land, the Israelites also had to content with all kinds of noise. There was the worship of Baal, its rituals, sacrifices, priests, and false prophets, all which sought to distract Israel's attention. And at times they had success drawing away the Israelites to marry those that were priestesses and followers of Baal of Peor for example (Numbers 25).

In the midst of world, then, the church exists and the Word of God exists. In the midst of giving thanks Paul thanks God constantly for the fact that the Thessalonians heard, received, and accepted the Word, and that it began to be lively in their midst, being at work in you believers (2:13). And so we must learn to do the same amidst so much spiritual, religious, and philosophical noise. We must learn to hear the Word of God as it comes through the words of a mere man, your minister, even as the Thessalonians heard Paul's words not as the word of men but as what it really is, the word of God (2:13). How do we do this?

Expectantly—"Lord, I expect you to speak"

How do we hear the Lord in a world filled with so much noise? We learn here to do so *expectantly*. We gather on the Lord's Day to hear the memoirs of the prophets and apostles, as Justin Martyr described in the ancient church.[1] These words not the mere words of men, they really are the Word of God. And if that is true, we come to worship with expectation that God himself will speak to us even as a friend speaks to us face to face. Our prayer, then, should be, "Lord, I expect you to speak."

This means that God still speaks. If anyone tells you that Reformed churches do not believe God speaks anymore, you need to tell them that God's voice is as clear and as fresh today as it was when prophets and apostles roamed the earth. When we hear the Word proclaimed we hear it not as the word of men but as what it really is, the word of God. When a minister preaches the Word, not the words of men, not his own words, not words of flattery and pretext for greed (2:5), he is God's voice. His words are not merely about God, but his words *are* God's words.[2] When a minister preaches sincerely to honor God, to preach Christ and not himself, we can be assured that it is the very Word of God that we hear. As our forefathers said,

> When this Word of God is now preached in the church by preachers lawfully called, we believe that the very Word of God is proclaimed, and received by the faithful; and that neither any other Word of God is to be invented nor is to be expected from heaven: and that now the Word itself which is preached is to be regarded, not the minister that preaches; for even if he be evil and a sinner, nevertheless the Word of God remains still true and good.[3]

The preaching of the Word is the Word because the Word "living and active, sharper than any two-edged sword, piercing to the division of soul and of spirit, of joints and of marrow, and discerning the thoughts and intentions of the heart" (Hebrews 4:12). In a word, Paul says there is a real presence of God himself in the preaching of the Word. Calvin described it in terms of "Christ offer[ing] Himself to us through the Gospel"[4] and elsewhere that the Father offers us Christ "clothed with his gospel."[5]

This means that we assemble not merely out of ritual or merely out of routine. God is no dead idol, but the living God. We have turned "from idols to serve the living and true God" (1:9). He is alive. He is active. Therefore he still speaks. Because of this we must come before him in worship expectantly, clinging to his every Word as heard from the mouth of the minister. We come to taste the sweetness of the Word, which is like "honey and drippings of the honeycomb" (Psalm 19:10b). To do this, the Thessalonians "looked beyond the minister, and lifted up their eyes to God in order to receive His Word," and so must we.[6]

This also means that we need to prepare ourselves to hear him speak his Word through his minister. We have to prepare our hearts all week long with a spirit of anticipation, knowing that we are going to enter the presence of God, knowing that something great is going to happen. We prepare ourselves to "go up to the mountain of the Lord, to the house of the God of Jacob" in the expectation "that he may teach us his ways and that we may walk in his paths" (Isaiah 2:3). By faith ascend into heaven when we assemble. We come to a heavenly mountain upon which Jesus Christ is speaking. We wake up and say, "Come, let us go the heavenly mountain, let us hear the Word of the Lord."

We need to prepare our minds for this reality, meditating upon what God has said to us the previous week. The Puritans recommended that their parishioners take notes so that they could review them.[7] This helps us hide the Word deeply within our hearts. We should re-read the passage that is behind us and read the one before us.

We must prepare our souls all week long by praying. As I have already said, in light of what Paul says about the reality of the gospel ministry, you need to be praying for the ministry of the gospel. Let me exhort you to pray that your hearts would be prepared like soil. Pray that the Holy Spirit removes the rocks, pray that he breaks it up, and pray that he waters it when you arrive. And as you do so, you will be ready to receive the little seed of the Word to be planted as you hear the Word.

Hungrily—"Lord, I need you to speak"

How do we hear the Lord in a world filled with so much noise? When the Lord's Day rolls around we must hear the Word *hungrily*, crying out to God, "Lord, I need you to speak." This means we have a hunger not just that God will speak in general, or that he will speak to someone else, but that he would speak to me. The Heidelberg Catechism describes this in terms of faith in Christ. It is a wonderfully personal answer about true faith:

> True faith is not only a sure knowledge, whereby *I* hold for truth all that God has revealed to us in His Word, but also a hearty trust, which the Holy Ghost works in *me* by the Gospel, that not only to others, but to *me* also, forgiveness of sins, everlasting righteousness, and salvation are freely given by God, merely of grace, only for the sake of Christ's merits (HC, Q&A 21; emphasis added).

"Not only to others, but to *me* also." Do you hunger for the Word like this? Why must I come hungrily? Why do I need God to speak to me through the words of a man, which are in reality the Word of God? It is because the Word of God, not merely written but as it is explained, exposited, and expounded is the food our souls. We live in a world of instant gratification. We have our iPhones, iPads, and our mobile devices, which we can pull out right after church to check email, to check scores, and to do so many other things. The world of instant gratification pulls us and it can easily become our world. This can have an effect on our spiritual life, as we begin to expect things to happen instantly, and if they don't, we move on to the next thing. Yet all that information we access and all that so-called Facetime doesn't last forever. It's here, it's a feeling, it passes, and it doesn't go on forever. It leaves us feeling empty. But the Word does not. The Word "endures forever" (Isaiah 40:8) and it is "living and abiding" (1 Peter 1:23). The Word satisfies the longing soul of the hungry. Like our forefathers in the wilderness had to learn, "man does not live by bread alone," but most importantly, "but man lives by every word that comes from the mouth of the Lord" (Deuteronomy 8:3). Since we don't live by bread alone, our lives are not characterized merely by what happens here and now; our lives are described by what happens in the then and there in heaven. That heavenly reality happens now as we partake of the food of the Word. Like the prophets of old, who were commanded to eat their scrolls to show the Israelites in a very graphic way that they must ingest the Word, we must partake of the Word (Ezekiel 3:1–2; Revelation 10:9–10). We need its nourishment.

What kind of appetite do you bring to worship? What sort of appetite do you have for the truth and the Word? Do you want the empty calories, the quick sugar fix and high of the devil's words? He gave that to Adam and Eve. He promised instant deification—"you will be like God" (Genesis 3:5). Do you want the world's promises, which seem so real and satisfying, but are only for the here and now? Do you want what *you* want? Thank God that he does not give us what we want, but what we need. Do you want a quick fix or do you want the Word? Do you want your ears tickled with promises of health, wealth, and happiness, or do you want to be "like newborn infants, [who] long for the pure spiritual milk, that by it you may grow up into salvation" (1 Peter 2:2). Candy tastes good—I admit it, I love it, but it is not nourishing. Milk may not seem to be the best thing to you, but it satisfies. It doesn't leave you feeling empty. It is healthy and doesn't destroy like sugar. It nourishes. It actually builds you up. That's what the Word of God does, so we must come with a soul that is hungry to hear the true Words, the very voice of God.

Attentively—"Lord, I will listen to you speak"

How do we hear the Lord in a world filled with so much noise? To make best use of the nourishment of the Word, we must listen and hear the Word of God *attentively*. During the sermon we must be praying, "Lord, I will listen to you speak."

Sermons seem to be a monologue. In reality, they are to be a dialogue. While the minister is preaching there is communication from God to us and from us to God in our hearts. We are to hear and affirm, hear and be challenged, and hear and grow. This means that every moment of every sermon we must be saying to ourselves in an attentive way, "These are not the words of my pastor, these are the Words of God. These are not the words of men but as they are in truth the Word of God." Since we recognize that God is in our midst speaking, we should be attentive. We should have our eyes open, looking up upon the minister but our ears perked up listening to the Lord.

As the Westminster Confession describes it, the "conscionable hearing of the Word" is an act of worship (WCF, 21.5). The best way I can describe what "conscionable hearing" is, is to say that it is the opposite of what a child may do in his stubbornness when his mom or dad tell him to do something. Maybe they do not want to listen at that moment, maybe they are doing something else and their mom and dad might say something that almost literally goes in one ear and as you know the phrase, it goes out the other. Conscionable hearing is the opposite of that. It means to hear the words; not merely the sounds that are created by the voice box, which go into your ears, and vibrate the eardrum to communicate to your brain. It's not merely the outward words, but with conscious awareness to hear them, to understand them, and to respond to them. This is why hearing the Word is an act of worship. We have heard, we have received, and we have accepted what God says. We give God our ears, we give God our hearts, and we give God our minds fully when we hear the Lord's Word. There is a wonderful illustration of this in one of Moses' last recorded sermons in the book of Deuteronomy. He exhorts the Israelites to recognize the profundity of what had just happened, saying, "For it is no empty word for you, but your very life ... " (Deuteronomy 32:37) The preaching of the Word through Moses was their life, was their bread.

That little phrase, "no empty word, but your very life," is a challenge to the minister of the gospel. He is not to preach in a way that is empty, that is vain, that is a cover for greed, or that is a pretext for flattery. This is also a challenge to you to think of preaching differently. Challenge yourselves to fight fatigue, to fight distracting thoughts, to fight the devil's temptations.[8] Think not how you can get instant gratification, but think of the profound nature of the Word as it is proclaimed—here God himself stands in our midst and preaches to us. Open your ears, your hearts, your minds, and your souls to God in your midst.

Faithfully—"Lord, I believe you when you speak"

How do we hear the Lord in a world filled with so much noise? He says for us to receive it *faithfully*. We come as believers to hear that our sins are already forgiven and to hear that message expound more and more. You have been forgiven; now give your ears to what God would say for your souls' nourishment. To hear the Word 'faith-fully', is to hear it with a full faith, with a whole-hearted trust, with a giving of ourselves and laying ourselves before God. It is to cry out to him when he speaks, "Lord, I believe; help my unbelief" (Mark 9:24). We must hear, praying, "Lord, I believe you when you speak."

We realize that this is difficult. If it were not, there would be no need to be exhorted to believe faithfully in hearing. It is difficult to hear because we see the man in front of us. It is a difficult thing to see merely the outward, and to be tempted to think that these are not God's words but merely his own. I know it is hard to believe that God actually speaks through me, but he does. You know that I am but a mere man; the Thessalonians knew Paul in all of his infirmities, in all of his weaknesses. You know that your minister is a sinful man, yet God uses sinful means to communicate his grace. Praise God.

The language Paul uses here, received, speaks of trust, acceptance, whole-heartedly giving oneself to appropriate something firmly in the hand. Because preaching is itself an act of faith and hearing it is also an act of faith, the devil is going to attack. He wants us to judge the minister with our eyes, seeing merely the man as the Corinthians judged the apostle Paul for his appearance: "For they say, 'His letters are weighty and strong, but his bodily presence is weak, and his speech of no account'" (2 Corinthians 10:10). How many people have judged a minister for wearing a preaching robe and therefore did not hear the Word that was proclaimed. This is to judge with the eyes and not to hear with faith. The devil wants us to judge and to be led astray by judging what we hear in our own hearts. We won't come out and say, "Well, I didn't agree with that. I didn't like what he said then. I'm not quite sure if I'm going to follow that part in what he said." Instead, the devil wants us to hold it in, to bear a grudge, to spite, and to store them up for weapons at a later time. This does not mean that a minister is inspired, or infallible, or inerrant—not even close. This does not mean that the minister is above criticism—he is not. What I am saying is that we can think so highly of ourselves and puff up ourselves in our minds and in hearts. We must be aware of the devil's subtle designs and temptations; his "flaming darts" (Ephesians 6:16).

We need to listen to what God says and focus our hearts on that, even though it comes through sinful and fallible men. And we need to rejoice that through the sinful and fallible words of a sinful and fallible man, God himself speaks. It's what Paul said of himself after he was converted and taught by Christ himself. Before he had been a great persecutor and enemy of Christ, so that when people first heard his preaching, they said, "He who used to persecute us is preaching the faith he once tried to destroy" (Galatians 1:23). They weren't judging, they weren't looking at the outward only and saying, "This can't be true, this can't be possible, I know him to well." Instead, Paul says this: "and they glorified God"—and notice there is no period there—"and they glorified God *because of me*" (Galatians 1:24). All my sins, all my faults, and all my failures—yet they glorified God all the more. By faith then come and believe, come and receive, come and accept the Word.

Obediently—"Lord, I will obey you when you speak"

How do we hear the Lord in a world filled with so much noise? Finally, we are to hear it *obediently*: "Lord, I will obey you when you speak." Notice the progression of the verbs in our text: they heard the Word, they received the Word, they accepted the Word, and then the Word is said to have been at work in you believers. John Calvin once described preaching like this: "The preaching of the Gospel has life when men are not merely told what is right, but are pricked by exhortation and summoned to the judgment-seat of God, so that they may not sleep in their errors."[9] The Word of God that pastors preach and that people receive can never be fruitless; it must always abound in fruitfulness. The prophet Isaiah described that for us where he says,

> For as the rain and the snow come down from heaven and do not return there but water the earth, making it bring forth and sprout, giving seed to the sower and bread to the eater, so shall my word be that goes out from my mouth; it shall not return to me empty, but it shall accomplish that which I purpose, and shall succeed in the thing for which I sent it. (Isaiah 55:10–11)

The Word is powerful. The Word is effectual. Is it in you? Are you a doer of the Word and not merely a hearer? (James 1:22) Is the Word of God at work in you, believer—brother, sister, friend in Christ? Paul can say this because it is God himself who is at work through the Word "both to will and to work for his good pleasure" (Philippians 2:13). Receive his Word, then, with the well-prepared soil of your heart that the seed of the Word that is planted may be watered by the Spirit that you might be fruitful. Hear his Word in an obedient way and follow through on what God says in it.

Conclusion

What we need more and more of as congregations is to learn how to fine tune our spiritual senses that we are enabled to hear and to discern the voice of the Word amidst a noisy world. We can do this as we listen expectantly, knowing that God is going to speak. We can do this as we listen hungrily, knowing that God is going to feed us. We can do this as we listen attentively, knowing that God is in our midst. We can do this as we listen faithfully, knowing that we must receive whatever God speaks. We can do this as we listen obediently, knowing that the Lord is the Lord, and that I am merely his servant. I challenge you brothers and sisters to do so that your life will be saturated with the Word in every part; that your life will be guided every step by that Word.

Let me close with a simple quote that encapsulates all this. One Puritan, Joseph Alleine (1634–1668), said this—and I pray that it is true of us as well. “Come off thy knees to the sermon; and come to thy knees from the sermon.”[10] Isn’t that wonderful?

9

Praise in the Midst of Persecution

1 Thessalonians 2:14–3:10

This is one of those passages that is difficult to preach. Pastors oftentimes wonder what they are going to say on a passage like this and might think of ways to skip it. It's difficult because it is a somewhat of a repetitive section of 1 Thessalonians and we've already seen what Paul is saying here about his pastoral heart towards these Christians. Paul and his assistants longed to see them; they longed to bring the Word to them to strengthen their faith and to establish them in things they may have been lacking. His lengthy thanksgiving for them comes to an end here (1:3; 2:13; 3:9). It's also a long section, much longer than what some are normally accustomed to preaching on for an epistle. Yet, the most difficult reason of all is that it does not seem to match our reality in the West.

Why? Paul is writing to a persecuted group of Christians. And he's writing to them, having himself experienced persecution in being run out of Thessalonica, being chased down to Berea and run from there as well. He writes as a Christian pastor who has suffered much affliction and writes to Christians who were suffering that same affliction. You see his great desire for them. You feel the sense of tension and angst that he feels for them. He knows what it is like to be tempted, so he knows what it was like for them to be tempted.

And here we are in peace and safety, and our experience is not even close to theirs. How can we sit in our comfortable church seats, with our nice clothes on, with our meals awaiting us back at home, and enter into the experience of this passage? We can because the principle remains the same. We learn from Paul's prayer, Paul's living example, and from the Thessalonians' example. What we learn is that we are to give God praise in the midst of persecution. No matter the persecution, whether it comes to us from the devil, from the world, or from our own flesh, we are to trust in and praise the Lord for it.

So what can we learn about praising God in the midst of persecution? Despite the somewhat lengthy passage before us, this one theme arises. And there are various reasons why we can give God praise in the midst of persecution.

Because it is God's Will

We are to give God praise in the midst of persecution *because it is God's will* for us. In all that Paul says here, focus on this verse: For you yourselves know that *we are destined for this* (3:3; emphasis added). This is a strong way of describing the will of God. God's purpose is behind this persecution. God's will brings it to pass; his hand turns the tide of history. He turns and leads us; he guides us even "through the valley of the shadow of death" (Psalm 23:4)—not around the valley, but *through* it. It is God's will that his people are persecuted for their faith. We are destined for this. Paul could say that not because he had some secret insight into God's mysterious will, but because he saw this throughout the Scriptures—and so can we.

We can see this from the testimony of God's people from the beginning in Genesis all the way to the end in Revelation. If it were not his will, why does it happen? Abel was persecuted by his brother Cain for offering an acceptable sacrifice to God (Genesis 4). This is why the apostle John could call Cain a murderer (1 John 3:2). As the first martyr of the church, Abel's blood cries out (Genesis 4:10; Hebrews 12:24). The Hebrews were enslaved and persecuted for hundreds of years by the Egyptians. The ancient prophets stood up to the false prophets, to unrighteous kings, and to illegitimate priests, preaching the Word of God. What was their payment? To be sawn in two (Hebrews 11:37). Our Lord Jesus Christ even said to his disciples that they would suffer much after he left:

> If the world hates you, know that it has hated me before it hated you. If you were of the world, the world would love you as its own; but because you are not of the world, but I chose you out of the world, therefore the world hates you. Remember the word that I said to you: "A servant is not greater than his master." If they persecuted me, they will also persecute you. If they kept my word, they will also keep yours. But all these things they will do to you on account of my name, because they do not know him who sent me. (John 15:18–19)

The world hates Christians. The longer we live in Christ the more we come to experience this, sadly. Think of your friends who do not go to church or believe in Jesus Christ. You call them friends and they call you friends. But they will come to realize and understand more and more that they hate Christians because they hate Christ. The world hates Christ and because of this hate persecuted and brought him to death, in the same way it will seek to do the same to us.

Paul's words draw all of this out: when I could bear it no longer, I sent to learn about your faith, for fear that somehow the tempter had tempted you and our labor would be in vain (3:5). The Thessalonians knew that they were destined for suffering. How did they know it? For when we were with you, we kept telling you beforehand that we were to suffer affliction, just as it has come to pass, and just as you know (3:4). Paul had preached it to them in his few short weeks among them. For example, just a few chapters prior to the story of the founding of the church in Thessalonica in Acts 17, we read that Paul and Barnabas were preaching throughout Asia Minor. As they came to Lystra, one of the things that summarized his message to them was that "through many tribulations we must enter the kingdom of God" (Acts 14:22).

I mentioned that this passage is difficult to preach because our experience does not match up to it precisely. We're so comfortable with our Christian experience. Unlike our brothers and sisters in this text, and unlike those throughout the world today, what relevance does this passage have for us if we are not suffering as they did? What can Paul say to us? Why not just skip the passage completely?

In the first place, when we read how it is God's will for Christians to suffer because of their faith we are exhorted by God, who challenges us and says to us that we must live our Christian faith in a way that we are able to be an object of suffering. We must live our life in a way that the world knows we trust in Christ. How do we do that? I recently heard a radio host explain how growing up as a Jew he knew how to determine the Jewish households from the Christian households: Jewish households had no Christmas lights and the Christians had Christmas lights and manger scenes. Is that how we hold our testimony of Jesus Christ? Is our witness that once a year we bring out of the attic or closets our Christmas lights? The Thessalonians were able to be persecuted because the world knew them to be Christians. If we are not honored in suffering and persecution, how are we ever to enter into Jesus' promises to support us in persecution? How can we ever give God praise if we are never persecuted as we are called to do?

We learn a second application from our passage, which is that every single moment of our life, through all the ups and especially the downs, we know that everything come to us from the hand of Almighty God himself. The Thessalonians were destined by God himself to suffer. We learn, as the psalmist describes, the blessedness of finding our protection "in the shelter of the Most High … in the shadow of the Almighty" (Psalm 91:1). We learn to "say to the LORD, 'My refuge and my fortress, my God, in whom I trust'" (Psalm 91:2). We learn that we can go to him, knowing he is the author of all things. We learn to say, "Although he may bring suffering into my life, it comes out of his good hands to mold me after Jesus' image." We are also encouraged here to empathize with our brothers and sisters who do suffer, even with those whom we may never know. As the book of Hebrews says, "Remember those who are in prison, as though in prison with them, and those who are mistreated, since you also are in the body" (Hebrews 13:3).

The older we get, the more our world gets bigger. The younger we are, of course, our world is only right in front of us. Let me encourage you to read and to learn about the Christian church across the world and pray for them. Christians suffer much. Christians are persecuted a lot. Christians are fighting a spiritual battle, and we must empathize with that and pray for them in their sufferings.

Because it is Satan's Strategy

We are to give God praise in the midst of persecution *because it is Satan's strategy*. This title of his, Satan (2:18), means adversary, which fits well with his strategy to persecute.[1] Paul also calls him the tempter (3:5). He is desperate, and persecution is his last ditch effort because he knows the end of the game, he knows the outcome of the story. He has only a few brief moments, from the perspective of eternity, to assault the people of God. He wants you to become desperate, to lose heart, and to lose faith.

And yet, we know that God uses him to purify the church as if he were God's gardener to pluck up the weeds among the wheat of the church. We can praise God because we know it is ultimately God's power that upholds us, and the Devil is merely his pawn. The Devil is merely a dog upon a chain that God allows to go out only so far to do only so much. He's God's devil. He is limited. And so we know that when he comes against us God is in control.

Notice *his strategy is powerful*—as powerful as death itself. These Thessalonians were being persecuted by their own countrymen, their own neighbors, their own family members, and their own friends because of their newfound faith in Jesus Christ (2:14–16). They were suffering just as their brothers and sisters in Palestine and Judea had suffered from their own loved ones, neighbors, and fellow synagogue members at their hands. And so Paul could say that in their persecutions they became imitators of the churches of God in Christ Jesus that are in Judea. For you suffered the same things from your own countrymen as they did from the Jews (2:14).

His strategy to bring death upon believers caused much despair. Yet, we know that this is ultimately that great struggle between the Devil and Christ, the church and the world, and the seed of the woman and the seed of the serpent (Genesis 3:15). Persecution began just outside the garden with Abel and Cain. It's been one of his strategies to bruise the heel of Christ and his Church. And yet, in the midst of such suffering, believers can praise their God because Christ is greater. The Devil may persecute, but Christ protects. While our Lord was being lifted up on the cross the very base of that cross was crushing the Devil's skull. The Book of Acts describes the church as being persecuted even by Paul himself, chasing them into homes, and destroying their lives (Acts 8:1–3). Speaking of the Jews Paul says here that they killed both the Lord Jesus and the prophets, and drove us out (2:15). The Book of Acts is nothing more than the book of the martyrs' blood being the seed of the church. The more the church was persecuted, the more the Word spread (Acts 2:41; 2:47; 4:4; 5:14; 6:7; 9:31; 12:24; 16:5; 19:20; 28:30–31). Even while the Christians were suffering in Rome under the diabolical Caesar Nero, who would use Christians as torches in his garden, Paul reminded them and encouraged them that "the God of peace will soon crush Satan under your feet" (Romans 16:20).

Notice also that *his strategy is personal.* It is not merely a principle, an idea that merely exists out there, but it is a personal strategy against the individual. It was so personal that Paul desperately desired to visit these Christians: but Satan hindered *us* (2:18). "But Paul was an apostle. He was an easy target of the Devil." But notice that Paul describes how the Devil's strategy was directed personally against this small little group of believers. That's why Paul was so concerned for them: for fear that somehow the tempter had tempted *you* and our labor would be in vain (3:5).

But what does it mean for us that the Devil persecutes and brings suffering? It means that we need to be aware that Satan is alive and well, that he is real, that he has real strategies, real power, and that he has a very personal strategy even towards us as believers.[2] He is not omnipresent, but it's as if he was because he has a hoard of fallen angels—demons—across the world. He has such an arsenal at his fingertips. And so we need to be aware of how he uses his craft, of how he applies his trade.

But why does God use him? Why not put that chain around his neck like the dog and put him in his doghouse and close the door? As Jesus told Peter, "Simon, Simon, behold, Satan demanded to have you, that he might sift you like wheat" (Luke 22:31). God uses Satan's persecution's to sift the church, to purify the church, to cleanse the church, and to weed out the unfaithful. Jesus uses his strategy against him. While the Devil sees persecution as causing believers to lose salvation, God sees it from the right perspective: to weed the garden of God.

That's a warning to any of you who may in a formal way say that you're a Christian. If you merely say with your lips that you trust in Jesus Christ, but you have no true faith, if you have no fruit to back it up, and if you have no lifestyle to give evidence of it, Satan's sifting is a warning to you. It should cause you to be in fear. "The devil prowls around like a roaring lion, seeking someone to devour" (1 Peter 5:8). That's not a wonderful promise, that's a fearful thing. And if you merely are just a formal professing Christian, merely going through the motions, merely to put a show up and put up a front before others, don't merely stay in fear, but you must turn away from that. And God offers his true salvation to you to flee from his wrath, to flee from his danger, to flee from his presence and to come to Jesus Christ to be saved, to run to Christ to be protected under his wings, to go unto him as a refuge, to fall upon him as a rock and be strong.

And for us who believe in Christ in true faith, the Devil's sifting is meant to purify us: "so that the tested genuineness of your faith—more precious than gold that perishes though it is tested by fire—may be found to result in praise and glory and honor at the revelation of Jesus Christ" (1 Peter 1:7). As Jesus said, God uses him to sift us like wheat. When everything goes through a sifter there is something left at the end. That is like what Jesus does. The Devil thinks we will fall through the holes, but we won't.

We can praise God in the midst of being sifted, in the midst of being persecuted by Satan himself because we know that our faith is a gift of God and that as a gift of God it is unassailable, it is invincible, it cannot be destroyed, it cannot be snuffed out. We can praise God for the Devil's temptations because they are signs to true believers of true faith. The Devil's temptations are signs to us that our faith is real. We can stand up in true confidence against the Devil. We know he wants our true faith to be destroyed, but it can't. Thus Paul even says confidently of the Jews who hinder[ed] us from speaking to the Gentiles that they might be saved: But wrath has come upon them at last! (2:16)[3] His confidence is shown in the past tense verb has come upon even though the final judgment is yet to come. We know that Satan persecutes and seeks to tempt us to lead us astray, and that's an evidence to us that we do belong to Christ. When we can stand up in confidence against him, even as we are in that sifter and we can sing with all of our hearts

And though this world with devils filled
Should threaten to undo us
We will not fear for God hath willed
His truth to triumph through us.
The prince of darkness grim,
We tremble not for him,
His rage we can endure,
For lo his doom is sure.
One little Word shall fell him.[4]

Because it is for Our Sanctification

And that leads to a final brief point. We praise God in the midst of persecution *because it is for our sanctification.* It is God's will for us by the means of the Devil for our good. As Calvin said, by persecution, believers are "polished beneath the anvil of God."[5] It is God's way of removing our rough edges and making us more holy. Persecution led Paul to send Timothy to these believers to establish and exhort you in your faith (3:2). Persecution led Paul to pray most earnestly night and day that we may see you face to face and supply what is lacking in your faith (3:10). Paul's earnest prayers for them were "a zeal for God and Christ [that] glowed so hotly in his sacred breast that in a measure it consumed all his other cares."[6]

You see, the pressures of persecution cause us to run to the Lord and to his means of grace. We see here that preaching and prayer are the outward means by which the church is purified, refined, and strengthened. The pressures of persecution bring us to that point where we rely solely upon the Lord in his Word and in prayer. "Lord, to whom shall we go?" (John 6:68) This is so vital for us to grasp. Our entire life is going to be one of spiritual trials and tribulations. We need to be receptive of the Lord's hand in this as well as recognize the devil's plan in this. We are in a constant spiritual war. But that's why we need to flee to the Lord constantly. And so these means of preaching and prayer, along with other means such as the sacraments, the fellowship of the church, the shepherding of pastors and elders, all are meant to sanctify us. We call these *outward* means because behind them is something much more profound. They're outward and visible because they point us to something that is spiritual and invisible—the Lord himself.

The essence of our sanctification is being molded according to Jesus' image, "to be conformed to the image of his Son" (Romans 8:29). He is the image of God *par excellence*, and the believer who is united to Christ goes through persecution, suffering, and anxiety all to conform us to Jesus. And we learn in this passage that the Thessalonians were being sanctified through suffering. Paul and Silvanus sent Timothy, our brother and God's coworker in the gospel of Christ, to establish and exhort you in your faith, that no one be moved by these afflictions (3:2–3). And Timothy's good news of was about their faith and love and that you always remember us kindly and long to see us, as we long to see you (3:6).

Sanctification is like God taking us, as he has molded us in rough form, and more and more scraping off some of the impurities and some of the outer things that are clinging to us to make us look like his Son. Preaching does this; prayer does this; the fellowship of the saints does this; the sacraments do this. Persecution is like the great and intense pressure that is upon a piece of coal over time, turning into a diamond. As coal, which is unattractive, becomes something that is one of the most prized possessions in life, so too our faith is conformed to Jesus' image by persecution.

In what areas of life do we grow more and more like Jesus through suffering? Paul speaks here in several places of faith (3:2, 6, 7, 10) and love (3:6). And note the connection here between what Paul is teaching the Thessalonians by this letter to them and that growth in faith and love. As Calvin said, "to the extent that we progress in the knowledge of God, the love of our brethren must at the same time increase in us, until it overcomes our corrupt love of self and takes possession of our whole heart."[7] As I like to say, a big theology leads to a big love! Our doctrine of suffering together as God's people leads us to believe it is all for our good (Romans 8:28), together, and to our practice of loving one another as God's people. God's work in the Thessalonians allowed him to pray, For what thanksgiving can we return to God for you, for all the joy that we feel for your sake before our God, as we pray most earnestly night and day that we may see you face to face and supply what is lacking in your faith? (3:9–10)

Conclusion

While our passage is not one that is easy to understand how it applies to us, it is the Word of God. It is profitable for us. Being a follower of Jesus Christ is not always easy. To belong to him is to enter a life that inevitably will experience persecution. As Jesus said, he came to "set a man against his father, and a daughter against her mother, and a daughter-in-law against her mother-in-law … And a person's enemies will be those of his own household" (Matthew 20:35–36). Being a follower of Christ was not easy for Paul, for the Thessalonians, for the prophets, for the people of God in the wilderness, for Abel. Yet, we know that God uses our experience of persecution for our good: "And we know that for those who love God all things work together for good, for those who are called according to his purpose" (Romans 8:28). As the ancient bishop of Rome, Gregory the Great (d. 604) said, "The evil things which bear down upon us here compel us to go to God."[8] Entrust yourself to God's will and praise him for it. Praise him, knowing the Devil's temptations are merely meant to bring you into more conformity to Christ. And live your life for his glory, blameless until the coming of our Lord.

10

God's Will for Your Sanctification

1 Thessalonians 3:11–4:12

Paul continues his relentless pastoral desire for the Thessalonians here. He prays earnestly that he would be led back to the city of Thessalonica: may our God and Father himself, and our Lord Jesus, direct our way to you (3:11). But most of all, he prays for their spiritual well being. He prays that the Lord would sanctify his people: may the Lord make you increase and abound in love for one another and for all (3:12). A pastor's desire is for his people to become more and more holy like Jesus. And we see that in chapter 4 as Paul's letter takes a turn to practical exhortation with the typical Pauline transition, "therefore," translated here then (4:1 cf. Romans 12:1; Ephesians 4:1). He also uses his typical strong verb for exhortation, translated here we … urge (*parakaloumen*; cf. Romans 12:1; Ephesians 4:1). And notice how 4:3 stands out at the center of this passage: For this is the will of God, your sanctification. Sometimes we as pastors, along with theologians, do so much talking about sanctification—how it relates to justification, what is its nature, how active are we in it—that we do not exhort our people to be holy and forget that we are called to seek to live before them as an example of holiness. Paul corrects us here.

So what is God's will for your sanctification? What does it mean that God wills us to be sanctified? How does God sanctify us? What purposes does God's will have in our lives and in the lives of others? I want to instruct your heads that your hearts may be enflamed with passion for the Lord and that your hands may be moved to serve him and each other in love. As we will see below, God's will for our sanctification has three relationships.

To Empower Us

First of all, God's will for our sanctification is *to empower us*. Let me from the outset explain that word sanctification (4:3; *hagiasmos*). In the simplest way possible sanctification is the process God uses to make us holy. It is the opposite of living for impurity (4:7; *epi akatharsia*). It is the work of God, who is like a master sculptor. He takes us and sets us next to his Son, Jesus Christ, *the* image of God. He then begins the process of whittling away from us our sinful thoughts, words, and deeds, in order to make us think, speak, and act like our Lord Jesus Christ.

It is God's will to do this in us. Now notice the heart of Paul's prayer at the beginning of our passage: that the Lord make you increase (3:12). It's fascinating that while he is praying that the Father and Jesus would direct him to them, he goes on to specifically attribute this work of increasing and abounding them in love to the Lord Jesus Christ. It is God's will for us to know that sanctification is a divine work. It is the work of Jesus Christ. This is seen where Paul prays that the Lord

Jesus would establish your hearts blameless in holiness (3:13). In the words of the Heidelberg Catechism, "Why must we do good works? Because *Christ*, having redeemed us by His blood, also renews us by His Holy Spirit after His image" (Q&A 86). As the Westminster Larger Catechism says, it is "a work of *God's* grace" (WLC, Q&A 75).

Like justification, then, sanctification is a part of the complete work of our Lord Jesus Christ as our Mediator and Redeemer. He is a complete Savior and we need to proclaim this whole gospel. But there are some differences. In justification Christ works *for* us in his life of obedience and death, while in sanctification Christ works *in* us to make us obedient and to die to sin. Justification is *outside* of us, while sanctification is *inside* of us. In justification we are *passive*, while in sanctification we are *active*. In justification we are *recipients* of Christ's work, while in sanctification we are *participants* with Christ's work. In justification Christ works *upon* dead men, while in sanctification Christ works *in and through* those who have been made alive (cf. WLC, Q&A 77).

This is why I said God's will in sanctification is to *empower* us. It is Christ's work in us by the power of the Holy Spirit to empower *us* to live a life of holiness in pleasing God. He empowers us. He enables us. He enlivens us to live for God's glory. This is why John Owen described sanctification not only as "an immediate work of the Spirit of God on the soul of believers, purifying and cleansing of their natures from the pollution and uncleanness of sin, renewing in them the image of God" but also as "enabling them from a spiritual and habitual principle of Grace to yield obedience unto God according to the Tenor and Terms of the New Covenant."[1] John Calvin wrote on the passage before us that "the purpose for which you are Christians, and … the aim of the Gospel, [is] that you may sanctify yourselves to God." How? Calvin went on to define sanctification in these terms:

"to renounce the world, put off the defilement of the flesh, and offer ourselves to God in sacrifice, for only a pure and holy offering is fit to be given to Him."[2]

To renounce; to put off; to offer. This means you are active in sanctification, you are a participant in this work, brothers and sisters. You actually have to live the Christian life. We are not passive. We are not to "let go and let God," as the bumper sticker theology asserts While it is the Lord who makes us increase and abound, it is we who then express love for one another and for all (3:12). John Chrysostom described the love Paul prays for and that should characterize our lives as an "excessive love" and "the unrestrainable madness of love."[3] Do you abound in love for your brothers and sisters? Do you exceed in love? As Paul goes on, it is we who walk … to please God (4:1). And just as you are doing you have to do so more and more (4:1). It is you who abstain from sexual immorality (4:3). It is you who must control [your] own body in holiness and honor, not in the passion of lust like the Gentiles (4:4–5). Christ empowers you by the power of the Holy Spirit. Now live an empowered life.

And whereas justification is a once and for all action that benefits us our entire lives, sanctification is also a lifelong benefit but involves lifelong activity. Notice that Paul prays that God would establish your hearts blameless in holiness before our God and Father, at the coming of our Lord Jesus with all his saints (3:13). Paul is praying that we would grow in sanctification more and more over the course of our lives until we reach perfection, at the coming of our Lord.[4] Sanctification never ceases until we reach glory. As John Stott said, "There is no greater stimulus to holiness than the vision of the Parousia, when Jesus comes in glory with his holy ones."[5]

To Please God

God's will for our sanctification is to empower us so we can live *to please God.* As I just mentioned, you see how in 3:12–13 Paul's prayer is for God's work to empower them. But with 4:1 he changes the mood of his writing, as he says, we ask, and then even stronger, we urge. Paul moves from telling us what God will do to what we must do in response, using here the strong verb for exhortation.

What does he urge us to do? To walk, which is a metaphor for the entire Christian life.[6] For example, in Romans 6:4 he says since Christ was raised we are to "walk in newness of life." In Romans 8:4 he says we are to "walk not according to the flesh but according to the Spirit." In Ephesians 4:1 he wrote, "I … urge you to walk in a manner worthy of the calling to which you have been called." And in Colossians 1:10 he connects our walk with pleasing God, saying, "walk in a manner worthy of the Lord, fully pleasing to him." That's what he does here: we ask and urge you in the Lord Jesus, that as you received from us how you ought to walk and to please God, just as you are doing, that you do so more and more (4:1).

This metaphor "walk" also communicates the idea that we are making progress during the entire Christian life. This desire to live in a way to please God (4:1) should make us careful to progress in the ways of the Lord. We should more and more take up the spiritual pursuits of godliness rather than the passing pursuits of this present evil age.[7] We should more and more walk according to the ways of the Lord than according to our own ways. As the psalms say, "Blessed is the man who walks not in the counsel of the wicked nor stands in the way of sinners, nor sits in the seat of scoffers; but his delight is in the law of the Lord, and on his law he meditates day and night" (Psalm 1:1–2).

So how are we to walk in a way that pleases God?[8] Note the issues Paul mentions of chief importance for our sanctification in the rest of our passage. We are to please God in our sexuality (4:3–8) and we are to please God in our love for each other (4:9–10). Isn't it amazing in our culture of promiscuous sexuality and selfishness that Paul's words still ring true? Sin is sin no matter the culture and since we live in a fallen world, the same issues Paul faced are the same issues we face today. The famous proverb is so true, the more things change the more they stay the same. "There is nothing new under the sun" (Ecclesiastes 1:9).

In fact, note well that after Paul says, For this is the will of God, your sanctification, he specifies that we abstain from sexual immorality (4:3).[9] How important is sexual purity in the life of the Christian to apostle Paul? Extremely. How important is sexual purity in the life of the Christian to God? Extremely. How important should sexual purity be in your Christian life? Extremely. Paul spoke of it like this in Romans:

> Besides this you know the time, that the hour has come for you to wake from sleep. For salvation is nearer to us now than when we first believed. The night is far gone; the day is at hand. So then let us cast off the works of darkness and put on the armor of light. Let us walk properly as in the daytime, not in orgies and drunkenness, not in sexual immorality and sensuality, not in quarreling and jealousy. But put on the Lord Jesus Christ, and make no provision for the flesh, to gratify its desires. (Romans 13:11–14)

We are to walk before the Lord in sexual purity. As Paul says, we are more and more (4:1) over the course of our Christian life to exercise control over our own body and to use it in holiness and honor in contrast to how the world wants us to use our bodies in the passion of lust (4:4–5).[10] St. Chrysostom described what God was calling us to as "go[ing] beyond the commandments and the statutes" and seeking to please God "no longer from the constraint of a teacher, but from [our] own voluntary choice."[11]

Let me be as practical as possible, yet remain reverent. Men, my brothers, we have to resist the not-so-subtle ways the Devil brings temptations through our eyes. Don't look in the rear-view mirror when passing by a woman. Don't gaze at the magazines as you checkout at the store. Don't believe the lie that pornography is fun, only fantasy, and fulfilling. In short, be aware of everything that leads you to lust, and resist. Be aware, and kill those urges. Turn off the show. Turn your head. Leave the room. Christian sexuality is different from the world. It was in the first century, and it is now. Listen to how the ancient Greek orator, Demosthenes described "normal" sexuality in ancient Greece: "We keep mistresses for pleasure, concubines for our day-to-day bodily needs, but we have wives to produce legitimate children and serve as trustworthy guardians of our homes."[12]

Woman, my sisters in Christ, resist the Devil's temptation to use your emotions. The man who gives you attention, who listens to you, who notices you more than your husband are schemes of Satan. Resist the false fantasies of the dream man. He doesn't exist.

Another way what he says here applies to both men and women. We are not to be unequally yoked as believers with unbelievers romantically. In 1 Corinthians 10 Paul lists various sins of the Old Testament church. He goes on to tell us that we are not to follow their example. One of the sins we are not to engage in is sexual immorality. Turn there with me and notice the example he uses? "We must not indulge in sexual immorality as some of them did, and twenty-three thousand fell in a single day" (1 Corinthians 10:8). Paul uses the example of Numbers 25. What's happened there? That's the story of when the Israelite men began to be unequally yoked with the daughters of Moab: "the people began to whore with the daughters of Moab" (Numbers

25:1). As Paul reminds us, in one single day "twenty-three thousand fell," that means, died. Why? Because to be unequally yoked with an unbeliever led them to lose their love for the Lord as they began to worship the Moabite women's god, Baal. Young people, to like, to be interested in, to "just be friends," to date, to be engaged to, and to marry an unbeliever is a spiritual problem. You may not think so now, but you will fall away from Christ and his church if you do so.

Notice Paul's conclusion to this in verse 8: Therefore whoever disregards this, disregards not man but God, who gives his Holy Spirit to you. Is it your heartfelt desire to listen to Lord's desire for you more than your own desires for yourself? Is it the passion of your life to be passionate for the Lord, his Word, his worship, and his people more than your own sinful passions? Oh brothers and sisters, the longer I pastor the more I pray for the things that really matter. I pray we are more and more grieved by our sins. I pray we are more and more desirous of holiness. When you are living in purity, you control your body, but when you are living in impurity, you lose control.[13] I pray we are more and more used by God as salt and light in the world.

To "Evangelize" the Lost

And that leads us to our final point, that God's will to empower us that we might please him leads us *to "evangelize" the lost*. Let me be clear. Here I am using the word "evangelize" loosely and improperly. Narrowly and properly to evangelize is to proclaim the gospel. As Paul told Timothy, "Do the work of an evangelist" (2 Timothy 4:5). This is so important because we can easily fall into the false trap, so memorably stated in a sound-byte: "Preach the gospel; use words if necessary." To evangelize is to speak the good news. But what I want to point out, though, is that our good works, our life of sanctification, and our desire to more and more (4:1) walk in holiness to please the Lord is used by God as a witness of his grace before the world. This is why Paul prays may the Lord make you increase and abound in love for one another and *for all* (*eis pantas*). As one commentator said, "The love of God poured into the believers' hearts by the Holy Spirit could not be reserved for members of their own fellowship; it must overflow to others without reservation."[14] *God* loves you. The infinite God's infinite love has come to you. Now it causes you, a finite creature, to overflow in love for him, for your brothers and sisters, and for the lost world around you.

You can see the connection Paul makes between God's work in us and our witness before the world in 4:3–5, where he says God's will for our sanctification is that we control ourselves to God's glory and do not live like the Gentiles (4:5). And note what he says about them, who do not know God. We once lived in passion, which is a sign of one who does not know God. But now we live in self-control, which is a sign that we do know God, that God knows us, and that he is at work within us. And again in 4:12 he calls us to walk properly *before outsiders* (4:12). The world is watching us. Now live like it.

It was Martin Luther who said so memorably that "God does not need our good works, but our neighbor does."[15] We see that illustrated here. Get busy being godly because your neighbor needs to see what it looks like to be known by God. Your neighbor needs to see light in the midst of the darkness of this world. Your neighbor needs to taste the salt that you are, preserving the world from complete destruction. Your neighbor needs to read you as a living epistle. Your neighbor needs to smell you are the savor of life. And when they do, and when they begin asking questions, we are to be ever ready to defend the faith and to speak words seasoned by grace to win them for Christ.[16] What an example of grace you can be to your neighbors. For those who had an up and down childhood, you know that sin is devastating and it affects us all. But like me, you may also remember in the midst of much family turmoil someone whose godly example impacted you. That person's godliness and enthusiasm, steadiness, simplicity, and stability was so attractive to you. And God used that person's godly lifestyle to plant seeds in your heart that eventually brought you to be converted to Christ. Evangelize the lost, my friends, and may your life match your lips.

Conclusion

So, will you desire more and more to live a Christ-empowered, grace-empowered, and Holy Spirit-empowered life? Will you seek to please God at every turn in your Christian walk? Will you live in such a way that you evidence your knowledge that God will use even you to bear witness to your neighbors and to prepare them to hear the amazing good news of the gospel? Will you? Will I? I pray we will. After all, this is the will of God, your sanctification.

11

The Hope of Christ's Coming

1 Thessalonians 4:13–18

We all know we live in an age in which the theoretical takes a back seat to the practical. Just watch your local "news" with its segments on cooking, marriage, and animal adoption, which drown out substantive political and cultural discussion. Sadly, this is no different than what exists in the visible Christian Church today. Important evangelical leaders have called for a new reformation, but one not of creeds but of deeds.[1] A recent study from the Barna Research Group has confirmed this.[2] One of the points this study mentioned was the following:

> *Growing numbers of people are less interested in spiritual principles and more desirous of learning pragmatic solutions for life.*

> When asked what matters most, teenagers prioritize education, career development, friendships, and travel. Faith is significant to them, but it takes a back seat to life accomplishments and is not necessarily perceived to affect their ability to achieve their dreams. Among adults the areas of growing importance are lifestyle comfort, success, and personal achievements ... we continue to separate our spirituality from other dimensions of life through compartmentalization.

Now, with that said, if there is any doctrine that actually *does* get modern Christians excited and interested, surely it would be the doctrine of the so-called "end times." As of the printing of this book, over 63 million copies of *The Left Behind* series have been printed.[3] How many conferences are there every year on the end times? How many sermon series have been given to get churches "back to the basics?"

But I want you to notice something about Paul's words before us. He's writing about these believers living sanctified lives in the areas of sexuality and love towards their neighbor. Then he immediately deals with a pastoral problem: there were some who thought those who died before the Lord's coming were lost forever. This is why Paul says he does not want us to grieve as others do who have no hope (4:13). Instead, he wants us to encourage one another with the comforting doctrine of Jesus Christ's second coming (4:18), because as he goes on to say later, this is intended to build up the people of God (5:11). Paul's doctrine of the Second Coming is practical. And our doctrine of Jesus' return must be just as practical.

Setting aside the details of Christ's coming for later, what I want to meditate upon here is the pastoral purpose of the Lord's coming again in terms of hope. How does Jesus' Second Coming give us hope in the midst of our world?

It Gives Hope in Grief

First, Christ's coming *gives hope in grief.* Paul tells us the reason why he writes about the coming of the Lord in verse 13. He did not want them to be uninformed … about those who are asleep, that is, who have died, because he did not want them to grieve as others do who have no hope.

What Paul is teaching us is the very practical and experiential truth that when we know that Jesus Christ is coming to earth a second time this transforms grief for the Christian. Notice, he does not say that we will not grieve, period. We *will* grieve in this life. To all of us who have lost loved ones we do not need to be ashamed for our grief, brothers and sisters. Grieving is a part of being human. But it is transformed for us as believers. In fact, as Psalm 56:8 says, God keeps our tears in his bottle. What Paul actually says here is that we must not grieve as *others* do who have no hope. What must it be like to grieve as those whom Paul describes elsewhere as "having no hope and without God in the world" (Ephesians 2:12), since they have no hope of heaven? Grieving is feeling sorry that a loved one's life was cut short. Grieving is feeling sorry for those left behind. Grieving is feeling sorry for oneself, as that spouse, friend, or family member will no longer be in your life. We grieve, but we do so in a Christian way, in a Christ-centered way, in a hopeful way. Listen to 2 Samuel 12:15–22 to see this:

> And the Lord afflicted the child that Uriah's wife bore to David, and he became sick. David therefore sought God on behalf of the child. And David fasted and went in and lay all night on the ground. And the elders of his house stood beside him, to raise him from the ground, but he would not, nor did he eat food with them. On the seventh day the child died. And the servants of David were afraid to tell him that the child was dead, for they

> said, "Behold, while the child was yet alive, we spoke to him, and he did not listen to us. How then can we say to him the child is dead? He may do himself some harm." But when David saw that his servants were whispering together, David understood that the child was dead. And David said to his servants, "Is the child dead?" They said, "He is dead." Then David arose from the earth and washed and anointed himself and changed his clothes. And he went into the house of the LORD and worshiped. He then went to his own house. And when he asked, they set food before him, and he ate. Then his servants said to him, "What is this thing that you have done? You fasted and wept for the child while he was alive; but when the child died, you arose and ate food." He said, "While the child was still alive, I fasted and wept, for I said, 'Who knows whether the LORD will be gracious to me, that the child may live?' But now he is dead. Why should I fast? Can I bring him back again? I shall go to him, but he will not return to me."

Notice the key to David's hope was eternity, what would happen after death. Of course he expresses his hope in an Old Testament way, which hope we now have in its fullness.

I remember the first funeral I attended in a Reformed church. I was in northwest Iowa for my summer internship back while I was a Seminary student. There was a tragic death of a 20-year old husband and father. Northwest Iowa was in tears. Yet what struck me the most was how the funeral was filled with so much hope. There were so many Scripture passages read. There were so many songs sung to the praise of God and his eternal kingdom. The reason for hope was knowing that believers go into the presence of God after death and that the Lord would raise their bodies on the last day. The coming of Christ gives hope in grief.[4]

It Gives Hope after Death

Our grief is transformed by the knowledge of the coming of the Lord as we have sure hope for what happens after death. Christ's coming *gives hope after death*. These Christians were grieving because they were uninformed, unsure about what happened to their believing loved ones who died before the coming of the Lord.

Notice how Paul describes our hope for what happens after death. He uses the euphemism of "falling asleep" for death that was common in the Old Testament (e.g., 1 Kings. 2:10). He did not want these believers to be ignorant about those who have fallen asleep (4:13). He went on to say that God will bring with him those who have fallen asleep (4:14). So does this mean that when we die, our souls go to sleep in an unconscious state until the coming of the Lord? This is how some have described this. But what does it mean to fall asleep?

First, it means that the body is dead. We speak to our children in this way when they've seen someone they loved who had died. What did they look like? It looked like they were sleeping, didn't it? To say they have fallen asleep is an observation of what the body looks like it is doing. But what about the soul?

Second, it means that the soul is at rest. To sleep is to rest and escape the cares of this world, from the toils of our day-to-day lives. When we die we rest because we are asleep in Jesus. Look at how the book of Revelation says this. Turn with me to chapter 14: "Blessed are the dead who die in the Lord from now on." 'Blessed indeed,' says the Spirit, 'that they may *rest from their labors*, for their deeds follow them!'" (Revelation 14:13) Now go back to Revelation chapter 6 with me:

> When he opened the fifth seal, I saw under the altar the souls of those who had been slain for the word of God and for the

> witness they had borne. They cried out with a loud voice, "O Sovereign Lord, holy and true, how long before you will judge and avenge our blood on those who dwell on the earth?" Then they were each given a white robe and told *to rest a little longer*. (Revelation 6:9–11)

But pause with me and ask this question, "Where are these souls of believers?" He doesn't want us to be uninformed about our loved ones, so where are they? Notice the reason for what Paul says: For since we believe that Jesus died and rose again—he died and then received life—even so—he's making a comparison here—through Jesus, God will bring with him those who have fallen asleep (4:14). The resurrection of believers' bodies is based on the resurrection of Jesus' body.[5] Just as Jesus died and was then given life so too those who have died, fallen asleep, are given life. Where is that here? God will bring *with him*. Those who die in the Lord go to be with the Lord so that with the Lord they can come to earth at the end. John Calvin described the hope the Christian has in death like this: "To sleep in Jesus means to retain in death the union which we have with Christ, for those who are ingrafted into Christ by faith share death in common with Him, in order that they may share with Him in life."[6] As Paul said elsewhere:

> For to me to live is Christ, and to die is gain. If I am to live in the flesh, that means fruitful labor for me. Yet which I shall choose I cannot tell. I am hard pressed between the two. My desire is to depart and be with Christ, for that is far better. (Philippians 1:21–23)

> So we are always of good courage. We know that while we are at home in the body we are away from the Lord, for we walk by faith, not by sight. Yes, we are of good courage, and we would rather be away from the body and at home with the Lord. So

> whether we are at home or away, we make it our aim to please him. (2 Corinthians 5:6–9)

Because our loved ones placed their hope in the Lord we have hope concerning them. In the beautiful words of the *Book of Common Prayer* in its committal of a body at the graveside:

> Forasmuch as it hath pleased Almighty God of his great mercy to take unto himself the soul of our dear brother (or this beloved child), here departed, we therefore commit his body to the ground; earth to earth, ashes to ashes, dust to dust; in sure and certain hope of the Resurrection to eternal life, through our Lord Jesus Christ; at whose coming in glorious majesty to judge the world, the earth and the sea shall give up their dead; and the corruptible bodies of those who sleep in him shall be changed, and made like unto his own glorious body; according to the mighty working whereby he is able to subdue all things unto himself.[7]

Jesus' coming gives hope for the life to come for all who die in faith.

It Gives Hope for Eternity

Finally, then, Paul teaches us of the coming of Christ that *it gives hope for eternity*. We grieve in hope when fellow believers die because after death their souls are with the Lord, and when the Lord returns all his people will remain with him for eternity. As Paul says at the end of verse 17, And so we will always be with the Lord. *Always*. What a wonderful promise. We will be in our Lord's eternal presence forever. As the psalms describe this:

> You make known to me the path of life;
> in your presence there is fullness of joy;
> at your right hand are pleasures forevermore. (Psalm 16:11)

> As for me, I shall behold your face in righteousness;
> when I awake, I shall be satisfied with your likeness. (Psalm 17:15)

My friend, if you are not trusting in Jesus Christ today, what do you expect will happen to you when you die? Do you have any hope of life after death beyond the grave? If so, will it be a good experience? Are you sure? Paul is writing to us as Christians about the hope that we have in the midst of grief when a believing loved one died. And that same hope can be yours. Jesus invites you to believe in him. He invites you to come with all your questions, all your doubts, all your uncertainties. Acknowledge your sins before him, call out to him for mercy, and he will accept you. And accepting you, he will use us as his people to instruct you, build you up, and guide you in a life that is pleasing to him.

Conclusion

Brothers and sisters, while the world around us grieves without solid hope, I pray you will know that Jesus is returning, and because he is, that you will have sure hope in the midst of tragedy and loss; sure hope for where believers go after death; and sure hope for eternity in the presence of Jesus. I pray that the promise of Jesus' coming again for your soul brings to your heart the assurance that we will always be with the Lord.

12

A Heavenly Reunion

1 Thessalonians 4:13–18

The Word of God is surprising. As I read this passage that I have read so many times before, something jumped off the page. The Word of God—God himself—surprised me. Notice verse 17 again: Then we who are alive, who are left, will be caught up together with them in the clouds to meet the Lord in the air, and so we will always be with the Lord. Did you hear it? Let me read part of it again: we … will be caught up together *with them* … to meet *the Lord.* The second coming of the Lord Jesus Christ will bring with it a heavenly reunion between us and the Lord. But here was the surprising thing. It will also bring a reunion between us and our loved ones who have died in Christ. What a precious thought.

I have to admit that I never saw that before. Sure, I saw the passage say those dead and those alive would be caught up together to go into the air to meet Jesus. But I never saw the full meaning of the fact that "we"—those grieving the loss of our Christian loved ones—and "them"—our dead Christian loved ones, will meet again. Have you thought of this before? I want us to focus in upon this theme that when Christ returns there will be *a heavenly reunion*.

With Our Loved Ones

We see here, first, that when Jesus returns we will have a heavenly reunion *with our loved ones*. We … will be caught up *together with them* (4:17). Here Paul echoes the Old Testament's teaching about the Day of the Lord in Zechariah, for example: "Then the LORD my God will come, and all the holy ones with him" (Zechariah 14:5). Note again how Paul is writing this section of his epistle to answer a difficult question the Thessalonians had about what happens to their loved ones who died before Jesus returns. He does not want them to be uninformed about those asleep that you may not grieve as others who have no hope (4:13). Those who have fallen asleep in verse 13 are the same as the dead in Christ in verse 16 and them in verse 17. This teaches us two important and comforting points about this reunion with our loved ones.

First, *this is a personal reunion*. Notice how Paul switches from those asleep and the dead in Christ to the personal pronoun, with *them*. Paul assumes the Thessalonians know of whom he is speaking—their own loved ones. It's as if he's saying to them, We will be caught up together with, now fill in the name of your departed loved ones here.

This is not just speculation about one passage in the Bible, though. Let me give just one other example from Scripture where we see the very personal side of eternal life in which people are recognized. In Matthew 17 we read of the story of the Mount of Transfiguration. On that mountain Jesus' disciples saw Moses and Elijah, who appeared among them, as well as the transfigured and glorified Lord, whom they still recognized. How personal is life after death? Those we will be reunited with have the same names and the same features that make them recognizable. Yes, there is change—as John said, "What we will be has not yet appeared" (1 John 3:2)—but there is also a degree of continuity, of sameness.

Does this comfort you? As the Scottish preacher, James Fergusson, once wrote, this was "a choice cordial [an invigorating liqueur] for comfort against all excessive sorrow."[1] What a great hope this should give to us now and for when we will face dying in faith in Christ. Let me also reference a brief section of a sermon from J. C. Ryle (1816–1900) on this subject. Ryle said:

> There is something unspeakably comforting, moreover, as well as glorious in this prospect. It lights up the valley of the shadow of death. It strips the sickbed and the grave of half their terrors. Our beloved friends who have fallen asleep in Christ are not lost, but only gone before. The children of the same God and partakers of the same grace can never be separated very long. They are sure to come together again when this world has passed away. Our pleasant communion with our kind Christian friends is only broken off for a small moment, and is soon to be eternally resumed. These eyes of ours shall once more look upon their faces, and these ears of ours shall once more hear them speak. Blessed and happy indeed will that meeting be!—better a thousand times than the parting! We parted in sorrow, and we shall meet in joy; we parted in stormy weather, and we shall meet in a calm harbour; we parted amidst pains and aches, and groans, and infirmities: we shall meet with glorious bodies, able to serve our Lord for ever without distraction. And, best of all, we shall meet never to be parted, never to shed one more tear, never to put on

mourning, never to say good-bye and farewell again. Oh! it is a blessed thought that saints will know one another in heaven![2]

The second practical point this reunion teaches us is that *this is a conscious reunion*. Our religion is not one that teaches that in the end we are unconscious for eternity, being absorbed into nirvana as Buddhism says, for instance. We will not only be able to put names to our loved ones' faces, but we will be totally aware, totally awake, and totally thrilled with them to be there with us. What conversations will we have with them. We will tell and retell what the hymn writer called, "The old, old story of Jesus and his love." We will fall down before the Lord side by side with those we loved most, to sing his praises. We will fellowship at the tree of life together, partaking of its healing leaves (Revelation 22:1).

But what about those we love who are not in Christ? What can we do? Here is a very, very serious and practical area of application you need to learn. Since Paul says we will be caught up together with *them*, that is, with the dead *in Christ* (4:16), we need seriously to labor in prayer, to labor in living godly lives, and to labor in bearing witness with our words to those we love most who are outside of Christ. God is omnipotent to save but he uses you as the means to bring people into the kingdom. In this life, then, with everything in us, we need to pray and bear witness. And in the end, trust in the Lord to do his work.

We will be reunited personally and consciously with our Christian loved ones. And while this brings us tremendous comfort, this is not all there is here. As that Scottish preacher, James Fergusson, said again, "yet the height of their happiness shall not consist in this, but in their blessed meeting with, and enjoying the presence of the Lord Christ, whose glorious face and fellowship will beautify all that famous general assembly of the firstborn, and make them lovely."[3]

With Our Lord

This leads to our second point, that Jesus' coming will bring a heavenly reunion *with our Lord*. We will be caught up with our loved ones to meet the Lord, to always be with the Lord (4:17).

Christian, is this your great desire? It should be. Is this your great hope? It must be. The apostle Peter movingly reminds us that, "Though you have not seen him, you love him. Though you do not now see him, you believe in him and rejoice with joy that is inexpressible and filled with glory" (1 Peter 1:8). If this is your response to him now—love, faith, and joy—what will be your response when you do actually see him? What a sight that will be!

When Jesus comes we will meet the Lord. Why is meeting our Lord such a great desire of ours? Because as we know all too well, in this life our sins experientially and emotionally distance us from our Lord. Yet when we meet him in the air all that distance between us and him will be removed. All the distance our own sins have caused between us will be removed. Do you know what I mean? All the distance created when we have failed the Lord by yelling at our wives and children will then be removed. All the distance created when we give in to lust shall will then be removed. All the distance created by our lack of prayer will then be removed. All the distance we have made for all our lack of faith, hope, and love will then be removed. Then, we will meet the Lord. Then, we will always be with him. Long for this, beloved.

Did you notice where this reunion will take place? Verse 17 says in the air, but where in the air? Don't miss this: Then we who are alive, who are left, will be caught up together with them *in the clouds*. All throughout the Old Testament the clouds were a visible demonstration of the presence of the Lord. Moses met with God in the cloud on Mount Sinai (Exodus 19; 24). Isaiah met with God in the cloud of his glory in the temple (Isaiah 6). And when our Lord appears, we will all meet with him in his glorious appearance.[4] In contrast to the Israelites, who at Mount Sinai were "afraid and trembled, and they stood far off and said to Moses, 'You speak to us, and we will listen; but do not let God speak to us, lest we die'" (Exodus 20:18–19), we will meet with him face to face, in joy and wonder.

I pray that if you do not have this assurance that you will meet the Lord on gracious terms when he comes, always to be with him and his love, that you will cry out to him now. Acknowledge your sins have separated you from your God and ask for his mercy. Ask for his grace. Ask for his love. And he will give it.

When Jesus comes we will always be with the Lord. We will have eternal fellowship and communion with him. As Thomas Aquinas once wrote, we will "derive constant enjoyment from Him."[5] We should not think of this eternal fellowship and communion with Christ as something so far off, so remote, so distant. It should affect us now. John Owen once said about this: "No man shall ever behold the glory of Christ by sight hereafter, who doth not in some measure behold it by faith here in this world … No man ought to look for anything in heaven but what one way or other he hath some experience of in this life."[6] Are you interested in eternal fellowship with Christ? Then show an interest in temporal fellowship with him now. Do you long for the eternal Word? Then read his Word now. Do you long to speak with him in heaven? Then pray now. Do you long to be stripped of all your infirmities? Then begin living a holy life now. I hope you get the picture. Owen made a stark contrast between wanting all the glories of heaven then, but doing nothing about it now, saying that heaven would be of no more advantage and delight than music to the deaf or paintings to the blind for those who have not exercised their spiritual faculties in contemplating now what our chief delight will be then.[7]

We will have a reunion with our Lord when he comes because we already have union with him today.

Conclusion

Brothers and sisters, I pray you are delighted with the surprising truth of God's Word in this passage. One day you shall be reunited with your Lord, and the blessing of that is so wonderful. But one day, you will also be reunited with your redeemed loved ones, with whom you shall once again pray, once again sing, and once again serve the Lord side by side.

13

The Coming of the Lord

1 Thessalonians 4:13–5:11

It's always helpful to pastors to read how the apostle Paul deals with weighty theological issues and problems in the context of pastoral necessity and concerns. This goes to show all of us that theology matters. While many today speak of theology as something that is man-made, of no concern to average Christians, or worse, artificially imposed upon the Bible, your theology—what you think about God—is like an anchor. Just like a ship needs a heavy anchor that will keep it stable amidst waves so too we need stability in life's many trials and tribulations. Theology is also like a window. The clearer this window is, the clearer you will be able to see the problems you face and the One who can solve them all—Jesus Christ.

In the passage before us, Paul deals with the weighty doctrine of the coming of the Lord. And he does so in the midst of the pastoral reality that we all face as humans: we all have loved ones who have died and we too will die one day. Even more, these Christians had lost Christian friends and family and were worried that they had missed the glories of heaven because they died before Jesus returned. As Paul said in 2 Thessalonians 2:1–2, he did not want them "to be quickly shaken in mind or alarmed either by a spirit or a spoken word, or a letter seeming to be from us, to the effect that the day of the Lord has come." And so Paul did not want them to grieve over the loss of their loved ones like the world of unbelievers grieves over their dead loved ones. You can see the hope Paul offers in that pastoral situation in 1 Thessalonians 4:14–15, and how that is connected with the doctrine of the second coming, as Paul speaks of the Lord bringing with him their loved ones at the coming of the Lord.

So what is this doctrine all about? What will happen when Jesus returns? His coming again brings with it several things.

It Brings Climax

First, the coming of the Lord *brings climax*. For the Lord himself will descend from heaven (v. 16). The time will come when the Lord will have seen his people grieve for so long that he will say, "Enough!" Like in the days of Israel's languishing in Egypt, when "the people of Israel groaned … and cried out for help" and "God heard their groaning, and God remembered his covenant … God saw the people of Israel—and God knew" (Exodus 2:23–25), so too the Lord knows what his people are going through in the world today. He knows your suffering, he knows your persecution, and he knows your struggle with sin. At the end, instead of sending an apostle, a prophet, or a pastor to comfort them in their grief, the Lord himself will come down out of heaven. Look closely at how Paul describes this climactic return of Jesus in verse 16 with three distinct terms. He could have just as easily had said, "The Lord is coming back." Instead, Paul heaps up a series of descriptions to captivate our imaginations with this climactic event: a cry of command, the voice of an archangel, and the sound of the trumpet of God.

The cry of command was a word used in the ancient world of a boat master crying out to his rowers to row in unison; it was used of a horseman crying out to his horse to speed up or slow down; it was used of a hunter crying out to his hounds; and it was used of an officer crying out in commands to his soldiers. It is the word of an authority to his subjects.[1] The Lord will come climactically with this authority and everyone will listen.

When he comes it will also be with the voice of an archangel. He comes not with just an angel's heralding, but with the heralding call of the chief of angels, the archangel. God often sent angels to proclaim his coming in the Old and New Testament Scriptures. Just think of the three men who appeared to Abraham and heralded the destruction upon Sodom and Gomorrah (Genesis 18:1–21). Just think of the heralds of our Lord's coming to earth (Luke 1:26–38; 2:8–14). When the Lord comes a final time it will be announced by the greatest of the angels of God.

The Lord will also come with the trumpet of God. In the Old Testament there are two things that are called a trumpet. There is the actual silver trumpet, but there is also the *shofar*, or, the ram's horn. The silver trumpet was used in ancient worship but the *shofar* was used at times of war and solemn celebration. The greatest example was the battle of Jericho (Joshua 6). Like at Jericho, when Jesus comes it will be as the Captain of the Lord's armies and with a war cry to gather his troops to himself and to execute his vengeance upon his enemies.[2] Paul speaks of this trumpet blast elsewhere with the fateful description of "the last trumpet" (1 Corinthians 15:52; *tē eschatē salpingi*).

Now let me be absolutely clear here about what Paul is saying when he speaks of the coming of the Lord (v. 15). The word Paul uses is *parousia*, which was used in ancient literature to describe the manifestation of a hidden god who acted in a powerful way. It was also used of an official visit of a high-ranking person to a city, with the leading citizens going out to meet him and escort him the rest of the way.[3] In the New Testament this word is used several times. In just the two letters to the Thessalonians it is used six times. Every time it is used by Jesus (Matthew 24:3, 27, 37, 39), Paul (1 Corinthians 15:23; 1 Thessalonians 2:19, 3:13, 4:15, 5:23), James (James 5:7, 8), Peter (2 Peter 3:4, 12), and John (1 John 2:28) it speaks of the once-for-all second coming of Jesus Christ. And just so that we get the message, this coming is climactic and dramatic, public and universal. Let me say this as clearly as I can but with love for you in my words: the hope Paul offers is not for a secret rapture. There was nothing secret about the Lord's coming upon Sodom and Gomorrah in judgment. There was nothing secret about the walls falling down in Jericho. There was nothing veiled about the birth of the Son of God upon earth. There is nothing hidden about what is going to happen when the Lord comes again. This hope is for a dramatic, public, and visible return of Christ. And like the ancient church fathers, we believe there will be a "rapture,"[4] but we believe this catching up into heaven to be with the Lord will be public. We believe the rapture is the second coming of our Lord Jesus Christ.[5]

This means we need to put our hope in the right event, especially in the time in which we live with so much hoopla about the rapture thanks to modern views of the end times as popularized in *The Left Behind* books and movies. And I know some of you may not understand this yet, or may not agree, but let me exhort you and encourage you as gently as I can, that your "blessed hope," as Paul calls it, is "the appearing of the glory of our great God and Savior Jesus Christ" (Titus 2:13).

It Brings Change

And what happens at that climactic event? Second, the coming of the Lord *brings change*. There will be a change in the mode of existence of God's people. As we get older we go through all kinds of changes. We change the kind of clothes we wear, we change our favorite things to do, and we even change in the way we look. This is normal and a part of life. Spiritually speaking, we also go through change. We change from unbelief to belief. We change throughout our life in the process we call sanctification. And one day, we will change again when we meet the Lord face to face.

Those who have already died in faith and are in the presence of God will be brought with the Lord, as we are told in verse 14. The Lord brings their souls from heaven to be reunited with the bodies that are raised, as we are told in verse 16. Then those who are alive, who are left, will be caught up (v. 17). Their mode of existence by faith will be changed to sight. Their mode of existence in this life will be changed to that of the life of the world to come. What is that going to be like? Listen to 1 John 3:1–3:

> See what kind of love the Father has given to us, that we should be called children of God; and so we are. The reason why the world does not know us is that it did not know him. Beloved, we are God's children now, and *what we will be has not yet appeared; but we know that when he appears we shall be like him, because we shall see him as he is.* And everyone who thus hopes in him purifies himself as he is pure.

When Jesus appears and when we are caught up, John says we do not fully know what that will be like. What we do know is that we will be like our Lord. We will be, as we say, glorified. It's what Paul says in 1 Corinthians 15, that "what is sown is perishable; what is raised is imperishable. It is sown in dishonor; it is raised in glory. It is sown in weakness; it is raised in power. It is sown a natural body; it is raised a spiritual body" (1 Corinthians 15:42–44). Like Jesus, we will have transformed bodies. Like our Lord, we will be freed from all sin.

We should be longing for this, brothers and sisters. Every time we are selfish should cause in us a longing to be selfless in the presence of the Lord. Every time we are angry should cause us to be self-controlled in the presence of God. Every time we lust should cause us to long for loving of our Lord and his people in the New Heavens and New Earth. Again, as Paul says, "Just as we have borne the image of the man of dust, we shall also bear the image of the man of heaven" (1 Corinthians 15:49). What a day that will be! What a hope we have!

And like John said, we should already begin to be living like this: "And everyone who thus hopes in him purifies himself as he is pure" (1 John 3:3). Let me give you one application of this before moving on. You have many chances to do this in the midst of the culture. How? Here in the United States many Christians are caught up with the culture in looking forward more to "Super Bowl Sunday" than to the Lord's Day on which it falls. How many of you reading this will choose to stay home from worship and sit in front of a television to watch an American football game or a "real" football match rather than sit in front of God's face? How many of you will be praying for your team to win rather than praying with your brothers and sisters to your Heavenly Father? If you are hoping for purification in heaven, get serious about living a pure life here in this life!

It Brings Comfort

Finally, the coming of the Lord *brings comfort*. I've mentioned this in the previous two chapters, but let me reiterate it like this. Notice why the coming of the Lord is comforting to the believer in verses 17–18: it's because when he comes he will change the experience of our relationship with him. Right now we meet him by faith, but then by sight. Right now we meet him through veils of Word and sacraments (baptism and Lord's Supper), but then unveiled face to face. Right now we are in and out of fellowship with him with all our earthly cares and concerns, but then we always be with the Lord (v. 17).

The coming of our Lord should cause in us as believers peace, not terror; comfort, not condemnation. "Since we have been justified by faith, we have peace with God" (Romans 5:1). Because we have been justified, "there is therefore now no condemnation" (Romans 8:1). One of the ways we experience this comfort now, as well as anticipate its fullness in eternity, is in the Lord's Supper. Listen to these beautiful words:

> … the remembrance of our Lord's death revives in us the hope of His return. Since He commanded us to do this until He comes, the Lord assures us that He will come again to take us to Himself. Hence, as we commune with Him now under the veil of these earthly elements, we are assured that we shall sometime behold Him face to face and rejoice in the glory of His appearing.[6]

While this coming of the Lord brings peace to believers, the apostle goes on to say just something very different just a few short verses later. At the coming of the Lord there will also be "sudden destruction" (5:3). At the coming of the Lord there will also be "wrath" (5:9). In his next letter, 2 Thessalonians, Paul reiterates this by saying that the coming of the Lord will bring "vengeance on those who do not know God and on those who do not obey the gospel of our Lord Jesus. They will suffer the punishment of eternal destruction, away from the presence of the Lord and from the glory of his might" (2 Thessalonians 2:8–9).

If you do not know God as your heavenly Father; if you do not obey the gospel by repenting of your sins and believing in Jesus Christ, I plead with you to come to Jesus in faith. If you do not, everything I am saying will not be for your comfort but for your condemnation. When Jesus comes again climactically, it will be to you like it was in the days of Sodom and Gomorrah—total devastation. He will come not to change you to have eternal fellowship with him, but he will confirm the choice you've made to serve yourself and not him by punishing you eternally. Instead of knowing today that you will be condemned, know the Lord's comfort. Come to him.

Conclusion

Beloved, do you see how doctrine is so practical? The coming of the Lord is not a theory, but it is a living and breathing reality. Many of you are downcast. The Lord speaks to you that you might lift up your eyes to heaven, that you might lift up your hearts. Hear the wonderful good news that Jesus is your Savior, and as your Savior, he is coming for you, to bring your life to its climax in his presence, to change you so that you can dwell with him forever, and to comfort you with the touch of his everlasting arms.

14

Staying Awake for the Lord's Coming

1 Thessalonians 5:1–11

In Titus 1:1 the apostle Paul speaks of what he calls "the truth that accords with godliness." What that means is that a biblical theology is consistent with a biblical piety. What we believe about God leads us—it should lead us—to live for God. This is why our forefathers defined theology as "the doctrine of living to God."[1] As Paul is seeking to give a theological answer to some serious pastoral questions about Jesus Christ's second coming, he is always showing us just how practical that theology really is.

Here in chapter five he continues to speak of the doctrine and benefits of the Lord's second coming. At the end of chapter four he was answering the Thessalonians' anxiety about the fate of their lost loved ones but now in chapter five he is answering their concerns about the timing of Christ's coming: Now concerning the times and the seasons (v. 1). Again, what he says theologically is so urgent for them practically. What we learn from these words is that knowing Christ is coming again should change our mindset—keep awake (v. 6)—and our lifestyle—be sober (v. 8)—as we await him. In this chapter we will meditate upon this first practical exhortation: a change of mindset. Whether those ancient Christians were being taught falsely about the timing of Christ's coming or were just worried about it with spiritual anxiety, the apostle Paul tells them that what they should be concerned with is how knowing he is coming soon changes their mindset during their time on earth.

Our Mindset Should Not be One of Speculation

First, *our mindset should not be one of speculation*. The Thessalonians were obviously troubled or curious about the times and the seasons of Jesus' second coming, but Paul says they had no need to have anything written to them (v. 1). Why not? Because Paul had already instructed (catechized) them well. He says you are fully aware that the day of the Lord comes like a thief in the night (v. 2). This day of the Lord (*hēmera kuriou*) was the day the Old Testament prophets longed for "when Yahweh would vindicate his righteous cause and execute impartial judgment."[2]

You see, just as Jesus taught his disciples, so too Paul was teaching his. And as a faithful pastor, he had taught them well and laid a solid foundation of the Word for them. As John Calvin said, "Believers do not seek to know more than they are permitted to learn in the school of God."[3] Because of that, he was able to point his people back to that foundational teaching. God help us have the same relationship.

The Thessalonians' anxiety or curiosity was nothing new. Remember Peter, James, John, and Andrew's question to the Lord, when Jesus said the temple would be toppled: "Tell us, when will these things be, and what will be the sign when all these things are about to be accomplished?" (Mark 13:4) Again, after Jesus' resurrection they asked him, "Lord, will you at this time restore the kingdom to Israel?" (Acts 1:6) We learn a lesson here about ourselves. We naturally are curious as human beings and as believers. We naturally want to know answers to questions. Our children ask us what we bought when they know we went out to shop for their birthday or for Christmas. And they feel tempted to sneak into the closet where the presents are so that they can have a sneak peek. Why do they do this? Because they are curious. In the same way we can be curious about spiritual realities such as the coming of the Lord. And if Jesus' inner circle of disciples were curious, we're going to be as well. But the problem of curiosity is that it can lead to ungodly speculation. And speculation leads us to try knowing what only God can know. God knows everything because he is God. And he has revealed some of that knowledge to us in his Word: "The secret things belong to the LORD our God, but the things that are revealed belong to us and to our children forever" (Deuteronomy 29:29). We need to spend our lives learning what he *has* revealed and not speculate about what he has not revealed. That's why in the two passages I just cited in Mark 13 and Acts 1, we read Jesus' responses:

> But concerning that day or that hour, no one knows, not even the angels in heaven, nor the Son, but only the Father. (Mark 13:32)

> It is not for you to know times or seasons that the Father has fixed by his own authority. (Acts 1:7)

Contentment, brothers and sisters, contentment with the Lord's goodness in the Word is what we need: "O LORD, my heart is not lifted up; my eyes are not raised too high; I do not occupy myself with things too great and too marvelous for me" (Psalm 131:1). Unlike some such as Harold Camping (1921–2013), who declared infamously that

May 21, 2011 was "Judgment Day," Jesus teaches us that this detail is not for us to know. We might ask why God does not want us to know? Isn't it obvious? Think about yourself. Think about your sinful tendencies. If God told us the day he was sending his Son, we would not keep awake and be sober (v. 6) as Paul exhorts us to do, but we would set our alarms and go to sleep spiritually speaking. We do not need speculation, then, but as Paul says, we already know what we need, a mindset of expectation.

Our Mindset Should be One of Expectation

Second, then, knowing that the Lord is coming *our mindset should be one of expectation*. Look at the two similes Paul gives to describe both the coming of the Lord and our mindset towards it in these verses.

First, the coming of the Lord is like a thief in the night (v. 2 cf. 2 Peter 3:10; Revelation 3:3). A burglar comes most often at night because while you think you are safe in your home and usually fast asleep, he can enter unexpectedly. Listen to how Jesus describes what should be our mindset of expectation:

> But know this, that if the master of the house had known in what part of the night the thief was coming, he would have stayed awake and would not have let his house be broken into. Therefore you also must be ready, for the Son of Man is coming at an hour you do not expect. (Matthew 24:43–44)

Second, the coming of our Lord is like having labor pains (v. 3). Notice how Paul describes the mindset of the world about the coming of the Lord. The world is too comfortable: people are saying, "There is peace and security" (v. 3). They will be like people during the days of Noah (Matthew 24:36–39) and during the days of the prophets, who cried out, "Peace, peace, when there is no peace" (Jeremiah 6:14; Ezekiel 13:10). The world is too unconcerned as they sleep (vv. 6, 7). The world is too oblivious in its selfishness: those who get drunk, are drunk at night (v. 7). But the Lord says our mindset is to be aware, because we know that when labor pains start, birth is near. One moment a pregnant woman is just pregnant, while the next she is in labor with painful contractions. In the same way, we now understand the reality that our Lord will come suddenly. Our Lord has not revealed to us the time or the season of his coming so that we would be eager for it.[4]

To the unbeliever who does not yet believe in Jesus Christ, I must say that he is coming back. It will be sudden. It will be climactic. There will be no second chances. There will be no warning. Can you face him? Can you stand before him and offer him your life? While he will then come "to judge the living and the dead" (Apostles' Creed), he now speaks to you as an Advocate. "Come to me and I will represent you. Come to me and I will plead your case. Come to me and I will acquit you of all your transgressions of God's law."

You don't need to be speculative, brothers and sisters, you need to be expectant. And here is a powerful exhortation to us today. Are we living like we are comfortable in our beds? Are we oblivious to the sudden labor pains that can come at any moment? What is your mindset towards the coming of the Lord? "Well, I don't want to be too heavenly minded that I am of no earthly good." The problem is that we are too earthly, too unspiritual that we don't even think of heaven and our Lord's return. We need to begin learning as a people to have the mindset of our forefathers in the first century. Can you say with Paul, "Maranatha—Our Lord, come?" (1 Corinthians 16:22) Do you believe James' words: "Establish your hearts, for the coming of the Lord is at hand?" (James 5:8) Do you have the same mindset as Peter: "The end of all things is at hand; therefore be self-controlled and sober-minded for the sake of your prayers?" (1 Peter 4:7) Do you believe Jesus' words at the end of Revelation: "Surely I am coming soon?" (Revelation 22:20) And can you say with full heart and mouth, "Amen. Come, Lord Jesus!" (Revelation 22:20) Or are you too busy trying to figure out which of your dozens of pairs of shoes match your new dress? Are you too busy filling in your NetFlix queue? Are you so earthly-minded and self-absorbed that you think people actually care to read about your every move on Facebook?

Wake up, O people of God! Jesus is coming!

Our Mindset Should be One of Realization

Because our mindset is one of expectation, *our mindset should be one of realization*. The Lord is coming like a thief in the night (v. 7). But, Paul says, you are not in the darkness (v. 4). If I can put Paul's words into modern idiom, what he is saying is the spiritual equivalent of, "Wake up and smell the coffee!" You need to realize who you are in Christ, beloved. You need to realize your ultimate, eternal destiny.

You are not in the darkness (v. 4). Darkness is an image of many things in Scripture and here Paul is using it to describe the darkness of unbelief. You used to be in the darkness of unbelief. That's why Paul says elsewhere that we "must no longer walk as the Gentiles do, in the futility of their minds. They are darkened in their understanding, alienated from the life of God because of the ignorance that is in them, due to their hardness of heart" (Ephesians 4:17–18). That's why Paul goes on to say here in our passage, We are not of the night or of the darkness (v. 5). And so, we should not be surprised by the suddenness of our Lord's return, so that that day does not surprise you like a thief (v. 4).

Instead, Paul proclaims who you are as a born again child of God. You are children of light, children of the day (v. 5). As the apostle Peter says elsewhere, Christ has called to us be a people who "proclaim the excellencies of him who called you out of darkness into his marvelous light" (1 Peter 2:9). God has taken you from unbelief to belief, from deadness to life, from unrighteousness to righteousness, and from having an unspiritual mind to a spiritual mind.

Do you realize who you are in Christ? You are not in the darkness, but in the light; you are not of the darkness anymore, but you are of the light now; you are no longer in your sins, but you are now in Christ. Embrace this rich promise today. Appropriate to yourself by faith your true identity. Revel in who you are. Stand in awe and wonder at what God has made you. And as you do this, become in practice what you already are in principle. Become who you were born again to be.

Conclusion

Paul tells us that our lifestyle should change because of what we know about Christ's coming. It's because you are of the light that he give two exhortations: Let us keep awake and let us be sober. Notice the connection between theology and piety. It's because of who you have become in Christ that you are enabled to go on to live out of Christ, for Christ. This is the truth that accords with godliness. This is how Jesus' second coming transforms our lives practically. How can it do anything less? Open your eyes to the light of Christ and begin walking on his lighted path.

15

Living in the Light of the Lord's Return

1 Thessalonians 5:6–11

"In case of Rapture, break glass." If you have spent any amount of time in an American evangelical church or even one influenced by American evangelicalism, you may remember seeing an encased Bible with that label on the front. "In case of Rapture, this car will be unmanned." Have you seen that bumper sticker? How about a good *Thief in the Night* movie night to get you scared into believing in Jesus? How about reading all the *Left Behind* books to learn about your great escape just before the tribulation period? If there is one thing evangelical eschatology, or end-times teaching, is known for, it is getting you ready to get out of here.

But remember what I said previously about the rapture, or the "catching up" (4:17). It is not a secret rapture but the glorious, public, and dramatic Second Coming of the Lord. These two different visions of the end affect how we live in this life. So how are we supposed to live before the cry of command, the voice of the archangel, and the sound of the trumpet of God? (4:16)

That's the question Paul is answering it here. And we see again how he answers by contrasting living in the darkness of unbelief with living by faith in the light the Lord's coming (5:4–5). We see Paul's answer in the contrast between living as if you are asleep with living in an awakened state (v. 6). We see his answer in the contrast between living as if you are drunk with living in a sober way (v. 7). All this to say as I said previously, Paul's purpose here is not speculation about the "times and the seasons" (5:1) of Jesus' return, but sanctification—our living a life of holiness—in light of his impending return.

What does living in the light of the Lord's return look like? You see it at the end of verse 8: Having put on the breastplate of faith and love, and for a helmet the hope of salvation. What does the Christian life look like in this age between Jesus' first and second comings? It looks like a struggle. It looks like a fight. It looks like a battle. So how do we live that way in the light of the Lord's return?

By Enduring

In the first place, we live in the light of the Lord's return *by enduring*, that is, by putting on ourselves the armor of God. Notice the key to all that he is saying about living in the light, living awake, and living soberly here is the verb having put on (v. 8). Why are we to live this way? Why do we need to listen to his twofold exhortation, Let us keep awake (v. 6), and, Let us be sober? (v. 8) The reason is that we have already put on the armor of God.

Now let me ask you a very simple question: what tense is having put on (*endusamenoi*)? It is a past tense verb. This means that Paul is describing something that has already happened in the past, right? To be a Christian who lives in the light of the Lord's return means that you have already put on the weapons of spiritual warfare—the breastplate of faith and love and for a helmet the hope of salvation (v. 8). And to live the Christian life means that we need to be sure that we have put on the armor of God. How? By trusting in Jesus Christ. Have you put your trust in him? If so, you have been endued with the armor of God.

Now notice something else about this verb. It is in what is called the middle voice. If it were in the active voice the focus would be upon action of the verb itself: the actual putting on. But as a middle voice verb the focus is not upon the action but upon the person, upon the subject. What this means is that there is a personal interest in putting on the armor listed here. Let me give you an illustration of this. In his comments upon the famous armor of God chapter in Ephesians 6, John Calvin once wrote this—and listen closely—"The Lord offers us arms for repelling every kind of attack. It remains for us to apply them to our use, and not leave them hanging on the rack or the wall."[1] He said this even more strongly in his sermon: "he also puts means into our hands and arms us; and yet we hang up our armour on a hook!"[2] We have put the armor on, as 1 Thessalonians 4 says, but we must continually put it on, as Paul says in Romans: "Let us cast off the works of darkness and put on the armor of light" (Romans 13:12).

What Calvin was getting at is what Paul implies here. We are to keep awake and be sober for the Lord's return because we have already been endued with the armor of God. But we have to constantly be endued; constantly awaken; constantly be sober. It is not enough for us merely to be watchful and awake, spiritually speaking, but we must be armed for battle.[3] To live the Christian life in the light of Jesus' return is a constant enduing of this armor. The great Irish Puritan, James Ussher (1581–1656), defined this spiritual warfare as, "The *daily exercise* of our spiritual strength, and armour, against all adversaries, with assured confidence of victory."[4]

Do you wake up every day, brothers and sisters, living in the light of the Lord's return? Are you conscious that he is coming quickly? Let me belabor this point for just another moment with one of the great examples of consciously living as if endued with spiritual armor. Patrick of Ireland (b. 387) is said to have wrote what is called the *Lorica*, the invocation. In this prayer, he began this way:

> I arise today
> Through a mighty strength, the invocation of the Trinity,
> Through the belief in the threeness,
> Through confession of the oneness
> Of the Creator of Creation.

He began with a confession of the God he served. He then went on to pray with a strong sense of being daily endued with the strength of God to fight the battles of faith that awaited him, and I pray you will do the same:

> I arise today
> Through God's strength to pilot me:
> God's might to uphold me,
> God's wisdom to guide me,
> God's eye to look before me,
> God's ear to hear me,
> God's word to speak for me,
> God's hand to guard me,
> God's way to lie before me,
> God's shield to protect me,

God's host to save me
From snares of devils,
From temptations of vices,
From everyone who shall wish me ill,
Afar and near,
Alone and in multitude.

Live in the light of the Lord's return by being endued with his strength.

By Engaging

But as Calvin said, it's not enough that we have the armor hanging in our proverbial spiritual closet or next to our front door just in case we need it. We must be wearing it. This leads to our second point: that we live in the light of the Lord's return *by engaging*—by engaging ourselves in battle wearing the armor of God. Paul assumes here that having put on this armor we are going to use the armor. We live in it. It is our daily clothing like it was for Christian in *The Pilgrim's Progress*. There is that great scene where Christian has been given his armor and then he meets Apollyon in the Valley of Humiliation. We read:

> Then did Christian begin to be afraid, and to cast in his mind whether to go back, or to stand his ground. But he considered again, that *he had no armour for his back*, and therefore thought that to turn the back to him might give him greater advantage with ease to pierce him with his darts; therefore he resolved to venture and stand his ground.[5]

Will you fight, Christian? Will you hear the call to take up arms? Paul calls them "the weapons of righteousness" (2 Corinthians 6:7) and "the weapons of our warfare" (2 Corinthians 10:4). Will you fight? Four times in Ephesians 6 when Paul writes about the armor of God he says, "Stand!" Stand in faith, stand in love, and stand in hope as Paul says here in our passage.

"But the armor is heavy. Can't I take it off for a while?" Too many of us want to do this. We want to hide our Christianity as we spend time among our family during holidays and special occasions. We want to live outside the church on the jobsite as anonymous Christians. We want to live among our neighbors without our armor. We want to be free to live among them without faith, love, or hope clearly upon us.

"But the armor is noisy. Can't I take it off while I am among the world?" You *are* in the world at all times. You cannot escape. You cannot live unnoticed. If you are a Christian your faith in Jesus Christ will make noise. Your love of the Lord and his people will clang. Your hope of eternal life in the presence of God will bang in their ears.

Are you catching what I'm saying, beloved? For our children, we need to explain it like this: When are you a Christian? On what day of the week are you a Christian? Hopefully they begin to think, "I was baptized and I can't be unbaptized. I belong to a Christian family and we read the Bible and pray every day." The devil, the world, and even our own sinful nature want us to be "Sunday Christians." They want us to be "secular Christians." They want us to go to church, but when we're done they want us to put our Bibles on a shelf, hang up our church clothes, and back out in the world without saying anything we heard preached. Can you live that way? Not unless we believe we are to be spiritually schizophrenic..

We have to engage the assaults upon our faith in Jesus Christ. False religions and philosophies, persecution from the world, and even all the things we experience daily that seek to shape our worldview are all assaults upon our faith. Isn't it interesting how in Ephesians 6 Paul says faith is our shield. There he is saying faith as an object gift of God—as he describes it in Ephesians 2:8–9—is to be our shield, repelling the devil's darts. But here in 1 Thessalonians Paul says faith is the breastplate (v. 8). It's not out there, but it's right here inside us. It's not just an objective gift from God, but it is our subjective response to God. What you believe must be held close to your hearts, beloved. We have to engage the assaults upon our love of the Lord and his church. The church is full of hypocrites, scandal, and sin: how can you ever love these people? We have to engage the assaults upon our hope. People say, "You believe in heaven? Have you ever seen it?" This world is all there is, we are told, and he who dies with the most toys wins.

Yet Paul calls us to engage the enemy with a breastplate of faith and love and a helmet of hope as we await the Lord's return.

By Enduring

Finally, Paul teaches us here that we live in the light of the Lord's return *by enduring* the battle until the Lord comes for us. It's a long battle. That's why Paul speaks of the Christian life not as a sprint but as a race, as a marathon in fact (1 Corinthians 9:24). It was at the end of Paul's life that he said, "I have finished the race" (2 Timothy 4:7). As Hebrews exhorts us, "let us run with endurance the race that is set before us" (Hebrews 12:1). That's why the Bible describes the Christian life not as stationary life, but as a pilgrimage.

Here is where verse 9 is so important. The Thessalonian's concern was for the eternal status of their lost loved ones (4:13). And they were anxious and ignorant for themselves about the times and seasons of Jesus' return (5:1). Yet Paul brings this entire section to a wonderful conclusion by saying, For God has not destined *us*, meaning, those who have died and those who are alive, those who are asleep and those who are awake (5:10). He has not destined us for wrath. God's eternal decree for the eternal state of his people is not to bring them into the wrath of God and then into hell. We've not been destined for that end, but for another more glorious end: to obtain salvation through our Lord Jesus Christ.

Conclusion

Until the Lord returns from heaven once and for all, how do we live? Until then, we endure. Until then, we engage. Until then, we endue ourselves with the armor of God. In a word, we live in the light of the Lord's return not by retreating from our surroundings, from our sins, and from Satan, but by entrenching against our surroundings, against our sins, and against the devil in holy war. And all the while, let us cry out for Jesus' aid, "Maranatha! Come, Lord Jesus."

16

The People and their Pastor

1 Thessalonians 5:12–13

With all the end-times hype in the evangelical Christian world there is precious little thinking, writing, or preaching on the connection between eschatology, the doctrine of the end of history, and Christian living. We've just spend a good time of time dealing with this connection, but notice that although our passage now takes up what we might describe as more mundane matters, the heavenly-oriented life of the Christian doesn't end with just thinking of and hoping for Jesus' return.

Wonderfully, as Paul now transitions into teaching on life together as a body of believers, he does so in the immediate context of the return of Christ. What we learn here is what my beloved college professor, who led me into Reformation teaching, used to say: "Theology that does not become biography is wishful thinking." It's because we hope for the Second Coming of our Lord that there must be a godly relationship between the people and their pastor (5:12–13), that there must be holy living in our relationships with each other (5:13–15), and that there must be fervency in our liturgical life of prayer and preaching (5:16–12).

Paul teaches us in verses 12–13 about the relationship between the people of God in a congregation and their pastor. What he teaches is that the people in the congregation must have a heavenly perspective in their relationship with their pastor. How do they—you—do this? Notice the two verbs used of the people here: to respect (v. 12) and to esteem (v. 13). Because Jesus is coming again you are to respect (*oida*) your minister. This verb is a common verb for know—to know this, to know that, to know him, or to know her. But it is used here in a specialized way to say don't just know who your minister is but take a personal interest in him by having an intimate knowledge of him and his work. And because of this intimate knowledge, acknowledge him with honor. Paul also says here that because Jesus is coming again you are to esteem (*hēgeomai*) your minister. Again, this is a common verb used of all those in high leadership positions. But Paul uses it here to say to us that because your minister is in this high position that you are to think highly of him, that you are to esteem him. And you are to do this in the highest measure, he says. The adverb very highly (*huperekperissou*) is only used three times in the New Testament. Earler in 1 Thessalonians 3:10 Paul used it of praying "*most earnestly* night and day" and elsewhere in Ephesians 3:20 Paul uses it of God who is able to do "*far more*" abundantly than we ask or think.

But the main question is why? Why are the people of God to

respect and to esteem most highly their pastor? There are several reasons given in this passage.

Because of His Person

First, the people of God are to respect and esteem their pastor *because of his person*. Notice that Paul does not speak in abstract ways here of "the clergy," of "the ministry," but of those. The Thessalonians knew exactly of whom Paul was speaking. They were not an inhuman group or a theoretical class found only in books, but actual people; their pastors and leaders.

We can understand this respect and esteem we are to have for pastors by meditating for a moment on the reality of God's purpose in setting men over us, and not angels. "But if God had set angels over us I'd have more respect and esteem for them than this pastor who is now over me." Of course you would. In *your* wisdom. But we are talking here of the wisdom of God. Yes, angels are sinless, but because of that they cannot know what it is to be touched with our weaknesses. Yes, angels are in the presence of God, but because of that they cannot know what it is to be earthly and to feel distant from God. Yes, angels have higher powers and abilities than us, but because of that they cannot know what it is to be merely creatures as we are. And so God in his infinite wisdom has decided to minister among his people through people like us; through men whom Paul describes as "jars of clay" (2 Corinthians 4:7); through men whom Paul describes as "fools for Christ's sake" (1 Corinthians 4:10).

So what does this mean for us? At the same time we respect and esteem the man whom God has set over us in his wisdom, we also recognize the reality that he is a person. Because I am a sinful man, I know I have disappointed my people. If I haven't yet, I will. I'm not going to call back as they had hoped. I'm going to forget things I should have remembered about them. I'm not going to be as sympathetic as they need and want. I'm going to sin right in front of them. I say this not as an excuse, but to highlight the realistic attitude that is needed. Respecting and esteeming are not the same as idolizing. I also say this that you might respond appropriately when your pastor doesn't deal with you precisely as he ought. Brothers and sisters, pray for him. Be patient with him. Be gracious towards him. I know you do and you have, and for that, your pastor is blessed to be among such a forgiving, loving, and hospitable people such as you.

Let me give you an example of this. John Newton (1725–1807), the English sailor and slave-trader, was converted, became an Anglican clergyman, and helped abolish the slave trade in England. He once wrote a letter to a friend about hearing sermons. In it he wrote these words about what to do when your pastor disappoints you with a lousy sermon:

> … when you hear a gospel sermon, and it is not in all respects to your satisfaction, be not too hasty to lay the whole blame upon the preacher. The Lord's ministers have not much to say in their own behalf. They feel (it is to be hoped) their own weakness and defects, and the greatness and difficulty of their work. They are conscious that their warmest endeavours to proclaim the Saviour's glory are too cold; and their most importunate addresses to consciences of men are too faint; and sometimes they are burdened with such discouragements, that even their enemies would pity them, if they knew their case. Indeed, they have much to be ashamed of; but it will be more useful for you, who are a hearer, to consider whether the fault may not possibly be in yourself. Perhaps you thought too highly of the man, and expected too much from him; or perhaps you thought too meanly of him, and expected too little. In the former case, the Lord justly disappointed you; in the latter, you received according to your faith. Perhaps you

> neglected to pray for him; and then, though he might be useful to others, it is not at all strange that he was not so to you. Or possibly you have indulged a trifling spirit, and brought a dearth and deadness upon your own soul, for which you had not been duly humbled, and the Lord chose that time to rebuke you.[1]

Oh, may the Lord be gracious to us both as people and pastor.

Because of His Position

Second, the people of God are to respect and esteem their pastor *because of his position*. He is over you in the Lord (v. 12). Does that sound shocking to you? He is over you? Does that upset your democratic, egalitarian, homogenous idea about life in the church? Good. Recently the well-known pastor, R. Kent Hughes, wrote a great book entitled, *Set Apart: Calling a Worldly Church to a Godly Life*. At one place he gives six anti-church trends among American evangelicals. Listen to these. Do they describe you?

1. *Hitchhiker Christians:* Those who let others do the work while they hitch a ride.

2. *Consumer Christians:* Those who view the church like their mall—it's what they get out and not put in that's the standard.

3. *Spectator Christians:* Those who think of the church like a football game, cheering from afar while they are in desperate need of engagement.

4. *Drive-through Christians:* "[These kind of people] get their 'church fix' out of the way by attending a weeknight church service or the early service on Sunday morning so that the family can save the bulk of Sunday for the all-important soccer game or recreational trip. Of course there is an unhappy price extracted over time in the habits and the arteries of a flabby soul—a family that is unfit for the battles

of life and has no conception of being Christian soldiers in the great spiritual battle."

5. *Relationless Christians:* Those who think the best church is the one that knows you least and demands the least.

6. *Churchless Worshipers:* Those who think worship is possible apart from the church.[2]

Instead, for the good of his church Jesus Christ has set apart some—not all—to be what we call office-bearers or officers over the people of God. There is authority from Christ and an official exercise of that authority within the church. There were twelve apostles—thirteen if we include Paul who described himself as one "untimely born" (1 Corinthians 15:8)—and then there were those they ordained like Timothy and Titus as evangelists who then ordained men to be pastors and elders. And so Paul speaks of the idea of office in the church in places like Ephesians 4 where we are told that Christ himself has given to the church apostles, prophets, evangelists, pastors, and teachers (Ephesians 4:11 cf. 1 Corinthians 12:27–28) so that everyone else is built up. And to prove that there are officers in the church, but that all are not those officers, Paul asked a simple series of questions of the Corinthians believers: "Are all apostles? Are all prophets? Are all teachers?" (1 Corinthians 12:29) The obvious answer is no.

The position of the pastor is not just over you because that's where Christ has placed him, but because the people recognize and receive this. Paul is speaking here of submission to leaders in the church who have an official function. Turn with me to Hebrews 13:17. Notice both their position and your reception of this: "Obey your leaders and submit to them." Why? "For they are keeping watch over your souls, as those who will have to give an account." Then the writer gives the practical guidance on how to do this: "Let them do this with joy and not with groaning, for that would be of no advantage to you." When we as pastors and elders make a policy decision and announce that to you, think before you speak. When we come to your home for family visitation and we exhort you in something, don't immediately put up your defense mechanism.

This idea of being submissive to those who are over you is totally contrary to life in evangelical Christianity. I know. Most of us know this. Let me exhort you, though, that if you profess faith in Jesus Christ, but you are not a member of a church and submissive to pastors, elders, and every other believer, you need to be. And let me speak to you of membership in the church. We as pastors and elders take our responsibility extremely seriously. We want you to be in submission to us because we care for your soul. We say that as those who will stand before Almighty God and give an account for every soul under our care.

Because of His Preaching

Third, the people of God are to respect and esteem their pastor *because of his preaching*. John Chrysostom said it like this: "For it is fit that those men who are sent forth from God, as ambassadors now coming from heaven, should enjoy great honor."[3] Notice how Paul links together the words respect and esteem with the words labor, admonish, and work. The people are to respect and to esteem their pastor who labors and works to admonish you (v. 12).[4] This is the work of preaching. And it is hard labor. He says to Timothy, "Let the elders who rule well be considered worthy of double honor, especially those who labor in preaching and teaching" (1 Timothy 5:17). He encourages Timothy to continue his work of a minister "by the grace that is in Christ Jesus" (2 Timothy 2:1). He compares the work of the minister in preaching to a soldier who fights in battle (2 Timothy 2:3–4). He compares it to an athlete who competes in a race (2 Timothy 2:5). He compares it to a farmer who harvests (2 Timothy 2:6). To the Galatians he compared his ministry to "the anguish of childbirth until Christ is formed in you!" (Galatians 4:19).

Imagine picking lemons off a tree to make juice. You pick a large lemon, cut it in half, then squeeze its juice out, only to get what seems to be a few drops. This often is what the ministry is like. We have a large arsenal of preaching and prayer, hospitality and visitation, sacraments and fellowship, but the results seem to be minimal. Yet when you do this over and over again, like with many lemons, that is when the fruit of labor shows. This is why the English preacher, John Boys (1571–1625), said, "The word work forbids loitering and the word ministry lording."[5]

Because of what Paul has already said in 2:13 about receiving the preaching of the Word not as the mere words of men but as the very Word of God, let me give you some practical ways to respect and esteem your pastor's preaching. As a caveat, what I desire from you to show your respect and esteem is not the annual pastor's appreciation day to be celebrated, or birthday and Christmas presents, or anything. What I desire from you is that you would receive the Word.

Before you come to worship, pray all week that your minister will study well and have the illumination of the Spirit. But also pray that you will hear a particular word for your soul. Like Simeon who did not depart this life until he saw the Lord's Savior (Luke 2:25–32), in the same way, do not be content with God's general promises but expect a particular and fresh revelation of his promises to you.

When you arrive expect God himself to speak and listen intently for him to speak. Like the Roman centurion who came before Jesus and appealed to him to heal his paralyzed servant, cry out, "Only say the word" (Matthew 8:8).

When you leave, seek to apply what you have heard. Like Mary, treasure up all the words of God you have heart and ponder them in your heart over and over again (Luke 2:19). Re-read the passage that was preached. Look at the sermon outline again. Review your notes. This is honoring and esteeming the Word.

Conclusion

John Calvin once made this comparison: "As the doctrine of the Gospel is to be held dear, so also it is fitting that we should regard its ministers with affection."[6] As pastors preach and as you listen, as ministers exercise authority and as you submit, and as your servants live among you as fellow sinners, I pray that you will have a heavenly perspective on your relationship with them, and that they will do the same with you.

17

The Father's Dysfunctional Family

1 Thessalonians 5:14–15

I've had several "aha" moments in my ministry. Two of the more vivid ones relate to the passage before us. The first came quickly after I was ordained and entered the gospel ministry. After seeing the ravaging effects of sin face to face in those to whom I ministered, I soon came to realize that every family, every couple, and every individual was "dysfunctional." Much later the Lord gave me the ability to accept that this is the reality of life together as a body in this life before our Lord returns. You see, I used to think, "We have such a small church, how can such a high percentage be so needy, so broken?" I've come to realize that we all are needy and broken, including yours truly, and that's life as the church this side of glory. There's a reason our great theologians made the distinction between the church militant—the church fighting sin in this life—and the church triumphant—the church that has overcome sin and is in heaven. That distinction is full of hope for this sinner!

In this life, the church is the Father's dysfunctional family. Sin brings all sorts of dysfunction, all sorts of brokenness into our lives and relationships. As we live together be aware of this. We live in a very transient world, so realize the impact you can have for a short time upon a person's life. We live in a very fragmented world with many of us having no family around and those that do oftentimes wish they didn't! Realize how valuable you can be to the body, which is a spiritual family. That's where our passage comes in today. The great twentieth-century Anglican pastor and commentator, John Stott, called this section in verses 12–28, "How to be a Gospel Church."[1] We saw previously how the gospel transforms our relationship as people and pastor. Here we see how it transforms our relationships within the body of believers. We are all dysfunctional, so how do we function together?

Recognize Your Family

How do we function together as a body of believers despite being a dysfunctional family? First, *recognize your family*. Just like you recognize all the differences and diversity within your own family recognize the nature of your spiritual family. We sing by faith, "Glorious things of thee are spoken, Zion city of our God,"[2] but what we have to come to grips with is the fact that the church of Jesus Christ—your local church—is full of spiritually battered, beaten, and broken people. We are a bunch of needy people. We have needs financially. We have needs physically. We have needs emotionally. We have needs spiritually. We see that in our passage as Paul urges the church in Thessalonica to recognize that there are idle people in their midst (v. 14). There are fainthearted people in their midst (v. 14). There are weak people in their midst (v. 14). There are people driven to seek revenge and to repay evil for evil in their midst (v. 15). And this is just the tip of the iceberg.

On a trip to the mountains I once saw a realistic picture of what this means for the church. As I was driving I saw a little storefront church with this name: "Hospital for Sinners." What a great name for a church! It gets at the heart of what the church is like—a hospital—and for whom the church exists—sinners. Of course, the church as a hospital is not like an earthly hospital. In our experience a hospital is a place you check into and when you are discharged you hope never to go back. The church, though, is a hospital that is preparing us to be discharged into heaven. We stay in this hospital our entire lives and receive the Great Physician's care and treatment until he takes us to heaven. The seventeenth-century Scottish preacher, James Fergusson, wrote this in his commentary upon this passage:

> The visible Church of Christ is constitute not of Angels or Saints made perfect, but men of sin and full of infirmities, and those of several sorts in several persons; and therefore the Church may well be compared to an Hospital full of sickly persons, labouring under a great variety of spiritual diseases, some under one sort, some under another.[3]

Let me offer two brief points of application before moving on. First, recognizing the church to be in reality a dysfunctional family means that there is no excuse for us not to unite ourselves to it. We've all heard, "But the church is so full of hypocrites." Yes, it is. And it includes those hypocrites who don't think they are hypocrites. Join us! You're the kind of person we're looking for.

Second, recognizing the church to be in reality a dysfunctional family means our expectations about the church need to change. You're going to be sinned against, offended, and rubbed the wrong way in every local church. Our natural response is to say, "I'm out of here. I'm transferring my membership." Why? So you can sin against another body or have someone in that body sin against you, only to start the cycle all over again? Expect to experience sin here, but I pray you also will expect to experience grace and forgiveness here as well.

Receive into Your Family

How do we function together as a body of believers despite being a dysfunctional family? Second, *receive into your family*. Receive sinners. Just like our children, who haven't been getting along very well with their siblings, are still their siblings, our spiritual family will always be our spiritual family. We need to learn to receive everyone who enters our churches with open arms whenever we see them.

Notice what Paul says here, especially in verse 14. As I said in my first point, Paul points out that there are idle, fainthearted, and weak brothers and sisters in our midst. But notice what he urges those who are not idle, fainthearted, or weak to do. Does he say they cannot become members? Does he say they cannot belong? Does he say they should be kicked out? No! Since these are idle, fainthearted, and weak brothers and sisters, they—we—are to admonish them not to be idle, encourage them not to be fainthearted, help them not to be weak, and to be patient with them all.

We as a church, beloved, need to be known for having a big theology; but for having just as big a heart. Think of our church as a large family table. On Sunday we're all sitting around and then someone new walks into those doors. That's like the doorbell ringing. What are you going to do? The table is set, the seats are full, and the place is full of the aroma of your favorite foods. What are you going to do? Answer the door and squeeze another chair around the table. We have to always be aware and be willing to be a welcoming church.

Why? Look with me at what Paul says in Romans 15 about this. Here is that great passage about the strong believer bearing with the weak. Then notice at verse 5 and following:

> May the God of endurance and encouragement grant you to live in such *harmony with one another*, in accord with Christ Jesus, that *together* you may *with one voice* glorify the God and Father of our Lord Jesus Christ. *Therefore welcome one another as Christ has welcomed you, for the glory of God.* (Romans 15:5–7)

When you know that welcoming another dysfunctional sinner is going to add difficulty to our family, welcome them as Christ has welcomed you and your difficulties. When you know that welcoming another dysfunctional sinner is going to add someone who is demanding, welcome them as Christ has welcomed you and your demands. When you know that welcoming another dysfunctional sinner is going to add someone who brings disappointment, welcome them as Christ has welcomed you and your disappointments. I, you, we, must receive them. There are no excuses. Why? Because Jesus welcomed you.

Respond to Your Family

So we recognize that the church is a dysfunctional family and we receive more and more dysfunction into our midst. Now what? Third, *respond to your family*. You need to help. Notice how verse 12 was an exhortation to the people in the church to respect their pastors. Now notice how in verse 14 and following Paul is urging the same group—the members of the congregation—to admonish, to encourage, and to help. As Stott wrote, "The existence of pastors does not relieve members of their responsibility to care for one another."[4] Paul is writing of what we call mutual discipline here and not the official church discipline that is spoken of the pastors and elders elsewhere. How can I respond?

First, respond by admonishing the idle. He's not speaking here of those who are enjoying a leisurely idleness, but of those who have become lazy. This word was used in the ancient world of soldiers who got out of formation. Hence the translation of the King James "unruly." As he said in 4:11–12, we need to work hard with our own hands and not be dependent on anyone so that we live properly before the world. And he goes on to say in 2 Thessalonians 3:10: "If anyone is not willing to work, let him not eat." Paul urges you to admonish as a brother in the Lord any who are living off others. Your admonition can be to give them a job, or to help them find a job, or to spur them on in their search.

Second, respond by encouraging the fainthearted. The fainthearted are literally those with "little souls" (*oligopsuchos*), meaning, they are so worried and anxious that their faith is small. Paul has written about those in the congregation that were anxious about their loved ones who had died in faith in 4:13–18. But Paul's urging here is for any sort of faintheartedness. The remedy is encouragement. Encourage like our Lord, of whom Isaiah said, "A bruised reed he will not break, and a faintly burning wick he will not quench" (Isaiah 42:3).

Third, respond by helping the weak. He's speaking here of spiritual weakness, for example, in Romans 14 with Jewish believers who could not bring themselves to eat pork, although Christ abolished the dietary laws of the Old Covenant, or in 1 Corinthians 8 with Jewish Christians who were stumbled because a Gentile Christian ate food that had been offered to idols, although Paul says it's just food and the idol is nothing. Whatever the spiritual weakness, Paul's remedy is to help, or literally, support them. To support, though, here, does not connote the image of beams that hold up a house, but the image of the supported holding onto the one needing support. You see the difference? Paul is not saying, "You who are strong let the weak hold onto you," but he is saying, in fact, that the strong holds onto the weak! You who are strong in faith hold the weak in faith, cling to the weak, and put your arms around them. They need to know others are right there with them and will not leave them. And just as the Lord is "slow to anger" (Psalm 103:8) and has been patient with us, do all of this with patience toward all kinds of dysfunctional believers.

Conclusion

The church is the Father's dysfunctional family. Recognize it; receive it; respond to it. And know that this is not bad news for us. I say that you and I are broken, needy, and dysfunctional not to crush but to console. After all, it is precisely because we are dysfunctional that we are the kind of people that Jesus Christ, the Great Physician of our souls, can exercise his spiritual cures upon.[5] As members of the church militant in this life, we can sing with expectation of our transformation into the church triumphant in the life to come:

'Mid toil and tribulation,
And tumult of her war,
She waits the consummation
Of peace forevermore;
Till, with the vision glorious,
Her longing eyes are blest,
And the great Church victorious
Shall be the Church at rest.[6]

18

The Joy of Being a Christian

1 Thessalonians 5:16–18

There's nothing like the experience of holding your newborn child. For those of you with kids, am I right? Besides pride, happiness, and relief, most of all it brings a feeling of inexpressible joy. To hold life itself in your hands! As one Psalm versification says, "He the barren woman takes, and a joyful mother makes."[1]

This is a great picture of the joy that God has when we are born again into his heavenly family. We know that the angels rejoice over sinners who repent (Luke 15:7). But even more amazing is that all throughout the Scriptures we are told that God is joyful in his people. The prophet Zephaniah says the Lord "will rejoice over you with gladness" (Zephaniah 3:17). Isaiah says this: "For as a young man marries a young woman, so shall your sons marry you, and as the bridegroom rejoice over the bride, so shall your God rejoice over you" (Isaiah 62:5). God is joyful in the children he upholds in his hands. The Christian faith and the Christian life are full of joy. And it's not just God who is joyful, but we are joyful in God.

But what is joy? Let me first tell you what it is not. It is not happiness. For example, the modern Pentecostalism that I lived among years ago has caused many believers to equate joy with happiness through phenomena like the "holy laughter movement." Do you think the prophets and apostles were laughing happily ever after as they were being martyred? But they were joyful. How? Because joy and happiness are not the same thing. Happiness is an emotion. Joy is a quality. Happiness comes and goes. Joy lasts: "Weeping may tarry for the night, but joy comes with the morning" (Psalm 30:5). So what is it? Listen to how James Fergusson described joy: it is "to be taken up with the sense and sweetness which floweth … from the consideration of the excellency of Christ himself … and of his usefulness unto [us] … together with [our] interest in him."[2] Joy is to have a deeply rooted sense of the sweetness of Jesus Christ to our souls. This is why the church fathers and Puritans turned to the Song of Songs to express the relationship of joy between the Lord and us: "I am my beloved's and my beloved is mine" (Song 6:3).

As Paul comes to the end of his first letter to the Thessalonians, he exhorts these persecuted brothers and sisters to remember the joy of being a Christian.

A New Relationship with God

First, the joy of being a Christian is found in *a new relationship with God.* Rejoice always, says Paul, but not just generically. As he says elsewhere in Philippians 4:4, "Rejoice *in the Lord* always: again I will say, Rejoice." We are to rejoice, that is, to express our joy in the Lord because we have a new relationship with him because of Jesus Christ.

Go back to 1:9 to see this. We once had a relationship with idols—chief of which is the idol of self—but now we have a relationship with God. We once had a relationship with dead idols, but now we have a relationship with the living God. We once had a relationship with false gods, but now we have a relationship with the true God. And our previous relationship was to serve them slavishly. Our idol of self and selfishness needed to be fed, it needed to be served, and it needed us. But now our relationship to God is one in which we serve him freely, willingly, and joyfully not because he needs us but because we need him; not because he depends upon us but because we depend upon him. As Paul said, "For you did not receive the spirit of slavery to fall back into fear, but you have received the Spirit of adoption as sons, by whom we cry, "Abba! Father!" (Romans 8:15). There's a wonderful line in one of the prayers in the *Book of Common Prayer* that speaks of God, saying, "whose service is perfect freedom."[3] We need to instruct those who have not yet committed their lives to Jesus Christ that a right relationship with God does not mean that we lose all our freedoms, but that we find our true freedom in serving him. And we are joyful in doing so.

And God is joyful in us doing so. Remember the story of the prodigal son. When he returned after squandering all his inheritance and his father received him joyfully and in celebration, the prodigal's older brother was incensed. Do you remember what the father told the older brother? "It was fitting to celebrate and be glad, for this your brother was dead, and is alive; he was lost, and is found" (Luke 15:32). And this is a parable of God's joy in us. And because of that we should be joyful. As the Puritan Thomas Watson wrote, "Who should be cheerful if not the people of God? They are no sooner *born of the Spirit*, but they are heirs to a Crown: God is their Portion, and Heaven is their Mansion, and shall not they rejoice?"[4]

"But why do I not always feel joyful? Why do I lack the ability to rejoice in the Lord from time to time?" Another of the Puritans, William Gurnall (1617–1679), best known for his huge exposition of Ephesians 6 and the armor of God, wrote, "The reason why many poor trembling souls have so little heat of heavenly joy in their hearts, is because they have so little light to understand the nature and tenure of the gospel-covenant."[5] When the joy in your hearts is running on empty, fill your minds with the precious promises that Jesus is sweet to your soul. Just here in 1 Thessalonians we learn that he has turned us from idols to God and that he will come again for us to reunite us with our believing loved ones and himself. The joy of the Christian life is found in a new relationship with God.

A New Satisfaction in God

Second, the joy of being a Christian is found in the ever-developing *new satisfaction in God.* I said at the beginning that joy was not the same thing as happiness. Let me give you an illustration. Can you tell me what the difference is between the sun and a light bulb? They're similar because they both give light so that we can see. But what is the difference? The difference is that the sun is always on while a light bulb is either on or off. Our joy in God is like the sun because it is always on. Sometimes it's covered by the clouds and you can't see it; but it's always there. Our happiness is light a light bulb because it's on sometimes and off at other times.

As Christians brought from slavery to sin to become servants of Christ, we have a new satisfaction in God. We know that our former way of life could never satisfy the desires of our sins, but now we know that Jesus Christ has satisfied the demands of God that we be perfect and that our sins are punished on our behalf. And so we rest satisfied in him. We are satisfied in him, so we can rejoice always (v. 16). We are satisfied in him, so we can pray without ceasing (v. 17). We are satisfied in him, so we can give thanks in all circumstances (v. 18).

Despite their being persecuted and all the hardships of being a Christian in first century Thessalonica, these believers were to become evermore joyful, prayerful, and thankful in the Lord. I think this is an amazing truth. The reality is that Christians do suffer and sorrow in this life. We are not immune to these since we have a new relationship with God. Jesus told his disciples, "Truly, truly, I say to you, you will weep and lament, but the world will rejoice" (John 16:30). Paul preached that "through many tribulations we must enter the kingdom of God" (Acts 14:22).

How do you respond to suffering, strife, and sorrow in your life? Do you say with Jesus, "But your sorrow will turn into joy?" (John 16:30) Do you say with James, "Count it all joy … when you meet trials of various kinds" (James 1:2). How can I say that? Because as a new creature in Christ with a new relationship with God you should be satisfied in God. And this satisfaction transforms our minds and hearts, the way we think of suffering and how we experience suffering. When you are satisfied with God, and in God, your soul is at rest and you know that everything God allows to come into your life is another reason for further rejoicing in the Lord. To quote James Fergusson again, the joy that comes from this new satisfaction in God is the "sovereign antidote" in trials.[6]

A New Passion for God

Finally, the joy of being a Christian leads to *a new passion for God.* Our passage says this passion is manifested in rejoicing, praying, and thanking. And this is God's will for our lives. To be joyful. To be prayerful. To be thankful.

Rejoice always. Despite the trials that come from within our own sinful hearts and that come from the world outside us, there are always reasons to rejoice. "Why are you cast down, O my soul, and why are you in turmoil within me? Hope in God; for I shall again praise him, my salvation and my God" (Psalm 42:5). Despite our sins we can say, "Be glad in the Lord, and rejoice, O righteous, and shout for joy; all you upright in heart!" (Psalm 32:11) The Welsh preacher, Walter Cradock (1606–1659), once said, "Take a saint, and put him into any condition, and he knows how to rejoice in the Lord."[7] Be passionate by rejoicing always.

Pray without ceasing. Go to the heavenly tabernacle, enter beyond the veil that has been torn, and come before the Holy of Holies—God himself—with boldness, with confidence, and with passion because he accepts you and listens to your pleas.

Give thanks in all circumstances. Every sin against you is an opportunity to grow spiritually. Every sorrow is a way to come closer to Jesus. Every trial, every temptation is another chance to think, speak, and act like Jesus Christ.

Conclusion

Experience the joy of being a Christian, of being held as one of God's newborn sons and daughters. Experience the joy of being a Christian, of being completely satisfied with him. Experience the joy of being a Christian, of being devoted to him as a servant.

19

Being a Spiritual Church

1 Thessalonians 5:19–22, 25, 27

When Spring arrives here in San Diego, California, the horizon becomes filled with the sight of hot air balloons on the weekends. The structural bodies of these large balloons lie flat on the ground until they are filled with air that is hotter than the air in the atmosphere, causing them to rise. Without the hot air, they go nowhere. This is like the church of our Lord. Like a balloon it is a structure, although a living structure of believers (1 Peter 2:5). Like a balloon it can go nowhere nor perform its proper function without something energizing it, something filling it. That something is in actuality someone, namely, the Holy Spirit. We need the Holy Spirit, brothers and sisters, to fill us and to enliven us.

We come to a text that may make us uncomfortable, in which Paul says, "Do not quench the Spirit." This is a rhetorical figure of speak called a litotes [*lie-tuh-tees*], that is, Paul is saying something negatively in order to affirm something positively. What he is saying is that instead of quenching the Spirit we are to be quenched by the Spirit; instead of extinguishing the Spirit in our lives we are to experience the reviving of the Spirit in our lives; instead of smothering his flame we are to be fanning his flame, even as Paul exhorted Timothy elsewhere, saying, "Fan into flame the gift of God, which is in you" (2 Timothy 1:6). Paul told the Ephesians, "Be not drunk with wine … but be filled with the Spirit" (Ephesians 5:18; KJV). John Calvin said that believers need to "fan more vigorously the sparks which God has kindled in them by daily progress."[1] So how are we as Christians and congregations to be quenched by the Spirit, revived by the Spirit, enflamed by the Spirit, and filled by the Spirit?

By Praying

First, we manifest our being a spiritual church *by praying*. We notice how Paul's exhortations, "Rejoice always, pray without ceasing, give thanks" (1 Thessalonians 5:16–18), are the immediate context that cannot be divorced from his next exhortation, Do not quench the Spirit (v. 19).[2] To quench the Spirit, as Aquinas said, is "by extinguishing the ardor for the Spirit either in himself or in somebody else."[3] This is why Paul exhorts us elsewhere to the contrary. Instead of being "slothful in zeal" we are to be "fervent in spirit, serve the Lord" (Romans 12:11).

How do we keep from quenching the Spirit and extinguishing the ardor for the Spirit and positively be "fervent in the Spirit," as Romans 12:11 can also be translated? By praying, that is, by an "offering up of our desires unto God, for things agreeable to his will, in the name of Christ" (WSC, Q&A 98). Why does Paul say prayer is a mark of a spiritual church? Let me offer two reasons.

First, because prayer is one of the *ordinary marks* of the child of God who has been born again by the Spirit. Listen to how J. C. Ryle explained this:

> … of all the evidences of the real work of the Spirit, a habit of hearty private prayer is one of the most satisfactory that can be named. A man may preach from false motives. A man may write books and make fine speeches and seem diligent in good works, and yet be a Judas Iscariot. But a man seldom goes into his closet, and pours out his soul before God in secret, unless he is in earnest. The Lord himself has set his stamp on prayer as the best proof of a true conversion. When he sent Ananias to Saul in Damascus, he gave him no other evidence of his change of heart than this, *"Behold, he prayeth"* (Acts 9: 11 KJV).[4]

How ordinary should prayer be to you, O child of God? It should be as ordinary as a child climbing up into its father's arms. God is our Father and we are his children. Are you close to him? Do you talk with him? The Puritan preacher, Thomas Watson, said this of prayer: "Prayer is the soul's breathing itself into the bosom of its heavenly Father."[5] It should also be as ordinary as a child crying. William Gurnall wrote:

> "Praying is the same to the new creature as crying is to the natural. The child is not learned by art or example to cry, but instructed by nature. It comes into the world crying. Praying is not a lesson got by forms and rules of art, but flowing from principles of new life itself."[6]

Prayer is a mark of a spiritual church because, second, prayer is one of the *ordinary means* the Spirit uses to build and bless his church. In a recent article, Joel Beeke defined what a biblical work of the Spirit is in what is called—dare I say it—revival. It is the sovereign work of the Holy Spirit. Beeke said it is "not miraculously different from the regular experience of the church. The difference is in degree, not in kind."[7] If I can put it this way, it is the Holy Spirit's extraordinary blessing on his ordinary means of preaching and prayer. What does this have to do with prayer? Two things. First, we need to pray, "O Lord, cause me to pray; cause us as a people to pray." We know God demands that we pray and desires that we pray, and we all pray to one extent or another. We pray, but do we really *pray*? Second, we need to pray, "O Lord, bless my prayers." He not only demands our prayers but delights in them and deigns to use them. As Paul says, Brothers, pray for us (v. 25), we not only need to pray but pray that our prayers will further the mission of God through the ministry of his preachers.

By Preaching

Paul's words, Brothers, pray for us (v. 25), lead us to our second point. We manifest our being a spiritual church *by preaching*. We keep from quenching the Spirit in our lives and in the life of our church by not despising prophecies (v. 20). Positively, we fan the flame of the Holy Spirit by cherishing prophecy. No doubt when you hear that you immediately think of some crazy charismaniac or some self-proclaimed prophecy expert like Harold Camping. But prophecy in Scripture is not only a foretelling, a prediction, but is especially a forth-telling, a proclamation. There were prophets in the New Testament period like Agabus, who foretold of a famine in Judea and of Paul's imprisonment (Acts 11, 21). But what do we see most of all in the New Testament? We see Peter forth-telling, proclaiming, and preaching from the Old Testament prophet Joel's words (Acts 2; cf. Joel 2). We see Paul forth-telling, proclaiming, preaching "from the Scriptures" with the Jews (Acts 17:2). We see Timothy charged to "preach the Word" (2 Timothy 4:2). We see those with the gift of preaching told to do so in 1 Peter 4 "as one who speaks the oracles of God" (1 Peter 4:11). Where is the prophet in today's churches? He is the one who stands up with conviction because he has been called to preach the Word of the Lord.[8]

"Do not despise prophecies" means for us that we do not despise preaching. Instead, as Paul said earlier, we are to positively receive the Word of God "not as the word of men but as what it really is, the word of God, which is at work in you believers" (1 Thessalonians 2:13). To be a spiritual church we need preaching. We need the Word. We need it read, as verse 27 says, "have this letter read to all the brothers." We need it preached, as he says here.

Now, I know this seems completely opposite to what so many of us are used to hearing. How many of us have been in churches that were being "led by the Spirit" in a service so much so that the pastor skipped reading and preaching the Word for more music, more singing, and more excitement? So, is it true that Pentecostal, charismatic, and evangelical churches have the Spirit while we as frozen chosen Reformed churches have the Word? Let me answer by saying this. I once heard a lecture by Sinclair Ferguson who was summarizing the theology of John Owen on the Holy Spirit. Here's what he said: "If you have the Word without the Spirit, you will dry up. If you have the Spirit without the Word, you will blow up. But if you have the Word and the Spirit together you will grow up."[9]

We need the Word and Spirit together. We need the Word as a means of bringing us into contact with the Spirit and the Spirit as "the Lord and giver of life" (Nicene Creed) by using the Word in our lives. "Well, the weak believers in our midst need the preaching of the Word. I've heard it all so I just come here to give moral support." That's an interesting theory. But notice that while he told us back in verse 14 to help the weak, to admonish the idle, and to encourage the fainthearted, here he does not qualify it. All of us need to pray. All of us need the Word. I keep coming back to the Scottish preacher,

James Fergusson, because his exposition of 1 Thessalonians is so good. Here's what he said about every believer needing the Word: "There is not any so far advanced in the way of grace and piety, but they stand in need of being helpt and bettered by the publick preaching of the Lords Word by his send Ministers."[10] And, "Constant attendance upon the Word preached by sent Ministers, is a singular help to beget and entertain the gifts and motions of the Spirit of God to good in our hearts."[11]

By Practicing

Third, we manifest our being a spiritual church *by practicing* a godly, spiritual lifestyle. In a word, as I've already said, theology that does not become biography is wishful thinking. All our praying to God and all our hearing from God must lead us to live for God.

We are to test everything (v. 21). We are to test all things we hear by the written Word just as a goldsmith tests what looks like gold by a touchstone. A touchstone is a small tablet of dark stone on which soft metals are rubbed. If it is gold, it leaves a visible trace; if it is not, it leaves no trace. The Word tests all things and finds them true or false. This is an exhortation for us as believers to know the Word deeply and intimately so that you can test what you hear. But let me caution the grumblers in the camp of Israel: you are not called to do this that you might sit in judgment over the ministry of the Word—God himself does that ultimately and he does that in this life through pastors and elders—or that you might complain and vent like your forefathers of old. You are called to test and try everything that you might find nourishment for your souls. That's why Paul says to hold fast what is good (v. 21) and to abstain from every form of evil (v. 22). We are to practice what we pray and what we hear from the very lips of God in the Word preached.

Conclusion

Oh brothers and sisters, the body of the church needs the Spirit that it might come to life and be filled. And we can experience what it is to be a spiritual, a Spirit-filled, and Spirit-empowered church if we are being led by and praying in the power of the Holy Spirit, if we are saturated and satisfied with the Word, and if we are living a life that is sanctified by the Spirit of holiness. God make us so in our generation.

20

Our Certain God

1 Thessalonians 5:23–24

We have come to the end of Paul's heart-opening letter to the Thessalonian believers. It still amazes me how he was only there for three weeks or at most a couple of months, according to Acts 17. This is a testimony of the bond that should develop between a pastor and his people. I pray, then, that you've heard Paul's passionate heart for his people. As we come to the end of this epistle, I want you to know that of all the things I desire for you as you read, of all the things I pray for you as a member of the body of Christ, of all the things I labor for in my preaching and teaching, there is one that is central. What my heart wants for you above all is to be certain. I want you to be certain about what God *has* done in your life, about what God *is* doing in your life, and what God *will* do in your life. In the words of

John Calvin, "There is certainly no purpose in promulgating doctrine, if God does not put it into our hearts." He went on to say "doctrine is useless until God engraves it with His finger on our hearts."[1] That's certainty. I want you to know God is at work on your hearts.

Why certainty? Because I am convinced it is the essence of being a Christian. The most perceptive insight into our faith as Protestant and Reformed Christians was by the Roman Catholic theologian, Robert Bellarmine (1542–1621). As the greatest Roman apologist of the sixteenth and seventeenth centuries, he said the chief difference between Rome and the Reformation was—ready for this—assurance.[2] Deep down our theology and life is about having the assurance that we are saved. I don't want you to know what the doctrine of election is, what the doctrine of limited atonement is, what our view of the sacraments are, what our theology of worship is … unless knowing this increases your certainty that you belong to Jesus Christ in body and soul both in life and in death (HC, Q&A 1).

We see this in Paul's final prayer for the Thessalonians. As he prays for them, notice that his prayer carries with it the theme of certainty. But don't miss this: the certainty is God himself. And it's because of our certain God that we can be certain as well.

The Certainty of God's Pacification

First, Paul proclaims here *the certainty of God's pacification*, that is, the certainty that peace has been made by him between us. What is the title Paul addresses God with? The God of peace (v. 23). We see him using this description of God elsewhere in the New Testament. For example, twice in Romans (Romans 15:33, 16:20) Paul addresses God as "the God of peace." Why? Think about the big picture of what Paul says in Romans. Central to all that he says in Romans is that God "justifies the ungodly" (Romans 4:5). Sinners are justified before a holy God. And Paul uses this title for God at the end of Romans because our God is the God who has made peace between sinners and himself. Listen to that great promise of justification in Romans 5:1: "Having been justified by faith we have peace with God." In Paul's prayer, then, we are built up in certainty because of the certainty of God's pacification.

But what makes justification by faith so certain that we are granted certainty because of it? This is so vital to grasp.

First, the certain peace we have with God in justification is an act of God in our lives. Notice that he's not praying for the Thessalonians to have peace. Notice also that he's not praying that they will "make their peace with God," as we so commonly hear it said today in the context of death. No, Paul prays to God in this way because peace with God—justification—is a certain fact. God *is* the God of peace.

Second, the certain peace we have with God in justification is a past act of God in our lives. He does not pray that we would be in the process of little by little becoming more justified in the present. Again, as Paul says, "Having *been* justified by faith" (Romans 5:1).

Third, the certain peace we have with God in justification is a once-for-all act of God in our lives. It is not a thing that we get, then can lose, and then can get all over again. It is not a perpetual action. It is not a process. It is once for all.

Now, before I move to or next point, let me say to you that you have to be certain that God has made peace with you or else nothing I say will be meaningful to you. As the God of peace, God reconciles you as a sinner to himself as a holy, perfect, and pure God. He offers his peace to you as a sinner. Turn away from your sins and turn to God. As he stands there with his arms wide open, embrace him and receive *the certainty of God's pacification*.

The Certainty of God's Purification

It's because we are justified that we are certain of being sanctified. Pacification leads to purification. As John Owen said, "Gospel truth is the only root whereon Gospel holiness will grow."[3] The second thing we learn here about God is *the certainty of God's purification*. This God of peace whom Paul addresses in prayer is also the God who will himself sanctify you completely (v. 23).

Let me point out two amazing passages in Paul's other letters where he describes this sanctification or purification. First, in Romans 8:29 we read: "For those whom he foreknew he also predestined to be conformed to the image of his Son."

Notice the purpose of our predestination is purification—to be conformed to the image of Jesus. When I say "sanctification" I want you to think of two pieces of wood standing side by side. One has been chiseled into an amazing statue: that's Jesus. The other is just a log that has been cut down. What God does in our lives is to begin tearing away all the bark, wiping away all the dirt, and then chiseling away at us to make us look more and more like Jesus. That's sanctification. It's God making us look like Jesus.

For the second passage about purification, listen to 2 Corinthians 3:18:

> And we all, with unveiled face, beholding the glory of the Lord, are being transformed into the same image from one degree of glory to another. For this comes from the Lord who is the Spirit.

Here Paul uses a different word to describe our purification. He uses the word for a metamorphosis, a change that occurs within us from the inside out. We are being changed into Jesus' image. We are becoming more and more like the Lord. And note well that it is the

Lord himself by the power of the Holy Spirit that is changing us: "For this comes from the Lord who is the Spirit." This is why Paul prays in our passage that God himself will sanctify you (v. 23).

So what is God purifying, sanctifying? Every part of us: completely. The prophet Isaiah says that from head to toe we are filthy (Isaiah 1:5–6). Sanctification is a lifelong process in which God, as it were, begins to scrub the spots on our filthy garment. And believers should know by experience that sometimes God scrubs a little harder than we would like to make us clean. Do you know why he does this? God would much rather see us with a hole in our garment than with a spot on our garment.

Do you have a deep-down desire to be sanctified and purified? Are you sick and tired of thinking the same sinful thoughts, saying the same sinful words, and doing the same sinful actions? Like Paul, then, one of the marks of a child of God is loathing of sin and longing for sanctification:

> Not that I have already obtained this or am already perfect, but *I press on* to make it my own, because Christ Jesus has made me his own. Brothers, I do not consider that I have made it my own. But one thing I do: forgetting what lies behind and *straining forward* to what lies ahead, *I press on* toward the goal for the prize of the upward call of God in Christ Jesus (Philippians 3:12–14).

As Hebrews says, "*Strive* … for the holiness without which no one will see the Lord" (12:14).

Are you more and more beginning to delight in sanctification? This is another sign that you are a child of God. It's not enough to say you're a sinner, it's not enough to ask God to sanctify you. You need to begin delighting in his work in you. As the Psalmist said of the man of God, "But his *delight* is in the law of the Lord, and on his law he meditates day and night" (Psalm 1:2). Do you delight in the Word of the Lord? "Lead me in the path of your commandments, for I *delight* in it" (Psalm 119:35). Do you delight to walk in the path of the Lord? And as Paul said, "For I *delight* in the law of God, in my inner being" (Romans 7:22). Delight today in *the certainty of God's purification.*

The Certainty of God's Preservation

Finally, the God who certainly declares pacification between us and who certainly works purification in us is the same God who certainly will accomplish preservation. Notice, then, *the certainty of God's preservation* in our text: and may your whole spirit and soul and body be kept blameless at the coming of our Lord Jesus Christ (v. 23). He will preserve us in this life from all the assaults and attacks of our worldly surroundings. He will preserve us in this life from all the temptations and trials of our sins. He will preserve us in this life from all the sorrows and sadness brought upon us by Satan. As John Chrysostom said, "For if He called you to salvation, and He is true, He will certainly save you, in that He wills it."[4]

How much do you love your children? And for those without children yet, imagine how much you will love them. We love our natural children as much as life itself. Now for those of you who have adopted or are contemplating adoption, that's a whole other level of love that is so amazing to me. You set your heart upon that child when all you had was a name, or a picture, or just an idea. And you spent lots of money, you prepared your home, you made up a room, and you went a great distance through many obstacles to make that child yours. You brought that child home. You teach that child how to speak, how to be obedient, and how to love. Will you give that child up? Out of the question, right? God loves us this much—and more! We are his adopted children. He took us from Satan's family into his own. He spared no expense by giving up his own Son for us. Now he is teaching us. Now he bathes us. Now he is raising us. And as Jesus said, he will not give us back:

> My sheep hear my voice, and I know them, and they follow me. I give them eternal life, and they will never perish, and no one will snatch them out of my hand. My Father, who has given them to me, is greater than all, and no one is able to snatch them out of the Father's hand. I and the Father are one. (John 10:27–30)

As Paul said,

> And we know that for those who love God all things work together for good, for those who are called according to his purpose. For those whom he foreknew he also predestined to be conformed to the image of his Son, in order that he might be the firstborn among many brothers. And those whom he predestined he also called, and those whom he called he also justified, and those whom he justified he also glorified. (Romans 8:29–30)

Conclusion

And how wonderful is the end of our passage? He who calls you is faithful—faithful to what? To himself; to his own promises—he will surely do it (v. 24). Paul's heart ached for the Thessalonians to have *the certainty of God's pacification, the certainty of God's purification,* and *the certainty of God's preservation*. So too my heart aches for all of God's children to be assured, to be confident, to be triumphant!

21

The Wonder of Sanctification

2 Thessalonians 1:1–4

I think many of us in churches that consider themselves "Reformed" are afraid. "Of what," you ask? I think that for so many of us who have come out of Charismatic and Pentecostal church backgrounds into a Reformed church we're afraid—get this—of God. I think we're afraid of God doing something in our lives and the life of our congregations that will upset our *status quo*. And I think we're afraid of doing anything for the Lord because we're so afraid that if we speak to someone about Christ we might mess up the words; if we do something to serve our church we might not do it the right way; if we do something to serve our community or try to get others in our church to join with us then we're considered legalistic and moralistic. I want to free you. I want to remind you that Jesus Christ frees us from sin that we might be free to serve.

Listen to how Paul elsewhere describes our freedom to serve Christ: "For you did not receive the spirit of slavery to fall back into fear, but you have received the Spirit of adoption as sons, by whom we cry, 'Abba! Father!'" (Romans 8:15) We are free to cry out to God as our Father. Paul told Timothy, "For this reason I remind you to fan into flame the gift of God, which is in you through the laying on of my hands, for God gave us a spirit not of fear but of power and love and self-control" (2 Timothy 1:6–7). Applying this to all of us, Paul is saying that you've been liberated; now love the Lord and your neighbor with all of your heart. You've been freed; now fight against sin with all of your spiritual might. You've been saved; now serve the Lord with all of your passion and zeal.

We come now to Paul, Silvanus, and Timothy's second letter to the church of the Thessalonians in God our Father and the Lord Jesus Christ (v. 1).[1] After the typical Christian greeting of grace … and peace from God our Father and the Lord Jesus Christ (v. 2), we read of the wonder of sanctification. As you read verses 3–4 I want you to be freed to stand in wonder at the Lord's work of sanctification, as the Holy Spirit makes you more and more into the image of Jesus. I want you to be in wonder at what you once were and what you have become. I want you to be in wonder at what the Holy Spirit is going to yet make you.

The Praise of Sanctification

First, the wonder of sanctification is seen in *the praise of sanctification*. Paul begins his prayer, saying, We ought always *to give thanks* to God *for you*, brothers, as is right (v. 3). When Paul thinks about the Thessalonians he offers praise. And he is constrained to do so—we *ought* always to give thanks … *as is right*—because of the powerful work of the Holy Spirit demonstrated in their lives.

This means that we recognize that sanctification is not a self-aggrandizing, self-congratulating exercise. He doesn't give praise *to* the Thessalonians, but gives praise to God, *for* them. What are people's attitudes towards holiness and good works? Some say we need to do good works in order to get more jewels in our heavenly crown. Some have a false humility that really says, "Look at me," with bumper stickers like, "Don't let the car fool you … my treasure is in heaven." The work of sanctification in us points outside of us to its source—God himself: We … give thanks *to God*.

At the same time we thank God for his sanctifying work in others, though, what we learn from Paul's praise is that we must have a personal interest, a personal appropriation in the Lord's work in our sanctification. So popularly we think of sanctification as, "Let go and let God," or, we rationalize that sanctification is so monergistic, so much the work of God alone, that we take that to mean it has nothing to do with us. Sanctification is participatory. "But doesn't that border on becoming Pelagian or Arminian or Neonomian?" Listen to what John Calvin said, and you tell me: "the godly should all hold to the principle of examining themselves each day and seeing the extent of their progress."[2] Like Paul with the Thessalonians, we need to be in awe of God's work in us and through us each and every day, even measuring our progress into conformity to Christ. As the Psalmist cried out at the wonder of the creation of man, "What is man that you are mindful of him, and the son of man that you care for him" (Psalm 8:4), so too with God's recreation of us in the image of Christ we need to stand back in awe and wonder at what he has done in our lives. Praise him for his sanctification.

The Power of Sanctification

Second, when we see our lives and the lives of others being more and more holy and—leading us to give thanks to the source of sanctification,

God alone—we come to see the wonder of sanctification in *the power of sanctification*. We ought always to give thanks *to God*.

I want to show you that sanctification has to be accomplished by the powerful working of God alone. Think about the very context in which Paul is writing. The experience of the Thessalonians is proof that sanctification finds its source in the power of God. They were persecuted, they were afflicted, they were mocked, they were despised, they were beaten, their missionaries Paul and Silvanus were run out of town, and their neighbors hated them. As our text goes on to say in verse 4, We ourselves boast about you in the churches of God for your steadfastness and faith in all your persecutions and in the afflictions that you are enduring. The power of sanctification has to be God's. How else is it that the more the world stains the church's outward beauty with blood the more her inward beauty shines? How else is it that the more the world persecutes the church with death the more the church grows? How is it that the more the world hates us the more we love God? It's the power of God at work in us that causes this!

Furthermore, the New Testament is saturated with verse after verse after verse that says everything about the totality of our salvation is found in God and his power—including sanctification. In 1 Corinthians 1:30 we read, "And because of him you are in Christ Jesus, who became to us wisdom from God, righteousness *and sanctification* and redemption." In 2 Corinthians 3:18 we read, "And we all, with unveiled face, beholding the glory of the Lord, are being transformed into the same image from one degree of glory to another. For *this comes from the Lord* who is the Spirit." In Titus 2:14 we read, "Who gave himself for us to redeem us from all lawlessness and *to purify for himself* a people for his own possession who are zealous for good works." Our passage in 2 Thessalonians 1:3 says our sanctification comes from God. The three passages above say it comes from Christ.

If you look at Ephesians 1:15–20 we read that it comes from God the Father, through Christ, by the Holy Spirit:

> For this reason, because I have heard of your faith in the Lord Jesus and your love toward all the saints, I do not cease to give thanks for you, remembering you in my prayers, that the God of our Lord Jesus Christ, the Father of glory, may give you a spirit of wisdom and of revelation in the knowledge of him, having the eyes of your hearts enlightened, that you may know what is the hope to which he has called you, what are the riches of his glorious inheritance in the saints, and what is the immeasurable greatness of his power toward us who believe, according to the working of his great might that he worked in Christ when he raised him from the dead and seated him at his right hand in the heavenly places.

Why is this so important? Let me illustrate by asking a question: how do you feel when you don't eat for a long time? Your stomach hurts, your head hurts, you feel tired, and you feel weak. Do you know why? It's because you need food to give your body what it needs to have strength and life. If you don't eat you die. What Paul is saying is so important because it teaches us that our Triune God himself is our spiritual food who gives us power to live for him.

I love how my favorite English Puritan, John Owen, described the power of sanctification: "This whole matter of sanctification and holiness is peculiarly joined with and limited unto the doctrine, truth, and grace of the gospel; for *holiness is nothing but the implanting, writing, and realizing of the gospel in our souls.*"[3] He went on to say, "There neither is, nor ever was, in the world, nor ever shall be, the least dram of holiness, but what, flowing from Jesus Christ, is communicated by the Spirit, according to the truth and promise of the gospel."[4]

Are you longing for the gospel to be implanted by the Holy Spirit in your soul? Are you thirsty for Christ to quench your soul with his grace to make you more like him? If you're a Christian, continue to look to your gracious Triune God for the power of your sanctification. If you're a Christian and you're struggling with some besetting sin, and you feel powerless to overcome it, the power is not found in you, in methods, in gimmicks—it's found in God himself. If you're not a Christian but you are coming to realize that you are a sinner but you feel that everything you've tried to change your life, to stop doing certain things isn't working, the answer is Christ. Come to him, believe in him and he will forgive you of your sins and begin to cause you to live a life as you were created to live—not for yourself but for him. Praise him for his power in sanctification

The Promise of Sanctification

And this leads us to see the wonder of sanctification in *the promise of sanctification*. As Paul continues in our text, Because your faith *is growing abundantly*, and the love of every one of you for one another *is increasing* (v. 3).

The promise of sanctification is that we will progress in this life in turning away from sin and turning to Christ in a life of holiness. This is vital to understand. We simplistically speak of faith in static terms, saying, "I wish I had your faith," or of love, saying, "I'm in love; I've fallen out of love," Instead, Paul describes the dynamic, vital, and progressive nature of our sanctification in terms of faith, hope, and love. He praises God for his power in their lives because their faith is *growing* abundantly and the love of every one of you for one another is *increasing* (v. 3). And here is what is so amazing about this little verse. Go back with me to 1 Thessalonians 1:2–3. Listen to Paul's prayer: "We give thanks to God always for all of you, constantly mentioning you in our prayers, remembering before our God and Father your work of faith and labor of love and steadfastness of hope in our Lord Jesus Christ." He went on to pray in 3:11–12 that they would increase and abound in love, and he urged them in 4:10 to love more and more, and he prayed in great confidence in 5:23–24 that all this would happen. Now notice our text. All of that is coming to reality! They were growing. They were increasing. They were abounding in all the ways of holiness and sanctification. In fact, Paul creates a compound word here to express the growth of their faith. It was growing abundantly, or literally, super-growing (*huperauxanei*).[5]

So what? So what! This means that we have the assurance that God himself will work in the hearts and lives of us his children. "He who began a good work in you *will* bring it to completion" (Philippians 1:6). "Now may the God of peace *himself* sanctify you completely … He who calls you is faithful; he *will* surely do it" (1 Thessalonians 5:23, 24). The perseverance of the saints in holiness in this life is an assured reality, not because it's some doctrine on a shelf, but because God has promised it. We … give thanks to God … because your faith is growing abundantly and the love of every one of you for one another is increasing (v. 3).

And notice something else that is really amazing here. God's promise to sanctify us by his power that deserves our praise is accomplished through the means of Paul's prayer. Paul prayed and God answered. In theological terms, this means that sanctification is our goal, which our forefathers called the final cause of our sanctification. Also, God himself is the one who accomplishes sanctification, which our forefathers called the efficient cause of our sanctification. But then we notice that it is prayer that is the way sanctification happened, which our forefathers called the instrumental cause of our sanctification. Think about that for a moment. Your prayers are the means through which God accomplishes the goal of your sanctification. This should encourage us to know that God promises in his Word and demonstrates in his Word that if we use the means he has given to us, he will bless those means accordingly. He always does. So praise your Triune God through prayer for his promise to sanctify you.

Conclusion

The devil wants you to be afraid. He wants you to be afraid of God and his working because the devil knows this is one way to distance us from God. Yet God wants you to praise him for his work.

The devil wants you to be afraid of God so you will trust in yourself and in your own efforts for sanctification. The devil knows this will lead you to despair. Yet God wants you to experience his power.

The devil wants you to be afraid of doing anything. He knows how easy it is to convince you to think that if you do something you might lose your salvation. But God wants you to rest in his promise, which enlivens you to pray more fervently. Be filled today with the wonder of your sanctification. Amen.

22

The Most Honest Sermon Possible

2 Thessalonians 1:5–9

I want to draw you in to the spiritual side of a preacher's preparation as he reads the above words, meditates upon them, and listens to what the Lord is saying through them. I knew these words spoke of God. I knew they spoke of Jesus' coming as judge. I knew they spoke of judgment and hell. But as I prepared, I was approaching these words impersonally, from a distance, only as doctrinal topics to be preached. What struck me was how these are open, sincere, truthful, and honest words from a pastor to his people. These words are the blunt truth we all say we want and need, but when we hear the blunt truth from a pastor concerning eternal things, we are offended. What Paul teaches us is that what we need to hear is not what we want, but what we need; not what we think we need, but what God says we need. As the old slogan said, "God said it, that settles it." This is why Paul said in his first letter to these Christians that true preaching "does not spring from error or impurity or any attempt to deceive … not to please man, but to please God" and not "with words of flattery … nor with a pretext for greed—God is witness." (1 Thessalonians 2:3, 4, 5)

Let me cut to the chase and say this portion of God's Word is *the most honest sermon possible* because it tells you about God, your condition before him if you do not trust in him, and your response to him if you do trust in him. What do we learn in this most honest sermon possible?

The Soberness of God

Paul's most honest sermon possible teaches us first of *the soberness of God*. When Paul speaks of God here he speaks with a soberness, a seriousness, and a reverence for him. We are so used to being bombarded with songs that sing, "What if God was one of us? Just a slob like one of us? Just a stranger on the bus? Trying to make his way home."[1] Paul speaks soberly of God because the very nature of God, the essence of God, the existence of God is a sober reality. When you read these verses as God intends, you should be struck with awe at who God is.

In verse 5 we learn that God's judgment is righteous. When believers are persecuted and nothing is done to the persecutors, we are shocked and dismayed at the lack of justice. But Paul is saying that this in fact *is* a visible token that one day there will be a final judgment. And that judgment will be according to God's perfect righteousness and justice. What Paul says here is what the psalmist says after listing all the sins of the wicked, especially their persecution of the righteous:

> He says in his heart, "God has forgotten,
> he has hidden his face, he will never see it."

Arise, O Lord; O God, lift up your hand;
forget not the afflicted.
Why does the wicked renounce God
and say in his heart, 'You will not call to account?'
But you do see. (Psalm 10:11–14a)

In verse 6 of our text we learn not only that God's judgment is righteous, but that God is a just God who will repay those who afflict his people. The idea is that the punishment meets the crime. How is that possible if an unbeliever persecutes a believer and is not persecuting God himself? When a Christian is persecuted, it is actually Christ behind the Christian who is persecuted. As Jesus said to Saul, the great persecutor of the early church, "Saul, Saul, why are you persecuting *me*?" (Acts 9:4; emphasis added)

In verse 8 we learn that God will inflict vengeance when Jesus returns. Does this sound like the nice little god who only wants to make your life happy? God is going avenge his people when he sends Jesus to the world to be its Judge. He will come in flaming fire (v. 8), which is a biblical image of the wrath of God.[2] This is why the New Testament tells us that we are not to be in the business of revenge: "Beloved, never avenge yourselves, but leave it to the wrath of God, for it is written, 'Vengeance is mine, I will repay, says the Lord.'" (Romans 12:19)

In verse 9 we learn that God will punish with eternal destruction. Be assured that the New Testament does not say that everyone makes it to heaven in the end. "Love Wins" out over justice is a sentiment that has no biblical basis at all.[3]

Do you have this sober vision of God? You need to. This is who the God of the Bible is. He is gracious and he is righteous. He is love and he is just. He is forgiving and he is avenging. You need to change your understanding about God from your opinions, your assumptions, what you have heard about what Christians believe, and even—and I say this to our shame as believers—from what you have seen us do in our inconsistent lives. You need to know God as he reveals himself to you in this Word.

That's some honest talk. That's some confident speech. That's some dogmatic speech, isn't it? But that's what you need to hear. Let me conclude this point with something interesting I read that illustrates the point. In a *New York Times* review of the Broadway show, "The Book of Mormon,"[4] the reviewer says the central theme of this play is that while religious stories are silly, religion can still do enormous good. The good comes from people who remember that religious teaching is to be taken metaphorically and it must be understood that all religions ultimately preach love and service. Listen to these sample lines from the review:

> Vague, uplifting, nondoctrinal religiosity doesn't actually last. The religions that grow, succor and motivate people to perform heroic acts of service are usually theologically rigorous, arduous in practice and definite in their convictions about what is True and False.
>
> The religions that thrive have exactly what "The Book of Mormon" ridicules: communal theologies, doctrines and codes of conduct rooted in claims of absolute truth.
>
> Rigorous theology provides believers with a map of reality. These maps may seem dry and schematic … but they contain the accumulated wisdom of thousands of co-believers who through the centuries have faced similar journeys and trials.
>
> Rigorous theology helps people avoid mindless conformity. Without timeless rules, we all have a tendency to be swept up

> in the temper of the moment. But tough-minded theologies are countercultural. They insist on principles and practices that provide an antidote to mere fashion.

This vision of the soberness of God is countercultural. And because it is, it leads us to our second point.

The Seriousness of the Lost

Paul's most honest sermon possible teaches us second of *the seriousness of the lost*. The fact that Paul had a sober vision of God was the reason he had a serious message for the lost. As Christians we believe there is one human race all derived from the same father, Adam (Acts 17:26). As Christians we believe we are all in the same predicament of our sins keeping us apart from fellowship with God (Romans 3:23). But we also believe we as humans are divided into two: Christians and non-Christians, believers and unbelievers, saved and unsaved, the forgiven and the unforgiven, God's friends and God's enemies, the church and the world. Why? Again, it goes back to God and who he is. Because he is perfect he cannot dwell with imperfection. Because God is righteous he must punish the unrighteous. Because God is holy he cannot look upon us in our sins (Habakkuk 1:13). This is why Paul speaks here of the serious condition of the lost.

Paul says those who afflict Christians will be repaid with affliction. If you are an unbeliever, let me ask you have you ever made fun of a Christian? Have you ever demeaned a Christian? Have you ever mocked a Christian for his or her beliefs? If you've done so you've made fun of, demeaned, and mocked Christ himself. And to do so is to take the name of the Lord in vain. And as the law of God says, "the Lord will not hold him guiltless who takes his name in vain" (Exodus 20:7). That is why the death penalty was commanded for it in the Old Testament (Leviticus 24:10–17; cf. HC, Q&A 100). That penalty will be fully meted out in eternity with eternal punishment.

Paul says those who do not know God will experience the vengeance of God and suffer eternal punishment. What does Paul mean by not knowing God when he says elsewhere that everyone does know him (Romans 1:18–21)? Let me illustrate this for you. In American schools we learn about the United States' first President, George Washington. He was a general in the British army (with apologies to my friends over the pond!) who then fought against the British for American independence. We are taught that George Washington was real. Did he really live? Of course, we say, although we have not met him. You see, we can know someone without ever truly *knowing* them. We can know someone existed, we can know he is real, and we can even know some things about him. But this is not the same as *knowing* him, that is, having a real living, face-to-face relationship with him. It's the same with God. God has made us all with a consciousness of his existence and with a conscience that knows right and wrong. The problem is that we constantly try to "suppress" that knowledge from coming to mind and from affecting us (Romans 1:18). And so the unbeliever knows God, but does not *know* God. And when that describes you, the serious reality is punishment.

Paul also says that those who do not obey the gospel of our Lord Jesus, meaning, who do not believe,[5] will experience the vengeance of God and suffer eternal punishment. This is a terrible situation to be in. You were born sinful and you continue to sin, suppressing God's knowledge and righteousness from your mind so that you can live on what you think are your own terms. But all you are doing, according to what Paul says in Romans 2:5, is "storing up wrath for yourself on the day of wrath." But God saves sinners. That's the gospel in as short a phrase as possible. God saves sinners. God has been merciful to the world in sending Jesus to the world to live perfectly, to die in the place of sinners, and to rise to demonstrate all this is true. He offers himself in your place so that you will not be cursed but blessed; that your sins will be taken away and placed on him so that his perfection will be placed on you instead. Then God can smile upon you and call you his child, his son or daughter. God saves sinners. But you reject it. Why? Come to Jesus with all your sins and he will forgive you. Come to Jesus with all your doubts and he will teach you. Come to Jesus with all your disobedience and he will lead you in a life of obedience.

If you are an unbeliever, you have a serious situation in which you find yourself today. But there is a God who offers you a serious solution to your sins.

The Service of the Church

What should be our response as believers when we read this passage? Paul's most honest sermon possible teaches us finally of *the service of the church*. Here we learn about our life in response to the soberness of God and the seriousness of the lost.

Obviously we should be ecstatic and exuberant that all this righteous judgment, affliction, and vengeance that we deserve has been satisfied by the life, death, and resurrection of Jesus for us, for you, for me. As one hymn celebrates it:

> Man of Sorrows! what a name
> For the Son of God, who came
> Ruined sinners to reclaim.
> Hallelujah! What a Savior!
>
> Bearing shame and scoffing rude,
> In my place condemned He stood;
> Sealed my pardon with His blood.
> Hallelujah! What a Savior!

Guilty, vile, and helpless we;
Spotless Lamb of God was He;
"Full atonement!" can it be?
Hallelujah! What a Savior![6]

But there's something of significance here in terms of our relationship to the world as churches. That significance can best be understood against the backdrop of our insignificant attitudes at times. We get all hung up over congregational budgets and certain line items. We can complain that our churches don't have cushioned seats. We can complain about the lighting. We can get hung up over not having a MOPS (Mothers of Pre-Schoolers) group, a junior high youth group, a high school youth group, or a college group. What are we doing? Where is our head? Where is our heart? This passage calls us back to why we exist. We exist to serve God but we also exist to serve the world. We must have an eager compassion for the state of the lost.[7] We must be praying fervently for opportunities to share the good news with the lost. We must be ever ready to explain our hope to a hopeless world. We have to be willing to invite seekers to church to be found by God himself. We must be hospitable and welcoming when the world arrives at our doorstep. This text calls us to service. We serve the Lord as we serve the world in its greatest need—bringing them face to face with the living God.

Conclusion

As you read this part of Paul's letter to the Thessalonians, I pray you can say, "That was an honest sermon." We cannot avoid what is clearly taught in the Bible. As St. John Chrysostom once said to his congregation, "Let us not avoid discourses concerning hell, that we may avoid hell. Let us not banish the remembrance of punishment, that we may escape punishment."[8] Hell and punishment are real, and when we speak of them, we acknowledge by faith our salvation; we acknowledge the world's need. What an honest God.

23

Jesus the Judge

2 Thessalonians 1:7–9

Jesus is coming again. This is a basic affirmation of New Testament Christianity: "Men of Galilee, why do you stand looking into heaven? This Jesus, who was taken up from you into heaven, will come in the same way as you saw him go into heaven" (Acts 1:9). This is a basic affirmation of catholic Christianity: "And He shall come again, with glory, to judge the living and the dead" (Nicene Creed). His Second Coming will have effects upon unbelievers, those who not know God … those who do not obey the gospel of our Lord Jesus (vv. 7–9), and upon believers, called "saints" and "all who have believed" (v. 10). Here I want us to meditate upon verses 7–9 only, and the effect of Jesus' Second Coming upon the unbelieving world.

As with the previous section, this is blunt, honest, and realistic truth about Jesus. This is not the so-called Jesus depicted in cheesy art, the mere man that liberal theologians and politicians describe as a maverick or radical, nor is it the Jesus who so neatly fits into our comfortable lifestyles. You know, the Jesus we say we believe is important to us—except on Sundays when we're out of town, when our kids have games or performances, or when I just need some "me time." This is God in the flesh who came the first time to be condemned but who is coming again to condemn; who came to be afflicted but who is coming again with affliction; who came to be judged but who is coming again to judge. This is *Jesus the Judge*. Notice with me what it means for Jesus and for the world for him to be the Judge:

The Revelation

The Recipients

The Result

The Revelation

First, Paul teaches us about *the revelation* of Jesus the Judge. Paul elsewhere calls the Second Coming of Jesus his "appearing" (2 Timothy 4:8) and his "manifestation" (Colossians 3:4), both which express the visibility of his Second Coming to the world; but here in 2 Thessalonians he calls it his "revelation," literally, his "apocalypse." This is a more dramatic word that expresses divine action. God will send him back to the world at his appointed time by pulling back the curtain of eternity to reveal the end of all things. And look at how Paul describes the circumstances of this revelation.

He will be revealed from heaven (v. 7). He will step out of eternity into time; he will come from heaven to earth; he will cease interceding for his people and intervene on their behalf. As Paul says in 1 Thessalonians 4:16 he will "descend from heaven with a cry of command."

He will also be revealed with his mighty angels (v. 7). He is, as the Old Testament says, the Lord of hosts, the Lord of all the armies of heaven. He will not come as the bleating lamb, but as the roaring lion. He will not come humbly on a donkey, but triumphantly on the white horse. As Paul said previously in 1 Thessalonians, Jesus will be heralded by "the voice of an archangel and the sound of the trumpet of God" (1 Thessalonians 4:16).

He will also be revealed in flaming fire (v. 8). Why is the imagery of fire so significant? Because in the Old Testament God himself is described as a "consuming fire" (Deuteronomy 4:24), but even more, whenever he would appear in a climactic way to his people it was often as fire. He appeared to Abram as a smoking fire pot and burning torch (Genesis 15). He appeared to Moses as a burning bush (Exodus 3). He appeared to the Israelites as a pillar of fire by night (Exodus 14). He appeared to Elijah and the prophets of Baal as fire (1 Kings 18). He appeared to Solomon as the fire that burnt upon the altar of the temple (2 Chronicles 7:1). The Psalms spoke this way, saying, "Fire goes before him and burns up his adversaries all around" (Psalm 97:3). When the prophets spoke of the coming of the Judge at the end of time, they spoke with the imagery of fire. Daniel said this: "A stream of fire issued and came out from before him; a thousand thousands served him, and ten thousand times ten thousands stood before him; a court sat in judgment, and the books were opened" (Daniel 7:10).

This is not "your own personal Jesus" that popular songs in our culture sing about. This is God in human flesh wrapped in the glory of eternity coming to wage war. Upon whom?

The Recipients

Second, Paul teaches us about *the recipients* of Jesus the Judge. Think about when you are looking down upon some ants or a small insect that you are about to squash. Looking down so far makes you feel so big, doesn't it? When we think and talk about God, his glory and his judgments, we should feel like those ants. We should feel the opposite of what we feel when we look down so far upon those ants. How little we are under the shadow of the Almighty.

And so Jesus is going to be revealed as Judge and the recipients of this aspect of his Second Coming are described as those who do not know God and those who do not obey the gospel of Jesus Christ (v. 8). When he comes again, he will come for all humanity. We saw this back in 1 Thessalonians 4. He will bring with him believers who died and went to be with him. Then he will raise their bodies and transform them to be like his glorious body. For those who believe in Jesus, his Second Coming finalizes everything about their salvation. This is why Paul said that we are not to grieve about the Second Coming but that we are to "encourage one another" with its glorious reality (1 Thessalonians 4:18). And here in our passage, he speaks of us glorifying him when he returns and marveling at his revelation. If you know God and have obeyed the gospel of Jesus Christ, be assured that his revelation is not to condemn you but to bring you ultimate consolation. For example, the Reformation statement of faith, the Belgic Confession, says,

> Therefore, with good reason the thought of this judgment is horrible and dreadful to wicked and evil people. But it is very pleasant and a great comfort to the righteous and elect, since their total redemption will then be accomplished. They will then receive the fruits of their labor and of the trouble they have suffered. (art. 37)

But for those who do not know God by having a relationship with him that is based on his grace in Jesus Christ, and who do not obey the gospel of Jesus Christ (v. 8) because they have not turned away from their sinful lifestyle and turned to Jesus for forgiveness, what

Paul says here should be terrible and dreadful. How will the unbeliever face Jesus on Judgment Day? All their sins will be exposed. All their thoughts will be made manifest. All their rebellion against God will be shown for what it is—a life of serving their own desires, their own pleasures, and their own wants. The Bible says some will try to hide:

> Then the kings of the earth and the great ones and the generals and the rich and the powerful, and everyone, slave and free, hid themselves in the caves and among the rocks of the mountains, calling to the mountains and rocks, "Fall on us and hide us from the face of him who is seated on the throne, and from the wrath of the Lamb, for the great day of their wrath has come, and who can stand?" (Revelation 6:15–17)

The Bible says others will try to impress him:

> Not everyone who says to me, "Lord, Lord," will enter the kingdom of heaven, but the one who does the will of my Father who is in heaven. On that day many will say to me, "Lord, Lord, did we not prophesy in your name, and cast out demons in your name, and do many mighty works in your name?" And then will I declare to them, "I never knew you; depart from me, you workers of lawlessness." (Matthew 7:21-23)

So how will you face him? What will you say to him? What will you present before him?

The Results

What will happen when the world of believers does face Jesus? And they will! Third, Paul teaches us about *the results* of Jesus as Judge. Let me be honest with you. This horrifies me. Why? Because Paul is describing the reality of the torments of hell. And it should horrify us that people are literally going there. This is the other side of the good news that, while we are afraid to speak of it, we must. If there is a heaven, there must be a hell. If there is grace, there must be justice. If there is good news, there must be bad news.

Hell is real. A whole generation has been catechized by John Lennon to deny the reality of hell, who sang,

Imagine there's no Heaven
It's easy if you try
No hell below us
Above us only sky
Imagine all the people
Living for today.

Here in our text what Paul says about hell is as real as the church that existed in Thessalonica. Hell is as real as the persecutions they were suffering. This is no allegory, no metaphor, and no figure of speech. There is nothing here that indicates he is speaking in any other way than to speak of a real, ultimate reality.

Hell is just. The Thessalonians' present persecution was an evidence of God's righteous judgment to come (1:5). In his justice he will repay those who afflict his people (1:6). In his justice he will inflict vengeance and cause his enemies to suffer punishment (1:8, 9). What is justice? It is perfect judgment. God is perfectly just and his law perfectly reveals his justice. When we violate his law we violate perfection. Violations must be perfectly and justly punished. This should horrify anyone who thinks he or she can stand before it. Every thought weighed in the balance. Every word weighed. Every deed weighed. Are they all perfect? Are they all pure? Are they all upright in accordance with justice and righteousness? His judgment is coming.

Hell is eternal. As Paul says, this punishment is *eternal* destruction (v. 9).[1] Some today have said that while heaven is eternal, hell is not. The context, though, compares this destruction with the presence of the Lord and the glory of [Jesus'] might, which are both equally eternal.[2] But if God is God, and he is who he is eternally, this means that both his grace and justice extend into eternity as his attributes. How long is "eternal?" As the Puritan, Thomas Brooks said, "The damned shall live as long in hell as God Himself shall live in heaven." How long is "eternal?" Another Puritan, John Flavel, said, "When millions of years and ages are past and gone, this will still be wrath to come. Ever coming as a river ever flowing."[3]

What will happen there in hell? Punishment "away from the presence of the Lord." Does that mean hell is the absence of God? Yes, and no. Yes if you mean the absence of the hope of grace, mercy, and love. No if you mean he is not there. He is omnipresent and even in hell. As the Psalmist said, "If I make my bed in Sheol, you are there" (Psalm 139:8). Hell is, as the Westminster Larger Catechism says, the reality of being "cast out from the *favourable* presence of God, and the glorious fellowship with Christ, his saints, and all his holy angels" (WLC, Q&A 89).

What will happen there? Punishment "from the glory of his might." Hell is a reality of being "punished with unspeakable torments, both of body and soul, with the devil and his angels forever." And this punishment will be eternal conscious punishment just as heaven will be eternal conscious paradise.[4]

Hell is a horrible place. Talk of hell should fill us with fear. For those who do not know Jesus Christ, we need to communicate in love their need for Jesus to escape punishment. For those who may be backsliding, "you who are spiritual should restore [them] in a spirit of gentleness" (Galatians 6:1). Help them awaken from their slumber. For those who know God and believe in Christ, who are strong and assured, allow God to work in you a heart of gratitude and allow God to work through you to enliven others with the good news.

Conclusion

Here is serious talk about Jesus. He came once as a lamb to be sacrificed but he is coming again as a lion to devour his enemies. Can you see the difference? If you have Jesus as a lamb, this means that he was judged. But if you have Jesus as a lion, this means that you will be judged. Don't be judged. Repent of your sins, believe in Jesus, and seek refuge for your soul by being baptized in his name and uniting yourself to his church.

24

The Glorification of Christ

2 Thessalonians 1:10–12

The Second Coming of Jesus Christ to this world is like a two-edged sword. For those who do not know God in a saving way by trusting in his Son, Jesus, it will be a day of condemnation. For those who do know God as the Father by faith in his Son, it will be a day of vindication. It will be a day of bane for many but a day of blessing for others. It will be a day of exposing guilt for many but a day of giving glory to others. It will be a day for punishing many but a day of praising for others: "Well done, good and faithful servant" (Matthew 25:21, 23). In the passage before us we want to meditate upon the results of Jesus' Second Coming for those who do "know God" and who do "obey the gospel of our Lord Jesus" (v. 8).

To do this we will focus especially on the idea of glory that permeates this passage. There are three senses in which the idea of glory or glorification is being used here. First, verse 9 speaks of the glory of Christ's might at this Second Coming, which verse 8 explained as his Second Coming "in flaming fire" in relation to the unbeliever. Second, verse 10 speaks of Jesus coming again to be glorified in his saints, which leads Paul to go on to pray in verse 12 that the saints would live in a way in which Jesus would be glorified in you. Third, there is another sense that you might have overlooked because the word itself is not used right in front of a sentence. Look again at verse 12: that the name of our Lord Jesus may be glorified in you, *and you in him*. He is saying that you [will be glorified] in him. This is what Paul elsewhere calls the doctrine of glorification (e.g. Romans 8:30).

It's these last two uses that we are concerned with here in verses 10–12. In these words Paul exhorts our minds and hearts to be focused upon *the glorification of Christ*—both his glorifying of us in verse 12 and our glorifying of him in verse 10.

Christ's Glorifying of Us

First, let us begin at the end of our passage, which speaks about *Christ's glorifying of us*. Here we read the goal of Paul's prayer for the Thessalonians is that Jesus' name would be glorified in them—that's our second point we'll come to in a moment—and that they would experience the ultimate goal of glorification, as you [would be glorified] in him (v. 12). Paul stated this great goal of God's redemptive work in us in terms of glorification most memorably in the familiar golden chain of salvation: "And those whom he *predestined* he also *called*, and those whom he called he also *justified*, and those whom he justified he also *glorified*" (Romans 8:30).

So what does it mean to be glorified? It means at least two things. First, it means to be granted entrance into the eternal and heavenly presence of God. As Paul says in 1 Thessalonians 2:12, we are to "walk in a manner worthy of God, who calls you into his own kingdom and glory." Elsewhere, the book of Hebrews speaks of God as the one "for whom and by whom all things exist" as the God who is also "bringing many sons to glory" (Hebrews 2:10). Glorification is the end goal of all of God's work for us in eternal election, in Christ's redemption in time on the cross, and in our personal life of sanctification. But how can we sinners ever enter into God's glorious presence in our sinful state? After all, the Lord told Moses "man shall not see me and live" (Exodus 33:20), and the Lord's glory was so great that the prophet Isaiah cried out, "Woe is me! For I am lost; for I am a man of unclean lips, and I dwell in the midst of a people of unclean lips; for my eyes have seen the King, the LORD of hosts!" (Isaiah 6:5) There is a second meaning to glorification, then. Glorification means to be made like Jesus. Look into the next chapter of 2 Thessalonians where we read:

> But we ought always to give thanks to God for you, brothers beloved by the Lord, because God chose you as the firstfruits to be saved, through sanctification by the Spirit and belief in the truth. To this he called you through our gospel, so that you may obtain *the glory of our Lord* Jesus Christ (2 Thessalonians 2:13–14).

When we enter into the eternal and heavenly presence of God we then become full partakers of and share in the glory of our Lord Jesus Christ. John Calvin described this blessing of salvation as "the chief and unique consolation of the godly."[1] We will be like our Lord. Let's delve into this some more. What is "the glory of our Lord Jesus Christ?" And what does it mean for us to have it?

Jesus' own glory is his existence as the eternal Son in unity with the Father and the Holy Spirit. Before his incarnation and birth as the God-man, the Son of God was in the eternal and glorious presence of the Triune God. In the words of Jesus' own prayer, "And now,

Father, glorify me in your own presence with the glory that I had with you before the world existed" (John 17:5). And here Paul is saying that we will obtain this glory of being united to our gracious God in eternity. Jesus also prayed, "The glory that you have given me I have given to them, that they may be one even as we are one" (John 17:22). The glory that we will obtain is the same glory God originally made Adam for. But that eternal fellowship with God was lost when Adam sinned. This eternal fellowship and glory is what none of us can have apart from Jesus Christ restoring it to us as the second Adam (1 Corinthians 15:45). When we turn away from ourselves and our sins and turn to Jesus Christ in faith we receive a new relationship with God that begins now in this life, and then lasts forever into eternity.

Jesus' own glory was also to be sinless. He was sinless in his mother's womb by virtue of being conceived by the Holy Spirit (Matthew 1:18). And he lived a sinless life, as Hebrews 7:26 says, "For it was indeed fitting that we should have such a high priest, holy, innocent, unstained, separated from sinners." To say that we will "obtain the glory of our Lord Jesus Christ" (2 Thessalonians 2:14) is to say that we will be like him in sinlessness for eternity. Looking back in 1 Thessalonians we recall that Paul prayed that the Thessalonians would increase and abound in love and that God would "establish your hearts blameless in holiness before our God and Father, at the coming of our Lord Jesus with all his saints" (1 Thessalonians 3:13). This should be the longing of our hearts. We should want to be freed from our sins so that we can be like Jesus, not partially, but fully. Are you sick and tired of sinning? Are you defeated? Do you long for holiness? Then cling to Jesus Christ the glorious Savior. Trust in him, rely on him, and cry out to him continually: "Wretched man that I am! Who will deliver me from this body of death? Thanks be to God through Jesus Christ our Lord!" (Romans 7:24–25a)

Jesus' own glory was to be resurrected in his body. Paul says he was "declared to be the Son of God in power according to the Spirit of holiness" (Romans 1:4). His title is "Son-of-God-in-power" and he received this by the Spirit of holiness. Again, Paul says that while "the first man Adam became a living being, the last Adam became a life-giving spirit" (1 Corinthians 15:45). By his resurrection he now is Lord of new life to sinners. We, too, will share in this resurrection glory. Our bodies will be sown in the ground perishable, but raised imperishable; sown in dishonor, but raised in glory; sown in weakness, but raised in power; sown a natural body, but raised a spiritual body (1 Corinthians 15:42–44). Paul tells us in Philippians 3:21 that Jesus himself "will transform our lowly body to be like his glorious body, by the power that enables him even to subject all things to himself."

What a gospel-blessing glorification is and will be. Paul describes it so simply, yet so profoundly: and you in him (v. 12). In the words of John Calvin, Paul prays here that "[God] may shine upon them with His glory and that they may partake of it."[2] Revel in Christ's future glorification of you.

Our Glorifying of Christ

This ultimate blessing of the gospel work of our Lord Jesus Christ should—must—cause us to respond. How? As Paul says in our passage: your life should be characterized by good works so that the name of our Lord Jesus may be glorified in you (v. 12). This is our second point, *our glorifying of Christ*. I need to stress the fact that our liberty in Christ does not lead to license in sinning (Galatians 5:13; 1 Peter 2:16); the certainty we have in him of glorification in the life to come does not lead to complacency in this life. Why do I say that? Let me explain it in terms that teenagers can understand. When the school year draws to its close do you stop doing your homework? Do you stop studying for tests? Do you stop working on final papers and projects?

Students know that as a semester or school year comes to an end how important it is to finish well to get the highest GPA possible so that their options are better when they finish high school. The point is that when you know school is almost done, you get excited and motivated to work hard. It's the same way with our spiritual lives. As we know Jesus is coming we are motivated to bring him glory and praise.

Now let me explain it by looking again at our passage. When Jesus returns "on that day" he returns to be glorified in his saints (v. 10). But notice—and this is so important to see in your Bible—in verse 11 he goes on to link what happens on the day we are glorified with how we live to bring him glory all the days of our lives. To this end is a strong purpose clause. It's because of the fact that Jesus will glorify us that Paul prayed always with that goal in mind (v. 11). Let me belabor this point by having you turn with me to 1 John 3. In verse 2 he says, "Beloved, we are God's children now, and what we will be has not yet appeared; but we know that when he appears we shall be like him, because we shall see him as he is." That's Christ's glorifying of us. Now look at what John says we need to be doing in response: "And everyone who thus hopes in him purifies himself as he is pure" (1 John 3:3).

So Paul exhorts us to glorify Christ in this present life that we live that we might bring him glory in the life that is to come. What are the means, that is, the ways we bring him glory? In the words of a medieval Latin aphorism that characterized the life of the monk, and that was later used by our Puritan forefathers, *ora et labora*, pray and work. Paul was praying that they would be working. Prayer and work are united in the Christian life.

Prayer brings glory to Jesus Christ most obviously because it is how we communicate to him our praise and our thanks. This is why the Heidelberg Catechism says prayer "is the chief part of thankfulness which God requires of us" (Q&A 116). Prayer also brings glory to Jesus Christ because by the very activity of prayer we acknowledge that we have come to the end of ourselves, that we are in desperate need of Christ, and that we depend upon Christ. So by prayer we go to God, but when we leave his presence by ending our prayer, we must not go without God. We go to God in order to go into the world with God. And that's what Paul is saying when he says he prayed that our God may make you worthy of his calling and may fulfill every resolve for good and every work of faith by his power (v. 11).

To be worthy of God's calling to glorify us on the last day means to live in such a way that reflects that truth. And we reflect his calling by resolving to do good and by actually doing good works in faith. How you live your life matters. Resolve to do good not only while you are around Christians and at home, but especially before the world when you are at the workplace and in your neighborhood. When we live to give Jesus glory now, we can be assured that on that [final] day he will be glorified in us (v. 10).

Conclusion

Let me conclude with this line from John Calvin, who said, "Those who have extolled the glory of Christ are to be glorified in their turn in Him."[3] Our glorification by Christ on the last day should cause our glorification of Christ today. This is the purpose of our lives. This is the devotion of our lives. This is the delight of our lives. Glorify him now and then for eternity you will enjoy him forever (WSC, Q&A 1).

25

False Prophets of the Second Coming

2 Thessalonians 2:1–3

The year 2011 brought the Christian church yet another "historic" event. Yet it is one we should not be proud of. This event was the latest from a long line of millennial cults. From the ancient Montanists to the Millerites and its Great Disappointment of 1844, to their off-shoot, the Seventh-Day Adventists, who reinterpreted 1844 as Jesus' entrance into the heavenly temple, to the Jehovah's Witnesses and their failed prediction of 1914, there has been ongoing millennial madness in church history. Even more recently the well-respected Chuck Smith (1927–2013) said the rapture of the church out of the world would be "any time before 1981," only to leave many people at Calvary Chapel Costa Mesa disillusioned.[1] As we meditate upon the text before us, one thing should be clear: the Second Coming of Jesus Christ is a *source of hope* and should not be used as a *subject of fear* for the believer. In the words of Thomas Manton, "The time of Christ's coming to judgment must be patiently expected, not rashly defined or determined."[2]

2 Thessalonians chapter 2 is the heart of this pastoral letter. Admittedly, though, this is one of those passages in Paul's writings that Peter very well may have had in mind when he said, "There are some things in [Paul's writings] that are hard to understand, which the ignorant and unstable twist to their own destruction" (2 Peter 3:16). Because of that, let me say that while I may have my own personal opinions about the meaning and application of certain things here, I want to model for you a responsible reading of Scripture by focusing on those things that are clear, that can be agreed upon, and that can be applied in our time. St. Chrysostom once used the illustration of a boat and its sail. If we open the sails, then we will be led under control by the wind; if not, we will merely float at the whim and wish of the sea and wind. Opening our Bibles is like opening our sails to the leading and illuminating work of the Holy Spirit as opposed to merely using our personal rudder of our own imaginations.[3] At the outset of this chapter, then, Paul warns the Thessalonians that there are certain *false prophets of the Second Coming* among them, who are speculating.

Their Message

First, Paul writes about these false prophets in terms of *their message*. He reminds the Thessalonians here, that, "When I was still with you I told you these things" (2 Thessalonians 2:5). What did he tell them? Going back to 1 Thessalonians we read:

> For the Lord himself will descend from heaven with a cry of command, with the voice of an archangel, and with the sound of the trumpet of God. And the dead in Christ will rise first. Then we who are alive, who are left, will be caught up together with

> them in the clouds to meet the Lord in the air, and so we will always be with the Lord. (1 Thessalonians 4:16–17)

Paul had clearly and comfortingly preached and taught the Thessalonians about the *parousia*, the coming of our Lord Jesus Christ (v. 1). He told them this would happen dramatically, climactically, and cataclysmically. Despite his clarity, these dear Christians had heard the confusing message of the false prophets, who said the day of the Lord has come (v. 2). The tense of this verb is key. The false prophets said the Lord has come. That's a perfect tense.[4] Paul even mentioned in another of his epistles two men, Hymenaeus and Philetus, who had taught that, "The resurrection has already happened" (2 Timothy 2:18). But Paul says throughout his epistles that the day of the Lord "is coming" (1 Thessalonians 5:2), or that it "is at hand" (Romans 13:12), or that it "is near" (Philippians 4:5). At its essence, the false prophets were preaching the Second Coming as a tactic of fear, while the true prophet of God preaches it as a part of Christian hope.

The false prophets' message was one that our Jesus himself addressed during his earthly ministry. He told his disciples in a substantive sermon that there would be false messiahs, saying,

> See that no one leads you astray. For many will come in my name, saying, "I am the Christ," and they will lead many astray. And you will hear of wars and rumors of wars. See that you are not alarmed, for this must take place, but the end is not yet. For nation will rise against nation, and kingdom against kingdom, and there will be famines and earthquakes in various places. All these are but the beginning of the birth pains … Then if anyone says to you, "Look, here is the Christ!" or "There he is!" do not believe it. For false christs and false prophets will arise and perform great signs and wonders, so as to lead astray, if possible, even the elect. See, I have told you beforehand. So, if they say to you, "Look,

> he is in the wilderness," do not go out. If they say, "Look, he is in the inner rooms," do not believe it (Matthew 24:4–8, 23–26).

So what was false about these prophets' message? Their false message was that Jesus' coming had already happened. And this heresy is the same sin as anyone throughout church history and even today who would set a date—even just the possibility of such a date—of Jesus' coming again. What is the sin of date setting? Prying into God's secret counsel that he has not revealed to us.[5] When Jesus' own apostles wanted to know the dates and times of his coming, he said to them, "It is not for you to know times and seasons that the Father has fixed by his own authority" (Acts 1:7). This teaching after his resurrection was consistent with his teaching before the resurrection: "But concerning the day and hour no one knows, not even the angels of heaven, nor the Son, but the Father only" (Matthew 24:36). This is the clear, unadulterated teaching of Jesus himself. This is not some theological gymnastics or some old confession of faith that is seeking to stifle the voice of the Spirit—this is Jesus saying this!

These false prophets' message was also sinful because it did damage to the faith of God's people.[6] Paul had to exhort these believers not to be shaken in mind or alarmed or deceived (vv. 2, 3). This was precisely the damage to the faith and consciences of the Thessalonians. They were unsettled, they were afraid, and they were led astray. As Paul told young pastor Timothy about Hymenaeus and Philetus, "They are upsetting the faith of some" (2 Timothy 2:18). A pastor is to strengthen true faith, not weaken it by attacking it at its foundation.

What do we learn from the false prophets' message in contrast to Jesus' message—that the date of his coming cannot be known—and in contrast to the apostles' message—that Jesus' coming "is at hand?" (Romans 13:12, James 5:8, 1 Peter 4:7) What we learn is that we are not to fix the time of his coming but also that we are not to put off the time. Instead, we are instructed to place our faith firmly on the Lord Jesus' coming. We are to expect in hope that he is coming for us. And our hearts are to be filled with love for our coming Savior.

Their Mission

Second, Paul writes about these false prophets in terms of *their mission*. All of our words not only mean something but are used to do something. Think about those people who stand on the sidewalk with signs about a business. They spin the signs, they throw the signs in the air, and they dance around with their signs. Why? Because they want you to see the words on the sign about a restaurant or a store and their mission is to get you into the restaurant or store. Words have meaning but also purpose. We see here that the false prophets' message had a mission for the Thessalonians. What was that mission? Very simply, as I've already alluded to, when Paul exhorts these believers not to be shaken, not to be alarmed, and not to be deceived, the implication is that this is precisely what the false prophets' words were doing (vv. 2, 3).

A false prophet's mission is to shake believers. This word is used of earthquakes and winds that blow reeds back and forth. All false doctrine and false prophets want to shake your faith.

A false prophet's mission is to alarm believers. What is interesting is how Paul uses the exact same words that Jesus used when he said, "And you will hear of wars and rumors of wars. See that you are not alarmed" (Matthew 24:6; Mark 13:7). The only other use of these words is when Jesus' disciples were frightened that Jesus appeared in their midst after his resurrection. All false doctrine and false prophets want to alarm your faith.

A false prophet's mission is to deceive believers. This is the same verb Paul goes on to use in 1 Timothy 2 when he describes the fact that the serpent deceived Eve in the Garden (1 Timothy 2:14). All false doctrine and false prophets want to deceive your faith.

When you hear anyone who presumes to speak in the name of the Lord, you need to use what Paul says here as three litmus tests of a false prophet. Ask yourself: "Does this doctrine shake the foundation of my hope? Does this doctrine alarm me from my hope? Does this doctrine deceive me to another hope?" And to guide you in your evaluation, you have the Word of God. Like the Bereans you are to examine the Scripture "to see if these things [are] so" (Acts 17:11). And as historically-informed Christians we recognize that we are not the only ones who have ever had to do this. And so we also have the ancient summaries of that Word in the creeds such as the Apostles', Nicene, Athanasian, and Chaldedonian. We also have the Reformation explanations of that Word in the catechisms and confessions of the sixteenth and seventeenth centuries.

Their Method

Finally, Paul writes about these false prophets in terms of *their method.* You can see here that Paul is describing their all out media blitz. Sounds familiar to the kinds of utilization of the media that we see and hear in our day, doesn't it? It always seems like the false teachers have access to all the media and are able to get their message out first, doesn't it? As the Puritan, Henry Wilkinson (1610–1675), said, "False teachers do use all possible means and diligence to prevail with persons to believe their false doctrines."[7] The Proverb said it like this: "The one who states his case first seems right, until the other comes and examines him" (Proverbs 18:17). Paul then goes on to speak of these false prophets as coming to the Thessalonians in a multi-faceted way: in spirit, in word, and in letter.

Paul exhorts these believers not to be shaken, alarmed, or deceived by a spirit (v. 2). He's not speaking here of *the* Spirit—the Holy Spirit—or of some ethereal "spiritual" things or of demonic spirits. Instead, he is speaking of the false teachers themselves who are professing to speak in the Spirit or for the Spirit.[8] Yet as Peter reminds us, the words of the actual Scriptures did not come from the will of man but from the will of God (2 Peter 1:20–21). These false prophets were not speaking for the Holy Spirit but were speaking false prophecy from their own delusional and depraved spirits.[9] It's what John said: "Beloved, do not believe every spirit, but test the spirits to see whether they are from God, for many false prophets have gone out into the world" (1 John 4:1). The spirits are the false prophets.

Paul also exhorts them not to be shaken, alarmed, or deceived by … a spoken word, or a letter seeming to be from us (v. 2). You can be sure of two things when it comes to doctrine: anyone who says they are an apostle or prophet and therefore has a word from the Lord doesn't and the actual apostles of the New Testament did have a word from the Lord. And again, as above, the difference is that false teachers speak their words, not *the* Word. That's why at the end of chapter 2 Paul says: "So then, brothers, stand firm and hold to the traditions that you were taught from us, either by our spoken word or by our letter" (2 Thessalonians 2:15). The apostolic doctrine that came in their sermons and their letters are what we look to in determining who is right and who is wrong.

Conclusion

So what does this mean for us to learn about the message, the mission, and the method of false prophets? Besides the fact that the world is full of them, you mean? Again, as I said at the outset, the Second Coming is a *source of hope* not a *subject of fear* for the believer. As one versification of Psalm 46 puts it:

God is our refuge and our strength,
Our ever present aid,

And, therefore, though the earth remove,
We will not be afraid;
Though hills amidst the seas be cast,
Though foaming waters roar,
yea, though the mighty billows shake
The mountains on the shore.[10]

Do not be shaken away from the truth of the apostles but be solidified upon their truth. Do not be alarmed away from the truth of the apostles but be assured of their teaching. Do not be deceived away from the truth of the apostles but be discerning towards false apostles, false prophets, and false teachers. Do not be led by the spirits of men but be led by the Spirit of God. Do not be followers of the words of men but of the Word of God. How?

First, by clinging ever so firmly to Jesus Christ by faith as if you were clinging to a buoy in a storm-tossed sea. Second, by learning to discern his voice amid all the noise of this world. You do this by reading his words in the Scriptures but especially by hearing his living Word proclaimed by the mouth of a minister who has been called and sent (Romans 10:14–17). Third, by uniting yourself to a true visible body of Christ. Become a living member of a local church where the Word is rightly proclaimed, where baptism and the Lord's Supper are rightly celebrated, and where godly discipline within a congregation is exercised—especially doctrinal discipline. When you do this, Christ himself will teach you that his Second Coming is a *source of hope* not a *subject of fear* for your soul.

26

The Great Apostasy

2 Thessalonians 2:3, 10–12

The heart of Paul's second letter to the Thessalonians is about the truth of Jesus' Second Coming. In contrast to the false prophets' doctrine that the Second Coming had already come (vv. 1–3a), Paul exposits the truth of this doctrine, saying that there are two things that must occur before Jesus returns again (vv. 3b–12). In the words of the end of verse 3, For that day will not come, *unless* (ESV; NASB) or until (v. 3; NIV) the coming of two things: first, the great apostasy, and second, the revealing of the man of lawlessness. And you see how the text is structured with this great apostasy mentioned in verse 3, then the man of lawlessness in verses 3–10, which leads Paul to come full circle and deal with the effects of the man of lawlessness on the great apostasy in verses 10–12.

In this chapter let us meditate upon *the great apostasy* in verses 3 and 10–12. Before doing so, what does our text mean by *apostasia*, which is translated by the ESV as rebellion, by the NASB as "apostasy," and by the KJV as "falling away?" It certainly is not used here for a political rebellion or falling away. Too many Christians believe this. Under the influence of modern Dispensationalism,[1] the man of lawlessness is understood by many to be a political leader[2] and the falling away will revolve around the modern political landscape of Israel. The word *apostasia* is not used for political rebellion, but is only used in the New Testament as well as the Greek translation of the Old Testament for *doctrinal* and *ethical* turning away from the Lord. We call this apostasy. For example, in Acts 21:21 James and the Jerusalem elders told Paul that the Jews who believed in Jesus as the Messiah were confused about what it meant for them to "forsak[e] Moses" while still remaining Jews. Apostasy, then, is a word that deals with the sacred realm of theology and not the secular realm of politics. So what is this great apostasy?

Its Content

First, as Paul speaks about the coming great apostasy, notice *its content*. Recognize, again, that Paul is not speaking about political issues in this passage, but doctrinal and ethical apostasy. It's certainly more exciting to have our newspaper or our favorite news website right next to our Bible, trying to figure out where everything we are reading fits into the biblical narrative. Yet Paul is not doing that. We read in verses 10–12 that the man of lawlessness is empowered by Satan to deceive, that God himself sends delusion, and that those who are apostatizing took pleasure in unrighteousness. These are theological and ethical categories, not political. And notice as an aside, that Paul does not reconcile these things to our satisfaction. How is it that God is the ultimate cause of this apostasy, that Satan and the man of lawlessness are the penultimate cause, and that apostate people are the antepenultimate cause? Only God knows. Let God be God. He is the potter; we are merely clay (Romans 9:20). The point is that this apostasy is a theological and ethical falling away from the one true God.

It is doctrinal apostasy: they refused to love the truth; they were deluded so that they may believe what is false in order that all may be condemned who did not believe the truth (vv. 10, 11–12). Paul doesn't define the truth here since he had already told them these things when he was with them, according to verse 5. We know from the Word of God that the Word itself is the truth. Psalm 119:160 says, "The sum of your word is truth, and every one of your righteous rules endures forever." We know from the Word that Jesus is the truth: "I am the way, the truth, and the life, no one comes to the Father except through me" (John 14:6). But most specifically, when Paul speaks of the truth, he speaks of the gospel message itself: "In him you also, when you heard the word of truth, the gospel of your salvation, and believed in him" (Ephesians 1:13). He says in Colossians 1:3–5: "We always thank God, the Father of our Lord Jesus Christ, when we pray for you, since we heard of your faith in Christ Jesus and of the love that you have for all the saints, because of the hope laid up for you in heaven. Of this you have heard before in the word of the truth, the gospel."

The day is coming before our Lord's return when there will be apostasy from the message of the gospel that God saves sinners by his grace in Jesus Christ. And the stark reality is that apostasy is only possible by those who have something to fall away from. Tragically, this great apostasy will occur within the church our Lord came to establish. Look at what Paul says elsewhere in 1 Timothy: "Now the Spirit expressly says that in latter times some will depart from the faith" (1 Timothy 4:1). This is a serious exhortation to us. Instead of falling away from the truth of the gospel, we need to cling to the truth of the gospel. We need to love the truth of the gospel. We need to pray like St. Anselm of Canterbury (1033–1109) prayed: "I pray you, Lord, make me taste by love what I taste by knowledge; let me know by love what I know by understanding."[3] It's not enough for your head to acknowledge the gospel, but your heart must embrace the gospel. It must be your lifeblood.

The great apostasy is also *ethical apostasy*: but [they] had pleasure in unrighteousness (v. 12). Notice the connection between doctrinal and ethical apostasy. They are rejecting the truth that they might embrace unrighteousness. They are suppressing the truth that they might live ungodly lives as Paul says in Romans 1:18–32. And because they "exchanged the glory of the immortal God for images resembling mortal man," Paul says "God gave them up in the lusts of their hearts to impurity, to the dishonoring of their bodies among themselves" (Romans 1:23, 24). We need to be aware of how often we twist the Word of God, how often we turn a blind eye to certain parts of the Word so that we can justify our behavior. And if we do this as believers, how much more so do unbelievers? Instead of taking pleasure in unrighteousness, we need to be taking pleasure in righteousness. Do you love the Father? Then you should love his law. Do you love Christ? Then you should love the cross-bearing life. Do you love the Holy Spirit? Then you should love "the holiness without which no one will see the Lord (Hebrews 12:14).

The content of this final and great apostasy is a rejection of the truth of the gospel for the purpose of embracing a life of unrighteousness. Doctrine and ethics go hand in hand. Therefore, we who believe in Jesus need to cling to the truth of his good news and the life God has given us.

Its Extent

Second, as Paul speaks about the coming great apostasy, notice *its extent*. Did you ever lose a friend as a child? Maybe you moved away or maybe they moved away. Maybe you started playing with another group or they started playing with another group. Maybe you just didn't get along anymore and you stopped being friends. Losing a friend was sad. In the church we sometimes lose a member like we lose a friend. Sometimes one of the people in the church will start believing something very wrong or living in a way that doesn't bring glory to God but shame to God's name. Eventually they leave and we as pastors and elders have to endure the long path to excommunication. It's very sad.

But this is just one person or maybe a couple of persons every once in a while. Imagine losing most of your friends, or imagine losing most of our church. The extent of the great apostasy is not merely an individual here or an individual there, but it is extended throughout the entire visible church. Why do I say this? John Calvin summed up the reason when he said that this apostasy "would not be confined to a single individual or even a few, but would spread far and wide among a considerably large number of persons. When the word apostasy is used without any addition it cannot be confined to a few individuals. Now the word apostates can be understood only of those who have enlisted in the service of Christ and His Gospel. Paul, then, is predicting a general defection on the part of the visible Church."[4]

Calvin's point was that Paul speaks here of *the* apostasy and does not qualify it with any other words. He is not speaking of a generic apostasy, or an apostasy of a small group of people, or that some will fall away over this little issue or that little issue. Instead, Paul is speaking of a specific, particular apostasy that will occur before our Lord returns. In fact, this is what our Lord taught in Matthew 24:

> And Jesus answered them, "See that no one leads you astray. For many will come in my name, saying, 'I am the Christ,' and they will lead many astray. And you will hear of wars and rumors of

> wars. See that you are not alarmed, for this must take place, but the end is not yet. For nation will rise against nation, and kingdom against kingdom, and there will be famines and earthquakes in various places. All these are but the beginning of the birth pains. Then they will deliver you up to tribulation and put you to death, and you will be hated by all nations for my name's sake. And then many will fall away and betray one another and hate one another. And many false prophets will arise and lead many astray. And because *lawlessness will be increased, the love of many will grow cold.* But the one who endures to the end will be saved. And this gospel of the kingdom will be proclaimed throughout the whole world as a testimony to all nations, and then the end will come … For false christs and false prophets will arise and perform great signs and wonders, *so as to lead astray, if possible, even the elect.* (Matthew 24:4–14, 24)

Let me draw out one application of this. Jesus links the great apostasy with "the love of many will grow cold." Many will go from being hot, to being lukewarm, to being outright cold, to being dead spiritually. Luke-warmness is a serious sin against the first commandment, according to the Westminster Larger Catechism (Q&A 105). Jesus threatened to vomit the Laodiceans out of his mouth because they were neither hot nor cold (Revelation 3:14–22). You think you can show up on Sunday morning but have nothing to do with the Word, with prayer, with fellowship with other believers from your church, with God himself the rest of the week. You are lukewarm! You think that because everything in your life is going better than normal—your marriage is better, your job is better, you are happier—then you can frequent the house of God less and less. You are lukewarm! Let me smash your idol of convenience and comfort. I would much rather upset your life in order to see you grow than never to say anything and you go on living your merry little, happy life where it's just all smiles and giggles. Here is an area in which we all need to grow. The church needs older, more mature members to be mentors, examples, and active disciplers of the younger in the church (Titus 2). Everyone is struggling with something. Everyone needs someone to talk to and give them godly advice. Everyone needs a shoulder to cry on. Everyone needs someone to model the Christian life. Instead of being lukewarm on the verge of cold and dead, our churches today need to be enflamed with love for Christ. In fact, did you know that our forefathers, the Puritans, were known as "the hotter sort of Protestants?" Are you?

Conclusion

What Paul teaches us here is that there is a great apostasy to come before the Second Coming of our Lord. Has it begun? Are we in it? Are we on the verge of it? Only God really knows. What we need to be concerned with is how we are living in the here and now. Let me conclude on this note.

The Puritan preacher, William Gurnall, once wrote: "None sink so far into hell as those that come nearest heaven, because they fall from the greatest height."[5] When we read of the great apostasy as believers, we are exhorted to not merely be near heaven. Don't merely be acquainted with the truth of the gospel. Don't merely be aware of what righteous living looks like in today's world. Don't merely be on the extended fringes of your local church. Be a living member of the heavenly kingdom here on earth. We read of those who will be deceived in the great apostasy described as refus[ing] to love the truth and so be saved (v. 10). Instead, you are exhorted to "give [your] heart to the love of [the truth]" and to be sure that you are saved. As John Calvin said, "faith is always connected with a seemly and spontaneous reverence for God, because we do not have a true belief in the Word of God, except when it is attractive to us and worthy of our devotion."[6] To keep apostasy away, recognize the attractiveness of the gospel. Give yourself in devotion to the truth of the gospel. Give yourself over to the righteous life that God calls you to. Be a living and active member of the church. Be a true Christian and therefore strong enough to withstand the temptation to apostasy.

27

The Antichrist

2 Thessalonians 2:3–12

St. Augustine of Hippo (354–430) is reported to have said, "He who loves the coming of the Lord is not he who affirms that it is far off, nor is it he who says it is near, but rather he who, whether it be far off or near, awaits it with sincere faith, steadfast hope, and fervent love."[1] In our current context with differing eschatological, or "end times" views, in evangelical churches, what this statement reminds us it that despite our position on the millennium, whether there is a secret rapture or the rapture is the Second Coming, and whether we believe in a personal antichrist or a movement of antichrists, the direction of our hearts should be faith, hope, and love in Christ's coming. Keep this in mind as we examine this unknown and strange passage.

What is this passage all about? *The Antichrist.* This passage follows the rest of the New Testament in teaching that there will be opposition to Jesus Christ, his kingdom, and his church until the day Jesus returns. Even more, here we learn that at the end of this age, just before Jesus' return, there will be one embodiment of this opposition known as *the* Antichrist. While some in the historical Reformed tradition—John Calvin being foremost—have said that "Paul ... is not speaking of one individual, but of a kingdom that was to be seized by Satan,"[2] I will be following the view that there will be one particular Antichrist before the end of the age. In the words of the apostle John, "Children, it is the last hour, and as you have heard that antichrist is coming, so now many antichrists have come. Therefore we know that it is the last hour" (1 John 2:18). The fact that there are many antichrists in this age that oppose Jesus Christ is evidence that it is the last hour of human history. Thus Satan is at work and is preparing the way for *the* final Antichrist. As one song describes Satan:

Rejoice then, oh ye heavens
But woe to the earth and the sea
For he is filled, filled with fury
He knows his time is brief
'cause he knows his time is brief.[3]

The passage before us speaks of the Antichrist in this way as well: For the mystery of lawlessness is already at work ... and then *the* lawless one will be revealed (vv. 7, 8). Paul also describes the Antichrist in parallel with Jesus' coming and revelation as he too will have a coming and revelation. So what does the Holy Spirit want us to know about the Antichrist?

His Revelation

First, Paul proclaims *his revelation.* Mark that word revelation. Not only does it speak of an unveiling, a making known something that previously was not known, but Paul uses this same root word to describe the "revelation" of Jesus Christ at the end of the age: "when the Lord Jesus is revealed from heaven" (2 Thessalonians 1:7). And now in chapter 2 he goes on to describe the revelation of the Antichrist in 2:3, 6, and 8. We begin to see a pattern emerging, in which the Antichrist mimics Christ. In the words of John Calvin, the Antichrist "puts on the mask of Christ."[4] Just as Jesus Christ will have a revelation at the end of history, so too will the Antichrist. Why? Because, as we will see, behind him is Satan, whom John called "the deceiver of the whole world" (cf. Revelation 20:3, 10) and whom Jesus called "the father of lies" (John 8:44). This means that for us "to recognize Antichrist we must set him in diametrical opposition to Christ."[5] Just like experts know what is counterfeit currency by knowing what is the authentic currency, so we know the Antichrist by knowing Christ. John Calvin went so far as to say about the Antichrist—albeit saying it about the Papacy of the Roman Catholic Church—that a ten-year old boy could recognize the revelation of the Antichrist.[6]

At this point, this question should begin to arise in your minds: when will the Antichrist be revealed? But notice that all Paul tells us is that the Antichrist's revelation will be after "what is restraining him now" (v. 6) and when "he who now restrains … is out of the way" (v. 7). The identity of this "restraint" and "restrainer" has been a mystery and a debated point of exegesis since the ancient church. Some have said it was the Holy Spirit while others have said it was the Roman Empire. The Puritans, following church fathers such as John Chrysostom, believed the latter view.[7]

In the words of St. Augustine, though, "For myself, I confess, I have no idea what is meant."[8] What we clearly do know is that he will be revealed sometime before the revelation of the Lord from heaven: For that day will not come unless [or, until] the rebellion comes first, and the man of lawlessness is revealed (v. 3).[9] But this has not been enough for many throughout church history, including today; so they create a whole story that they add to Scripture and make millions of dollars selling their end times books. Remember, the primary reason for Paul saying all of this was to assure these believers that the Day of the Lord had not yet come, and so they were to look forward to his coming in faith, hope, and love.

His Action

Second, Paul proclaims *his action*. Paul gives the Antichrist the titles man of lawlessness and son of destruction (v. 3), but it is his actions that are the key. We are told that the Antichrist opposes and exalts himself against every so-called god or object of worship (v. 4). The word opposes has the prefix, *anti*, which can mean "against" or "in the place of." The Antichrist will be the one who opposes himself against everything holy, especially God and the Lord Jesus Christ. But he's no atheist; he's no agnostic. He also exalts himself above God and the Lord Jesus. How does he do this?

Note what his opposition and exaltation leads to: so that he takes his seat in the temple of God, proclaiming himself to be God (v. 4). Here Paul is using seat and temple metaphorically. There was no seat in the temple. To sit is a symbol of authority and power. Just as Paul says elsewhere that Jesus "sits at the right hand of God," meaning, he has the authority and power of God. As well, throughout the New Testament, the language of the temple describes the church.[10] For example, Paul addresses the issue of division in the church, saying of he and Apollos, "For we are God's fellow workers. You are God's field. God's building" (1 Corinthians 3:9). Then he goes on to say:

> Do you not know that you *[pl.]* are God's temple and that God's Spirit dwells in you *[pl.]*? If anyone destroys God's temple, God

> will destroy him. For God's temple is holy, and you *[pl.]* are that temple. (1 Corinthians 3:16–17)

Again, Paul addresses the Corinthians as the temple of God when he addressed the issue of Christians being unequally yoked with non-Christians: "What agreement has the temple of God with idols? For we are the temple of the living God" (2 Corinthians 6:16). He says this again to the Ephesians, where he says the union of Jews and Gentiles in Christ "grows into a holy temple in the Lord" (Ephesians 2:21).

What is Paul saying? He is saying that the Antichrist, this man of lawlessness, this son of destruction will arise *from within the visible church* and take a position of ultimate authority, in opposition to Christ, who alone is the head of the church, and in exaltation above God, who alone is Lord.[11] This is why, for example, the original Westminster Confession of Faith said, "There is no other head of the Church but the Lord Jesus Christ: nor can the Pope of Rome in any sense be head thereof; but is that Antichrist, that man of sin and son of perdition, that exalteth himself in the Church against Christ, and all that is called God" (25.6).

What does this mean for us? Certainly, again, Paul is writing to the Thessalonians to assure them that Jesus has yet to come, and so he's not writing this to add to our vain curiosities to speculate who is the Antichrist. We need to be content to speak very simply as Scripture does and not to build an entire end-times theology on a verse here or a phrase there.

At the same time, knowing what Paul says here, we do need to be aware of the many antichrists already in the world and the rise of the final Antichrist. This is what Jesus said:

> See that no one leads you astray. For many will come in my name, saying, 'I am the Christ,' and they will lead many astray … And many false prophets will arise and lead many astray … Then if anyone says to you, 'Look, here is the Christ!' or 'There he is!' do not believe it. For false christs and false prophets will arise and perform great signs and wonders, so as to lead astray, if possible, even the elect. See, I have told you beforehand. So, if they say to you, 'Look, he is in the wilderness,' do not go out. If they say, 'Look, he is in the inner rooms,' do not believe it. For as the lightning comes from the east and shines as far as the west, so will be the coming of the Son of Man. (Matthew 24:4, 11)

This is also what Paul said throughout his New Testament letters. For example, we read in Paul's final address to the elders of the church in Ephesus:

> Pay careful attention to yourselves and to all the flock, in which the Holy Spirit has made you overseers, to care for the church of God, which he obtained with his own blood. I know that after my departure fierce wolves will come in among you, not sparing the flock; and from among your own selves will arise men speaking twisted things, to draw away the disciples after them. Therefore be alert. (Acts 20:28–31)

We do need to develop the spiritual ability to be discerning. We do this by becoming theologically alert to trends and new ideas. Of this ability to discern truth from error theologically, Martin Luther once wrote to Pope Leo X concerning the truth that we are justified by faith alone and not works: "Therefore, whoever has this knowledge can easily and without danger manage those countless rules and commands of the pope, bishops, monasteries, churches, princes, and magistrates."[12] In the same way we can be armed with the truth of the Word about the Second Coming of Jesus and stand against the curiosities, traditions, and fictions of what many modern Christians believe about this.

His Inspiration

Third, Paul proclaims *his inspiration*. What will lead the Antichrist to act as Paul says he will? What will motivate him? As Paul says so simply, yet profoundly, The coming of the lawless one is by the activity of Satan (v. 9). The Antichrist is not Satan himself "but some man, that admits [Satan's] fully working in him."[13] Again, we see the pattern that just as Jesus did miracles when he came, so too the Antichrist mimics him: with all power and false signs and wonders (v. 9). As Chrysostom once said, "He will copy the Son of God."[14] He will be inspired by Satan. But to do what?

Note well the inclusion of the phrase, and with all wicked deception for those who are perishing (v. 10). The devil doesn't just do his powers, signs, and wonders through the Antichrist to dazzle, but to distract. Just like in the Garden when he used a serpent to distract Adam and Eve (Genesis 3), so too at the end of human history Satan will attempt, again, to lead all humanity away from their Creator God. Satan's inspired Antichrist wants your attention off of your Creator who sent his Son to be the Savior of the world, and onto a false object.

What does this mean for us today? We need to be well grounded in the Word so that the waves and winds of false apostles do not toss us and blow us away from Christ (Ephesians 4:14). Our eyes need to be firmly fixed on Jesus, not looking to the right or to the left to be distracted by false signs and wonders. We must be like Christian in the great book, *The Pilgrim's Progress*. When Christian passed through the Valley of the Shadow of Death he walked on a narrow path with a pit down on his right and a quagmire down on his left; but he kept moving forward, one sure-footed step at a time. We as churches do not need to be ashamed that we do not offer the so-called signs and wonders of Pentecostalism or the so-called miracle of the Mass of Roman Catholicism. Why? Because we have Jesus Christ! As Paul said, "For Jews demand signs and Greeks seek wisdom, but we preach Christ crucified [but don't forget he goes on to say], a stumbling block to Jews and folly to Gentiles, but to those who are called, both Jews and Greeks, Christ the power of God and the wisdom of God" (1 Corinthians 1:22–24).

His Destruction

Finally, Paul proclaims *his destruction*: whom the Lord Jesus will kill with the breath of his mouth and bring to nothing by the appearance of his coming (v. 8). Recognize that the Antichrist has a revelation like Christ. Recognize that the Antichrist exalts himself as an object of worship just as Christ is exalted and the object of worship. Recognize that the Antichrist does signs and wonders even as our Lord has done. The Antichrist is the final earthly manifestation of the seed of the serpent that seeks to wage war against the seed of the woman (Genesis 3:15). And what's the result of this age-old conflict? The Antichrist's destruction.

It is interesting to note that the means our Lord uses to kill and bring to nothing the Antichrist is the breath of his mouth. Here Paul is using an Old Testament image to describe our Lord. In Isaiah 11 the prophet spoke of the coming Messiah, saying that he would be anointed with the Spirit of the Lord. This Spirit is then described as "the Spirit of wisdom and of understanding, the Spirit of counsel and of power, the Spirit of knowledge and of the fear of the LORD" (Isaiah 11:2). Then the prophet describes how he would apply his anointing:

> He will not judge by what he sees with his eyes,
> or decide by what he hears with his ears;
> but with righteousness he will judge the needy,
> with justice he will give decisions for the poor of the earth.

> He will strike the earth with the rod of his mouth;
> with the breath of his lips he will slay the wicked. (Isaiah 11:3b–4)

The Messiah, our Lord Jesus Christ, would judge not by the means of earthly, political princes but by means of his Word. While John Calvin interpreted this passage in his context as teaching "the victory of the Word" over the Roman Papacy,[15] we can apply what he said about the Word's victorious power over all the forces of darkness, including Satan and whomever his Antichrist ends up being. Until Jesus returns, it is our responsibility as pastors to preach and our responsibility as people to support the Gospel. One hymn celebrates this, saying, "May Thy Gospel's joyful sound conquer sinners, comfort saints."[16] Until Jesus returns, it is our responsibility as the people of God to pray for all Satanically-inspired Antichrist influence to be destroyed. When we pray, "Thy kingdom come," we pray that God would "destroy the works of the devil, every power that exalts itself against Thee, and all wicked devices formed against Thy Holy Word, until the fullness of Thy kingdom come, wherein Thou shalt be all in all" (HC, Q&A 123; cf. WLC, Q&A 191).

Conclusion

Let me conclude with a contrast. It's in this description of the heinousness of the Antichrist that we get a picture of the beauty of Jesus. Antichrist's revelation will seemingly be climactic as he arrives on the scene of human history. Jesus' revelation was humble. He was born in little Bethlehem, not the royal palace of Jerusalem. He was "enthroned" in a manger. He was wrapped in the "royal" vestments of swaddling cloths. Antichrist's actions will be self-aggrandizing and exalting himself. Jesus' were self-emptying. As Paul said,

> ... though he was in the form of God, did not count equality with God a thing to be grasped, but made himself nothing, taking

> the form of a servant, being born in the likeness of men. And being found in human form, he humbled himself by becoming obedient to the point of death, even death on a cross. (Philippians 2:6–8)

Antichrist's inspiration was Satan, and Satan's plans are always to short-cut God's plan, whether with Adam in the Garden or with Jesus in the wilderness. Jesus' inspiration was his eternal plan with the Father and the Holy Spirit to became the humble mediator who would enter back into glory only after he had first been betrayed by a friend, suffered tremendously despite having no sin, and been crucified for our sins. Antichrist's destruction will be by Jesus. Antichrist is a foil for Jesus. Only Jesus can save from sin. Come to him today.

28

God Chose *You*

2 Thessalonians 2:13

"My soul clings to the dust; revive me according to your word! (Psalm 119:25; NASB/NKJV) This is how the Psalmist expressed the languishing of his life because of his sins. Our sins weigh us down. Our sins crush our spirits. Our sins burden us. But as the psalmist came before the Lord in prayer he also expressed his longing to be revived by means of God's Word. Why do I mention this? Because this is what we come to receive as we meditate on the Word. We come with souls that cling to the dust. We come before the God who revives, longing to hear his Word. As John Owen said, "The enjoyment of Christ in and by the ordinances of his worship [meaning preaching, sacraments, and prayer], is the immediate fountain and spring of all our refreshments and consolations in this world."[1]

Here in 2 Thessalonians 2:13 Paul revives the Thessalonian Christians, whose souls clung to the dust because of their persecutions, with these refreshing words: But we ought always to give thanks to God for you, brothers, beloved by the Lord, because God chose you. Here he is resuming his thanksgiving that he began in 1:3. After detouring to discuss the coming of Christ in the end of chapter 1 and the coming of the Antichrist in the beginning of chapter 2, he picks up where he left off to refresh and console these brothers and sisters. Why? Remember, again, that they were being persecuted from enemies outside the church (2 Thessalonians 1:4) and preyed upon by enemies within the church, who said, “the day of the Lord has come” (2 Thessalonians 2:2). And how does he seek to revive their souls, refresh their spirits, and console their hearts? With the phrase, God chose you (v. 13). He does so with the doctrine of election or predestination.

We normally associate election or predestination either with speculation that is too high for us as ordinary believers or with a doctrine that is impractical for our daily lives. But obviously Paul thinks otherwise; and so should we. Predestination is practical. Paul sought to comfort these Christians with the doctrine of election, telling them, *God chose you.*

God Chose You Sovereignly

First, *God chose you sovereignly*. What does that mean? It means that we've done nothing while God has done the choosing. It is his sovereign power that chooses his people. Notice that Paul gives thanks *to God* (v. 13). Notice that Paul calls the Thessalonians, beloved *by the Lord* (v. 13). Notice that Paul then says why he gave thanks: Because *God* chose you (v. 13).[2]

Now some might say that God cannot choose some to salvation. To say so is to say God is not God. Others say that God would not choose only some to salvation. They say this either because God waits to see how we might respond to him before he takes action or because for God to choose some and not others is unjust; it's just plain wrong. Turn with me to Romans 9. Notice that it was Paul's desire for his brothers, his kinsmen according to the flesh to be saved. In fact, he even was willing to be "accursed and cut off from Christ" for their sake (Romans 9:3). Paul is answering the question of why don't all the Israelites believe in Jesus as their Messiah. So has God's promise in the Old Testament, then, failed? This is the implied question in verse 6. His answer is no and he goes on to explain this from the doctrine of election: "Jacob I love, but Esau I hated" (Romans 9:13). But this would mean that God is unjust, right? That's the next question in verse 14. He answers this question from the sovereignty of God: "I will have mercy on whom I have mercy, and I will have compassion on whom I have compassion" (Romans 9:15). This leads to the final question: "You will say to me then, 'Why does he still find fault? For who can resist his will?'" (Romans 9:19) You understand the question there, right? It's the age-old reply to God's sovereign election that it makes us robots or that it means it doesn't matter what I do because God has already figured it all out. Note Paul's brilliant answer: "But who are you, O man, to answer back to God? Will what is molded say to its molder, 'Why have you made me like this?' Has the potter no right over the clay, to make out of the same lump one vessel for honorable use and another for dishonorable use?" (Romans 9:20–21)

I don't know about you, but my languishing soul needs this. I need salvation to be taken out of the whims and wishes of my mind. I need salvation to be taken away from my sin-stained hands. I need salvation to be removed from my stony heart. I need a God who chooses. As the hymn writer said:

'Tis not that I did choose Thee,
For Lord, that could not be;

This heart would still refuse Thee,
Hadst Thou not chosen me.
Thou from the sin that stained me
Hast cleansed and set me free;
Of old Thou hast ordained me,
That I should live to Thee.

'Twas sov'reign mercy called me
And taught my op'ning mind;
The world had else enthralled me,
To heav'nly glories blind.
My heart owns none before Thee,
For Thy rich grace I thirst;
This knowing, if I love Thee,
Thou must have loved me first.[3]

Be refreshed as you read 2 Thessalonians 2:13 because it teaches that God chose you sovereignly.

God Chose You Lovingly

But election is not just a sovereign act of God's omnipotent will. Notice a second point about it: *God chose you lovingly.* We see that as Paul described these believers as beloved by the Lord (v. 13). What caused God to choose one and not another? The deep, deep love of God himself. Note as well how Paul says in Ephesians 1:4–5, "*In love* he predestined us."

But why? Why has God chosen one and not another? For sure, it is not because the one is better than, more holy than, or more worthy than the other. As Paul said in Romans 9:11 of Jacob and Esau, "though they were not yet born and had done nothing either good or bad—in order that God's purpose of election might continue, not because of works, but because of him who calls." This should humble us to the core. "But for the grace of God, there go I," we should be saying every moment of our lives.

So why did God choose one over the other? Why does he call these believers beloved by the Lord (v. 13) while later in 3:2 he says, "For not all have faith?" Turn with me to Deuteronomy 7. Here the Lord tells the Israelites that when they entered the land of promise, Canaan, they were not to marry unbelievers. Why?

> For you are a people holy to the LORD your God. The LORD your God has chosen you to be a people for his treasured possession, out of all the peoples who are on the face of the earth. *It was not because you were more in number than any other people that the LORD set his love on you and chose you, for you were the fewest of all peoples, but it is because the LORD loves you* and is keeping the oath that he swore to your fathers, that the LORD has brought you out with a mighty hand and redeemed you from the house of slavery, from the hand of Pharaoh king of Egypt. Know therefore that the LORD your God is God, *the faithful God who keeps covenant and steadfast love with those who love him and keep his commandments, to a thousand generations.* (Deuteronomy 7:6–9)

Why does God love us? Because he decided to love us! Why do we as parents love our children in a way that we do not love their friends? Because we have made a decision to be parents and that decision included loving our children even before they came out of their mother's womb. God chose to love us. He not only chose to love us despite our sins, but he chose to love us in full view of our sins.

How should we respond to the love of God? Listen to how John Owen described our response:

> They know nothing of the life and power of the gospel, nothing of the reality of the grace of God, nor do they believe aright one

> article of the Christian faith, whose hearts are not sensible of the love of Christ herein; nor is he sensible of the love of Christ, whose affections are not thereon drawn out unto him.[4]

God's love to us in election, which is revealed to us in Christ, must cause us to love in return. "In this is love, not that we have loved God but that he loved us and sent his Son to be the propitiation for our sins … We love because he first loved us" (1 John 4:10, 19). How? We must place our "most intense affections of our souls on the person of Christ." We must "lov[e] him with all our hearts because of his love." We must be "overcome [with his love] until we are sick of love."[5] As you experience that kind of love from Christ, return that kind of love to Christ. As the hymn says,

> I find, I walk, I love, but oh, the whole
> Of love is but my answer, Lord, to Thee!
> For Thou were long beforehand with my soul,
> Always Thou lovest me.[6]

> Be refreshed as you read 2 Thessalonians 2:13 because it teaches that God chose you lovingly.

God Chose You Eternally

His choosing of us was not in response to our choosing him, as he chose us sovereignly; his choosing of us was not because we were so good, as he chose us lovingly. This is amazing. And to add to that amazement that causes us to love him passionately is a third fact about election in our text: *God chose you eternally*. Again, as Ephesians 1:3 says, "Even as he [God] chose us in him [Christ] *before* the foundation of the world." Paul states this elsewhere in 2 Timothy 1:9: "who saved us and called us to a holy calling, not because of our works but because of his own purpose and grace, which he gave us in Christ Jesus *before* the ages began." What about in 2 Thessalonians 2:13? The ESV reads, Because God chose you *as the firstfruits*.

Most of our Bibles probably have some sort of footnote here, mentioning that there is a textual variant between God chose you as the firstfruits (*aparchēn*) and God chose you from the beginning (*ap' archēs*).[7] Let me say that both ideas of us being firstfruits and us being chosen from the beginning are biblical. Let me also say that in the thousands of manuscripts of the New Testament we do have textual variants that occurred due to copyist error over the ages. Yet in all of these variants there is no new teaching added to the Scriptures or any essential teaching taken away. That said, while commentators disagree as to which reading is the original, it seems to me that the most likely reading is the traditional reading behind the King James Bible, "from the beginning." Why? Let me give you four reasons:

First, while "firstfruits" is a concept used for believers often in the New Testament, especially in Paul's letters (James 1:18; Revelation 14:4 cf. Romans 8:23, 11:16, 16:5; 1 Corinthians 15:20, 23, 16:15), it is never connected with election. And grammatically, when it is used, it ordinarily is connected with a follow-up phrase in the genitive case that defines it.[8] We are described as the firstfruits *of something*.

Second, these Thessalonians were not the firstfruits of either the province of Asia (Romans 16:5) or the region of Achaia (1 Corinthians 16:15).

Third, Paul's text here traces the theme of the Thessalonians' salvation from the past ("he chose you from the beginning") and to the future ("so that you may obtain the glory of our Lord Jesus Christ"). As James Denny said of these verses, they "are a system of theology in miniature. The apostle's thanksgiving covers the whole work of creation from the eternal choice of God to the obtaining of the glory of our Lord Jesus Christ in the world to come."[9]

Fourth, Paul is seeking to comfort those who thought the day of the Lord had come, so he tells them that despite all that rages on around them, God chose them before time even began.

In conclusion, John Calvin summarized this discussion in these words: "Let us, however, retain the more generally accepted reading, viz., that the Thessalonians have been chosen from the beginning."[10]

> Be refreshed as you read 2 Thessalonians 2:13 because it teaches that God chose you eternally.

Conclusion

How can you know if you are one of those that God has chosen? It is the duty of a minister to give you assurance.[11] You as a sinner can know that you were chosen by God not by trying to know the secret mind of God.[12] Instead, our text tells us how we know: God chose you … through *sanctification* by the Spirit and *belief* in the truth (v. 13). This is why John Calvin said of our text, "since it is not our business to penetrate into the secret counsel of God, there to seek the assurance of our salvation, he designates the signs or tokens of our election, which should give us sufficient confidence in it."[13] What are these outward signs? First, do you believe the truth of God's Word? In contrast to those who are led by the spirit of Antichrist to hate the truth, do you love it? Second, are you being sanctified by the Holy Spirit? Ask yourself this question: are you more concerned to live righteously than the world around you that takes more pleasure in unrighteousness? The outward signs that God has elected us are not ethereal and hard to grasp or mysterious and hard to understand. Instead, they are evident in and around you. As you believe in Jesus Christ and the doctrines of his Word and seek to live a godly life day by day, you will come to know God's electing love more and more. He promises you this. And as you believe it, be refreshed in your soul.

29

Obtaining Jesus' Glory

2 Thessalonians 2:14

"It is impossible that he who never meditates with delight on the glory of Christ here in this world, who labours not to behold it by faith as it is revealed in the Scripture, should ever have any real gracious desire to behold it in heaven."[1] That's how the great English theologian, John Owen, described the connection between meditating, thinking, and believing in Jesus' glory now and our experiencing his glory then, in the life of the world to come. We should be delighting to spend time with Jesus in prayer and in contemplation of him as we read of him in his Word. Why? Because the goal of our lives is to obtain the glory of our Lord Jesus Christ in eternity. But what is his glory?

Recall from chapter 1 that Paul said when Jesus returns he will be glorified in us—meaning, he will be praised and exalted by our lives and lips—and when he returns "you [will be glorified] in him" (2 Thessalonians 1:12). The word we have translated as "glory" can mean praise. Because something is so worthy it is praised. God is worthy because he is God and so we praise him. But the word also speaks of the one being glorified. It speaks of the weightiness and the worthiness of a king or of God who therefore is glorious and deserving of glory. And when it is used of us, of course, it is speaking of our being made worthy, our being glorified from sinner to saint.

So what is Jesus' glory? I said before that Jesus' glory—his inherent worthiness—is expressed in three things. First, his glory is expressed in his *pre-existence*. Before he, as the Son of God, took upon himself our human nature he existed in the ineffable and incomprehensible glorious presence of the Triune God. This is why he prayed in John 17:5, "And now, Father, glorify me in your own presence with the glory that I had with you before the world existed." Second, his glory is expressed in his *person*. The invisible Son of God became visible by taking to himself humanity: "And the Word became flesh." As the God-man he was conceived sinless and lived sinless. John continued to say, "And we have seen his glory, the glory as of the only begotten, full of grace and truth" (John 1:14). Third, his glory was expressed in his *power*. At his resurrection he was "declared to be the Son of God in power according to the Spirit of holiness" (Romans 1:4).

Here is the promise of God for you: if you are trusting in Jesus to save you from your sins, if you are resting in Jesus and not in your self-confidence to save yourself from your sins, you will obtain the glory of our Lord Jesus Christ.

Our Purpose

First, obtaining the glory of our Lord Jesus Christ is *our purpose*. You can see the grammar of Paul here is what we call a purpose clause:

so that (v. 14). This explains the purpose of all that has gone before in Paul's statement in verses 13–14. Again, Paul is comforting these brothers and sisters who were persecuted from enemies outside the church and who were being persuaded by enemies from inside the church, who said "the day of the Lord has come" (2 Thessalonians 2:2). And besides addressing the error of those false prophets head on in verses 3–12, Paul comforts them with the saving acts of the Triune God. You can see in our text this one saving plan worked out by the three distinct persons of our adorable God.

This comfort was found in the fact that their salvation was from eternity past: "God chose you" (2 Thessalonians 2:13). This comfort was found in the fact that their salvation was an experience in the present, as they were being sanctified by the Spirit and were believing in the truth (2 Thessalonians 2:13). Paul even explains further that they came into possession of this salvation through God's calling of them through the preaching of our gospel (v. 14). This comfort was also found in the fact that their salvation was unto eternity future. But notice that he doesn't just say that. Instead, he says the past and present aspects of salvation are all preparatory for our future aspect. God chose you, God called you, God is sanctifying you so that you may obtain the glory of our Lord Jesus Christ (v. 14).

Here is your ultimate purpose. God made our first parents in his own image, crowning them with glory and honor (Psalm 8). He made them, as the Heidelberg Catechism states, to "live with Him in eternal blessedness, to praise and glorify Him" (Q&A 6). He made them, and us, with the "chief end" of "glorify[ing] God, and fully to enjoy him forever" (WLC, Q&A 1). But because of Adam's sin, "all have sinned and fall short of the glory of God" (Romans 3:23). And the ultimate purpose of Jesus Christ's gospel is to restore to us that experience of and fellowship in God's glory. Do you want to live with

God forever? Come to him through Jesus Christ. Do you want to experience your ultimate purpose in existing? It's not to serve yourself and your selfish desires; it's to have communion with your Creator and Redeemer forever. And you can have that if you trust in Jesus.

What does this mean for us as believers in this life? You might be thinking, "I agree, this is my ultimate purpose; but I live in the here and now." So let me give you one way this is so beneficial to us now. Another English Puritan, Thomas Goodwin (1600–1680), said that all the grace of God we are receiving in this life brings us in communion with God; but it does more. It is also preparing us to see God face to face in glory.[2] This means you and I need to live our lives in the expectation of eternal life. When you hear that your sins are forgiven, you should be longing to hear that from Jesus' lips in heaven. When you experience God's gracious Word as you read it at home as individuals and as families, you should be preparing to hear the very voice of God speak to you in eternity.

Our Privilege

Obtaining the glory of our Lord Jesus Christ is also *our privilege*. Let me just mention this briefly, but I hope you are seeing in this text the reality that all of God's amazing acts are acts of his grace. We are beloved *by* the Lord. That's grace. We are told that "God chose you." That's grace. He chose us to be saved. That's grace. He saves us through sanctification of the Spirit and belief in the truth. That's grace. We are told that he called you (v. 14). That's grace. And now he says our ultimate purpose is to be glorified in Jesus' presence. Isn't that grace? Paul even says that our being glorified in Christ is "according to the grace of our God and the Lord Jesus Christ" (1 Thessalonians 1:12). What privileges we have! What gracious privileges God has given to us as his dear children!

This should affect us and cause us to shout out, "Amen! Praise the

Lord!" (Psalm 106:48) This should cause us to sing with exuberance in public and private. This should cause us to awaken out of any spiritual slumbers we might be in and to realize the immense privilege God has given not only to others but also to *me*.

This should also affect us in how we live, shouldn't it? Jesus has forgiven you, now you forgive seventy times seven (Matthew 18:21–22). Husbands, your believing wife—you know, the one your eyes keep straying off of—is purposed for glory. Love her alone and look at her differently. Wives, your believing husband—you know, the one who doesn't match your unattainable expectations—is purposed for glory. Submit to him. Children, your brothers and sisters also belong to Jesus. Should you hit them, yell at them, take from them, or be mean to them? No, love them as Jesus does.

Our Participation

Finally, obtaining the glory of our Lord Jesus Christ is *our participation*. I've shown you what this glory of Jesus is in his pre-existence, person, and power. I've shown you that it is our purpose to obtain it. I've shown you that it is our privilege by grace to obtain it. But what does it mean to obtain it? How do we participate in this glory? We participate in Jesus' glory by faith now and by sight then, in eternity.

Faith Now

We participate in Jesus' glory by faith now. Thomas Goodwin asked the question we are asking, "What is it to have Christ dwell in the heart by faith?" His answer was, "It is to have Jesus Christ continually in one's eye, a habitual sight of him. I call it so because a man actually does not always think of Christ; but as a man does not look up to the sun continually, yet he sees the light of it, so here faith is called the seeing of Christ."[3] We participate in Jesus' glory now when we fix our eyes upon Jesus by faith. As the hymn says,

Turn your eyes upon Jesus,
Look full in His wonderful face,
And the things of earth will grow strangely dim,
In the light of His glory and grace.[4]

How do I do this? Turn your eyes upon him in his own Word every day as you read it and every Lord's Day as it is read and proclaimed. Turn your eyes upon him in baptism and the Lord's Supper every time they are celebrated. These are not meant to be shows to gaze at, but actions and ceremonies you participate in by faith. Turn your eyes upon him in daily prayer individually, as couples, as families, and corporately as congregations. Turn your eyes upon him in your fellowship with your brothers and sisters inside and outside of public worship; love and support one another in good times and hard times.

Do you have a habitual sight of Jesus by faith? This sight by faith should cause in us a restlessness to have more. As John Owen wrote, "For being once touched by the love of Christ, receiving therein an impression of secret ineffable virtue, [believers] will ever be in motion, and restless, until they come unto him, and behold his glory."[5] May God grant us who have rest in Christ this godly restlessness. Be assured of having Christ now by faith, but long for more; long for him in his fullness.

Do you have a habitual sight of Jesus by faith? This sight by faith should cause in us an earnestness to have more. Again, John Owen wrote of Moses' request to God, "Show me thy glory," saying this: "the nearer any one is unto God the more earnest will be his desire after the full fruition of him."[6] May God grant us this earnestness.

Sight Then

And that final rest and final fruition will come to reality when our faith turns to sight in eternity. So what will it mean to have sight of

Jesus in his glory and to finally obtain the glory of our Lord Jesus Christ? We certainly will not have pre-existence as Jesus had, because we are creatures who had a beginning; but we will have an eternal existence into the future. We certainly will not have the glory of his person, being both God and man, divine and human, because we are mere humans; but we will put off our sin nature and actually sinning. We certainly will not have the same divine power as him, who was declared to be the Son of God in power (Romans 1:4), but we will be raised in glory and honor; our bodies will be made like unto his glorious body (Philippians 3:21).

So what will our glory be? Thomas Goodwin said, "We shall be made one with Him so far as the creature is capable of being made one with Him, and we shall have the next union to that which God and Christ have with one another."[7] We will be as much like Jesus as a creature can be. As the apostles John wrote, "Beloved, we are God's children now, and what we will be has not yet appeared; but we know that when he appears we shall be like him, because we shall see him as he is" (1 John 3:2). The apostle Paul used the metaphor of a husband and a bride, saying, "Husbands, love your wives, as Christ loved the church and gave himself up for her, that he might sanctify her, having cleansed her by the washing of water with the word, so that he might present the church to himself in splendor, without spot or wrinkle or any such thing, that she might be holy and without blemish" (Ephesians 5:25–27).

There is mystery here, beloved. There is still the aspect of hoping for what is not yet seen. John Owen said that we speak of Christ's glory "in a poor, low, broken manner" and that "we teach them as they are revealed in the Scripture," but then he said, "when we come into a steady, direct view and consideration of the thing itself, our minds fail, our hearts tremble, and we can find no rest but in a holy admiration of what we cannot comprehend."[8] One day our eyes will see what our faith longs for now.

Conclusion

Will you meditate with delight on the glory of Christ by faith now? Will you persevere in love to behold him in eternity? Will you hope more and more to see him face to face as a friend forever? If so, know that you will obtain the glory of Jesus by sight with your glorified eyes in the eternal glories of heaven.

30

Stand Firm, Hold On

2 Thessalonians 2:15–17

In a world so full of chaos and change under our feet we must stand firm upon the solid foundation of the Word of God. We must hold on with a tight grip to the Word of God like a light in the midst of a dark and dying world as we await the coming of Jesus Christ. As one hymn expresses this:

How firm a foundation, ye saints of the Lord,
Is laid for your faith in His excellent Word!
What more can He say than to you He hath said,
You, who unto Jesus for refuge have fled?[1]

To begin with, I want to explain 2 Thessalonians 2:15; then I will offer three points of application that this verse gives to us. Paul begins with so then, which should indicate to you that he is bringing his argument to a conclusion with a practical exhortation. He is concluding all that he has said up to this point. These believers were being persecuted for their faith, which he addressed in 1:3–12. These believers were being led astray by false teachers concerning the Second Coming of Jesus, which he addressed in 2:1–12. And you see how all this is linked together with Paul's thanksgiving in 1:3, which he resumed in 2:13. So he wants them to stand firm in the presence of persecution, but especially in the face of false teachers. You see that in the connection between 2:2 and 2:15. I said a while back that "a spirit" was a way of speaking of the false teachers themselves. Now Paul says to listen to us in verse 15. And these false spirits sought to lead the Thessalonians astray by the "spoken word" and their written "letter." But now Paul says listen to our spoken word and our letter.

So then, what? So then, they were to stand firm and hold on to the apostles' traditions. Paul uses the verb stand firm elsewhere in his letters to exhort believers to stand firm in the Lord (Philippians 4:1), to stand firm in faith (1 Corinthians 16:13), to stand firm in one Spirit (Philippians 1:27), and to stand firm in freedom (Galatians 5:1). It means, then, to be immovable upon the spiritual foundation we have in Christ and his holy gospel. He also uses the verb hold when he exhorts believers to hold on to Christ (Colossians 2:19) while the letter to the Hebrews exhorts believers to hold on to their confession (Hebrews 4:14) and to hold on to their hope (Hebrews 6:18). This means, then, that we are to be clinging on to Jesus Christ as we would cling to life itself.

So then. But what are they to stand firm upon and hold to so firmly? The traditions (*paradoseis*). But note well that this has nothing to do with Roman Catholic or Eastern Orthodoxy's concept of extra-biblical authority.[2] Let me show you what it is not first. Jesus spoke of "the tradition of the elders" (Matthew 15:2; Mark 7:5), "your tradition" in reference to the Pharisees (Matthew 15:3, 6; Mark 7:9, 13), and "the tradition of men" (Mark 7:8). It obviously has a negative connotation because these leaders were adding to the Word of God with their own interpretations and impositions upon the people of God. Paul also spoke negatively of "human tradition" that was wrapped up in "philosophy and empty deceit" and was "not according to Christ" (Colossians 2:8). He also spoke negatively of his pre-conversion zeal for "the traditions of my fathers" (Galatians 1:14).

But Paul also spoke positively of "tradition." In 1 Corinthians 11 Paul commended the Corinthians because they "maintain[ed] the traditions even as I delivered them to you" (1 Corinthians 11:2). He further defines this tradition as that which Christ gave him to deliver to them concerning the Lord's Supper (11:23). In fact, Paul uses in 11:2 and 11:23 the same form of the verb "delivered," showing us the link between these verses and that the tradition is what Christ taught and the apostles passed down. Paul speaks of tradition positively in only two other places, both here in 2 Thessalonians. In both 2:15 and 3:6 he speaks of the tradition that you were taught by us. But note how in 2:15 he further qualifies this with by our spoken word or by our letter. So what it Paul saying? In contrast to the traditions of the scribes and Pharisees who blotted out the true Word of God for the sake of their own opinions, believers are to follow the Word of God as it has been passed down by Jesus Christ through his apostles to his Church.[3] Remember, who caused the riots in Thessalonica so that Paul and Silas had to flee to Berea? The Jewish leaders. So Paul was saying to the Thessalonian believers that they were to flee their extra-biblical traditions for the true tradition as it has been passed down in two forms: apostolic preaching and apostolic writing.

So what does this mean for us by way of application?

We Need to Know the Apostles' Tradition

First, in order for us to stand firm and hold to the traditions *we need to know the apostles' tradition*. The world around us is like a raging sea. As the Psalmist said, "The floods have lifted up, O LORD, the floods have lifted up their voice; the floods lift up their roaring" (Psalm 93:3). In the midst of that sea the apostles' doctrine is like a rocky island that we can stand firm upon. It is like a lifeline that we can cling onto in the midst of that sea. But do you know there is a rock upon which you can climb? Do you know that there is a line to cling to? If you do not know the Word you cannot be safe in the world.

You notice while Paul is explaining the coming of the Lord, the great apostasy, and the Antichrist, he pauses and says, "Do you not remember that when I was still with you I told you these things?" (2 Thessalonians 2:5) They had forgotten. So Paul has to remind them again to stand firm and to hold on to this Word. It is so easy for us to forget for several reasons. First, like Vanity Faire in *The Pilgrim's Progress* the allure of the world's promises of pleasure leads us to focus our energies on everything else but the Word. Second, our sinful nature inherited from father Adam causes us to think and act waywardly against the Word of God to put our own words in its place. Third, the constant spiritual temptations of the devil cause us to trip up in our faith in God's trustworthy and enduring Word.

There should be nothing we long to see more than the Holy Spirit work mightily in our lives, our families, our churches, and our societies. We should want to see the Spirit cause in us a longing for the truth of the Word. We should hunger for him to teach us. We should long for the words of Psalm 119 to come alive: "revive me according to your Word." But are we longing for this? Are we crying out to God for this? If you've ever spent any amount of time in a foreign mission setting, you have seen this with your own two eyes. The things you heard and saw in that foreign setting make you feel like crawling into a hole in the ground and throwing dust on your head in repentance before God. We complain about driving to hear the pure Word a mere thirty minutes. I've met people who traveled for days by boat to hear the Word; I've met people who weekly travel two hours *one way* by bus to get to church in the morning and then have to do it again to get back home. Yet here I am complaining how worship is so inconvenient to my plans.

We Need to be Convinced of the Apostles' Tradition

But why would we be so desperate for the truth that we should go to such extremes? Second, *we need to be convinced of the apostles' tradition*. You can have all the right doctrines, all the right explanations, and all the right jargon in your head, but it can make no difference to your life. Remember what James said: "You believe that God is one; you do well. Even the demons believe—and shudder!" (James 2:19) Mental knowledge is great, but you have to be convinced of it in your heart of hearts. Everything Paul was saying to these believers in 2 Thessalonians about the truth of Jesus' coming again meant nothing unless these believers were convinced of his words to them.

What does it mean to be convinced? Go back to 1 Thessalonians 2:13. There he praised these believers because "when you received the word of God, which you heard from us, you accepted it not as the word of men but as what it really is, the word of God." Being convinced of the apostles' tradition is a matter of the heart. Is your attitude that you are coming to church or it is, "Come, let us go up to the mountain of the LORD, to the house of the God of Jacob, that he may teach us his ways and that we may walk in his paths" (Isaiah 2:3). Is your attitude that you are coming to hear what the Pastor has to say or is it, "Speak, Lord, for your servant hears" (1 Samuel 3:10).

Are you convinced that it is God with whom you meet and that it is God who speaks to you in the preaching of the Word?

If so, then you have something to stand firm upon and to hold on to. And if you are convinced, if we as churches are convinced, then our attitudes need to change. Every time you come to public worship you should be expecting the Word to change your life. Come expecting baptism and the Lord's Supper to encourage and comfort your soul. Come expecting your prayers and those of your entire congregation to be answered. Are you convinced of the apostles' tradition? Then be changed. Are you convinced of the apostles' tradition? Then be an agent of change. Come to the assembly of God's people expecting God to provide you an opportunity to minister to another brother's or sister's needs. Say hello to someone. Ask how someone is doing. Find out how you can pray for someone. Get involved in someone's life. The gospel changes us and enables us to be instruments of change.

We Need to Experience the Apostles' Tradition

That leads to our final application, which I've already been hinting at. Third, *we need to experience the apostles' tradition*. Notice the connection between verse 15 and then verses 16–17. We are exhorted to stand firm and hold to the apostles' tradition. Then Paul prays our Lord Jesus Christ himself and God our Father (v. 16) to enable us to do this. And just as he loved us, just as he gave us eternal comfort, and just as he have us good hope through grace, so too he will comfort your hearts (v. 17). But notice what else he says. He will also establish [your hearts] in every good work and word (v. 17). John Calvin explained what this meant when he said, "We shall hear nothing but an empty sound if doctrine is not endued with power by the Spirit."[4] We need the Word that was once inspired by the Holy Spirit (2 Timothy 3:16) and we need the ongoing illuminating and convicting work of the Spirit to bring that Word home to our hearts and lives (Ephesians 1:16–19).

We learn here how standing upon the Word and holding on to the Word leads to action. It leads to service. It leads to sanctification. We need to experience the power of the apostles' tradition. It has to be at the center of our soul. It has to be so a part of us that we cannot hold it in. Jeremiah said the Word was so in his heart like a burning fire and so in his bones that he could not hold it in any longer (Jeremiah 20:9). Jesus said that we *are* the light of the world and therefore cannot put a lampshade over us (Matthew 5:13–16). It's as if the world was a dark room with no lights on. Our light should be so shining that if we opened our eyes in that room we would see each other surrounded in a glow of light.

Let me make two further applications of this as I draw to a close. I want to apply this to worship and then to the duties of parents.

First, if we know the apostolic tradition concerning worship and if we are convinced of it, then it needs to start trickling down into our experience. We say that worship at its essence is a meeting with the living God of the universe. We say that God speaks and we respond in a beautiful covenantal dialog. We say that worship is a foretaste of heaven. We say that God speaks in the preaching of the Word and that God comforts in the use of the sacraments. If this is what we stand upon and hold on to then we have to live it out. You need to show respect to God by showing up on time. If you can make it on time to work at 7am, or to school at 8am, or to an appointment at 9am, then you can make it on time to meet with God himself at 10am. You need to show respect to God by not getting up and using the restroom and by not talking in the narthex as if you were at a movie or some school event. Parents, take your kids to the restroom before you come to church and if you need to again, before the service begins.

Second, if we know the apostolic tradition and if we are convinced of it, then it needs to start trickling down into our experience of how we model the Christian faith to our children and how we train them as members of his covenant family. The greatest fear for those of us with children is that they will not believe in Jesus as we do. So we read the Word with them, we sing the Psalms and hymns with them, and we memorize the teachings of the Word as found in historic catechisms with them. But our children need more than Catechism and Bible reading. They need to see the power of the gospel in us. They need to see the power of the Word in us. Let me put it to you like this: what good is it if we say Jesus is the center of our lives but then we demonstrate in our experience that he's really only one thing among many in our lives? Tell me, how important is Jesus in the eyes of our children when we let them spend more time playing video games and playing on the computer than reading Scripture, memorizing catechism questions, and reading edifying books such as biographies of godly men and women of the past? What are you communicating to your children about the importance of Jesus, the Lord's Day, and the church when you come to church sporadically or rush out after the service to play sports or do other activities, to go to parties, and list goes on? Our kids need to see the radical discipleship that Jesus commanded: take up your cross and follow him (Matthew 16:24). Die to yourself and live for him. Die to the world and live for Christ. As the hymn says,

> Were the whole realm of nature mine,
> that were a present far too small.
> Love so amazing, so divine,
> demands my soul, my life, my all.[5]

Conclusion

Beloved, we must not only stand firm and hold on to the Word of God once in our lives or when it is convenient for us. We must stand in the midst of the raging sea of the world and we must hold on in the midst of the onslaught of Satan's temptations as we await the coming of our Lord. We must do so with our minds. We must do so with our hearts. We must do so with our actions.

31

Praying for the Ministry

2 Thessalonians 3:1–5

The story goes that five students had traveled to London to hear Charles Haddon Spurgeon preach. As they arrived early and were waiting for the doors to open a man came up and welcomed them. He asked if they would like him to show them around the Metropolitan Tabernacle before the service. They said yes. As he took them around he asked if they wanted to see the heating plant (what we call a boiler room) of the church? Of course they didn't but they didn't want to be rude so they said yes. The man took them and opened the door. They saw 700 people praying for the service that was about to begin. The man said to them, this is the heating room of this church. As he closed the door he introduced himself to the students—it was Charles Haddon Spurgeon.

What this account illustrates is that prayer is absolutely vital to the ministry of the gospel. It's the most important way we show ourselves thankful to God for his blessings to us in Christ. That's not only what our Heidelberg Catechism says (Q&A 116). That's also what Scripture says. Psalm 116 says it in this way:

I love the LORD, because he has heard
my voice and my pleas for mercy.
Because he inclined his ear to me,
therefore I will call on him as long as I live.
What shall I render to the LORD
for all his benefits to me?
I will lift up the cup of salvation
and call on the name of the LORD,
I will pay my vows to the LORD
in the presence of all his people. (Psalm 116:1–2, 12–14)

We saw the importance of prayer for the Christian back in our exposition of 1 Thessalonians 5, where Paul said this—and note the things he connects together here: "Rejoice always, pray without ceasing, give thanks in all circumstances" (1 Thessalonians 5:16–18). Our joyful and thankful lives are expressed in prayerful lives.

So how important is prayer to you? But more specifically, note well how the Word of God specifies for us in 2 Thessalonians 3 that we are to be devoted to *praying for the ministry*. How often do you pray for the ministry of the Word in your church? How devoted are you to praying for the success of the Word in your church's services? I want to explain this duty and blessing by answering a simple yet profound question. The question is this: why should we pray for the ministry of the Word if it is the ministry of the Lord himself?

Because God Commands Us to Pray

Why should we pray if the ministry of the Word is the ministry of the Lord himself? First, *because God commands us to pray*. Finally, brothers, *pray* for us (v. 1). Simple enough, isn't it? Let me press home this point for a moment. Beloved, it is a truism that Christians pray. It's such a self-evident truth that we shouldn't even need to be reminded of it. As John Owen said, without prayer "there can be no religion at all."[1]

Yet setting aside all the commands and examples of prayer in the Old Testament, all of Jesus' commands and his example of praying, and all the other commands and examples of all the other apostles, let me just focus on the apostle Paul. Besides all the examples in his letters of his prayers for the churches, he commands the churches on at least eleven other occasions to pray. This means it is a big theme in his letters and a big burden on his heart as a pastor. He commands us to pray in general:

> Rejoice in hope, be patient in tribulation, be constant in prayer. (Romans 12:12)

> Do not be anxious about anything, but in everything by prayer and supplication with thanksgiving let your requests be made known to God. (Philippians. 4:6)

> Continue steadfastly in prayer, being watchful in it with thanksgiving. (Colossians 4:2)

> Pray without ceasing. (1 Thessalonians 5:17)

> First of all, then, I urge that supplications, prayers, intercessions, and thanksgivings be made for all people. (1 Timothy 2:5)

> I desire then that in every place the men should pray, lifting holy hands without anger or quarreling. (1 Timothy 2:8)

Paul also commands us to pray for the ministry:

> I appeal to you, brothers, by our Lord Jesus Christ and by the love of the Spirit, *to strive together with me in your prayers to God on my behalf.* (Romans 15:30)

> ... praying at all times in the Spirit, with all prayer and supplication. To that end keep alert with all perseverance, making supplication for all the saints, and also for me, *that words may be given to me in opening my mouth boldly to proclaim the mystery of the gospel, for which I am an ambassador in chains, that I may declare it boldly, as I ought to speak.* (Ephesians 6:18–20)

> At the same time, pray also for us, *that God may open to us a door for the word, to declare the mystery of Christ*, on account of which I am in prison. (Colossians 4:3 cf. 2 Corinthians 1:11; 1 Thessalonians 5:25)

You and I are commanded by our sovereign Lord who has saved us from all our sins to fall down on our knees and to pray for the ministry of the Word. Let me apply what this means by rejecting four false opinions and attitudes that hinder us from prayer. First, God is so sovereign that we do not need to pray, right? No. May this never be our attitude. In his sovereignty he commands us to pray. Second, the ministry of the Word is effectual because it is the Word of God, therefore we do not need to pray for the success of preaching, right? Again, absolutely not. The Word and prayer go together. Third, since we believe public worship is the most important thing we do, our public prayers are enough, right? No. No. No. We must pray without ceasing, publicly *and* privately. Fourth, we're not those kind of evangelical Christians who have daily devotions and prayers and so we don't need to pray privately, right? Do I even need to respond to this? Finally, brothers, *pray* for us (v. 1).

Because God Connects the End with the Means

Why should we pray if the ministry of the Word is the ministry of the Lord himself? Second, *because God connects the end with the means.* What does Paul want in this exhortation to the church? What is his end? That the word of the Lord may speed ahead and be honored, as happened among you, and that we may be delivered from wicked and evil men (vv. 2–3). And how does Paul say this end will happen? By the means of the Thessalonians' prayers. God is sovereign and doesn't need our prayers. But he desires and delights in our prayers. He has bound his purposes to our prayers in his inscrutable wisdom. As John Calvin said, "Though the Lord gave him powerful support, and though he was unsurpassed in his passion for prayer, he still has regard for the prayers of believers."[2]

If this does not encourage you to pray, nothing will. Think about how a father has a plan to do something with his son. He loves his son so much that when he tells him the plan, he even asks his son to tell him what he likes about the plan. He even asks what his son wants to do. So too God our Father actually wants us to pray to him and he actually uses our prayers to bring about his plan in our lives. Do you hear what God is saying here? He actually uses our prayers to accomplish his purposes. Oh, this should cause our hearts to be inflamed, this should cause our knees to bend, this should cause our eyes to be raised, and this should cause words to come forth from our mouths. God is encouraging you here that he has attached a promise to your prayers, that when you pray for the ministry, the ministry is actually extended—it speed[s] ahead—and the ministry is successful—it is honored.

He connects the end with the means. So what end is Paul asking the Thessalonians and us to pray for?

First, pray for the extension of the ministry. Pray that the word of the Lord may speed ahead and prepare our neighbors' hearts, our friends' hearts, our loved ones' hearts, and the hearts of those we have never met. Pray that it would extend into more and more lives every Lord's Day and every day until our Lord comes again.

Second, pray for the success of the ministry. Pray that the Word of the Lord would be honored, as happened among you. Just as the Thessalonians received the word as the Word of the Lord (1 Thessalonians 2:13), just as you honored the Word when God converted you, so too pray for many, many others to hear, receive, and honor the Word.

Third, pray for the freedom of the ministry. Pray that we may be delivered from wicked and evil men. Pray that no government hindrances are erected. Pray that no persecution arises. Instead, as with praying for the Word to speed ahead of its actual preaching, pray that hearts are softened and opened to hear and receive its message.

There is also a fourth thing, mentioned in Paul's other letters that I read in our first point: pray for the words of the minister. Paul exhorted the Ephesians to pray "that words may be given to me in opening my mouth boldly to proclaim the mystery of the gospel … that I may declare it boldly, as I ought to speak" (Ephesians 6:18–20). Pray that God would give your pastor a message to declare to you with boldness. To the Colossians he said, "pray also for us, that God may open to us a door for the word, to declare the mystery of Christ" (Colossians 4:3). And isn't it fascinating that Paul called upon the Romans to "strive together with me in your prayers to God on my behalf?" (Romans 15:30) This is a part of your spiritual warfare. The world, our own flesh, and the Devil himself hate the ministry of the Word and want to frustrate it by every possible means. But you strive for its success.

Because God Causes Us to Grow through Prayer

Why should we pray if the ministry of the Word is the ministry of the Lord himself? Third, *because God causes us to grow through prayer*. It was John Calvin who wrote that God commands us to pray not for his good, but for our own good.[3] You can see this in the connection Paul makes between the church's prayer for him and his ministry and their spiritual growth. They prayed for Paul to be delivered from the faithless that they too would know and experience that the Lord is faithful to them against the evil one (v. 3). They prayed for Paul's ministry that they would find themselves growing by doing … the things we command (v. 4). This growth in godliness in sanctification that culminates in our glorification is "the glory of the Gospel."[4] They prayed for the lost that they too would experience the love of God, which is God's love for us, and the steadfastness of Christ, which is Christ's steadfastness (v. 5).[5]

So how does God use our prayers to cause us to grow? First, he elicits from our renewed hearts prayer to him, which he then uses to align our imperfect will with his perfect will. Paul willed for the Thessalonians to pray to the Lord, and their prayer was their aligning their wills to God's. Second, prayer evidences our dependence upon the Lord. He is God, we are not. Everything good comes from him, not us (James 1:17). As we pray, then, we pour out our hearts before the Lord in utter dependence (Psalm 62:8). We pray to him because we've come to the end of ourselves. And as we pour out our hearts to God our Father through Christ in dependence on the Spirit, we reciprocally experience the pouring out of the love of God towards us (v. 5). Prayer is a means of our thankfulness to God and his graciousness to us (HC, Q&A 116).

Conclusion

Let me conclude by returning to my opening questions to you. How important is praying for the ministry to you? How often do you pray for the ministry of the Word in your church? How devoted are you to praying for the success of the Word in your church's services? I plead with you to make prayer for the ministry a priority in your personal prayers. If you want to see your church be both a place where sinners are saved and the saved are sanctified, then you need to pray. If you do not pray for the ministry of the Word, your church will be like a cold room. But when you pray your church will be warmed by the presence of God. And I pray that we can say of wherever we pray for the ministry, "This is the heating room of this church."

32

A Pauline Work Ethic

2 Thessalonians 3:6–18

We've come to the end of Paul's two letters to the ancient Thessalonian Christians. As we come to the end, let me go back to the beginning. This had been a recent church plant of Paul, Silas, and Timothy in the church of Antioch's second missionary journey (Acts 17:1–15). According to Paul's custom, he went to the local synagogue and "on three Sabbath days he reasoned with them from the Scriptures, explaining and proving that it was necessary for the Christ to suffer and to rise from the dead, and saying, 'This Jesus, whom I proclaim to you, is the Christ'" (Acts 17:2–3). The new church plant was made up of "some" of those from the synagogue, some "devout Greeks," and many "leading women" from Thessalonica (Acts 17:4). This caused those Jews who rejected Jesus as the Messiah to form a mob and storm the house of Jameson (Acts 17:5). When Paul and Silas were not found, they hauled Jameson and some believers before the magistrate and uttered some of the most famous words that described the early church: "These men who have turned the world upside down have come here also" (Acts 17:6). Their charge got the authorities' ears perked up: "They are all acting against the decrees of Caesar, saying there is another king, Jesus" (Acts 17:7). The church, then, sent Paul and Silas "away by night to Berea" (Acts 17:10). The Jews followed them there, causing Paul to flee to Athens while Silas and Timothy stayed behind (Acts 17:14–15). Because this church was born into persecution, Paul's great pastoral desire was that they would persevere in their faith, hope, and love. He didn't want them to grow weary in doing good, but wanted them to rekindle their zeal even as we need to.

As we come to the end of 2 Thessalonians, then, recognize that Paul has been dealing with two major issues. First, there were those enemies outside the church who were brining the pressure of persecution on the church, which Paul mentioned in chapter 1. Second, there were those enemies inside the church, of the church, who were trying to persuade the rest of the congregation through false doctrine concerning Jesus' Second Coming, which Paul mentioned in chapter 2. But there was another pastoral problem. Aren't there always in the church on this side of glory? Here in chapter 3 we see that there was a third group troubling the Thessalonian Christians. As you ought to know by now from experience, so too in Thessalonica there were members inside the church who were not practicing the Christian life. One lesson we need to learn from this is how important it is for us as church leaders to realize that it's not enough for us to have orthodoxy in our doctrine; we must also apply that doctrine so that there is orthopraxy in our life together as congregations so that all the glory goes to our great God.

We see that idea of applying doctrine to life here at the end of

2 Thessalonians 3 in the area of work. Some believers were not living Christianly. How so? They were not living a godly life in terms of their work ethic.

We Are Called to a Life of Imitation

First, *we are called to a life of imitation*. After his command to keep away from the idle (v. 6), Paul explains that he and his companions worked hard in the short time they were among the Thessalonians (vv. 7–10). We were not idle when we were with you (v. 7), they did not eat anyone's bread without paying for it, but with toil and labor we worked night and day, that we night not be a burden to any of you (v. 8) Why did they work so hard? They did so that they would be an example to imitate (v. 9 cf. v. 7).

Imitating the apostle Paul is a recurring theme in Paul's epistles. For example, he wrote to the Corinthians, "I urge you, then, be imitators of me" (1 Corinthians 4:16). He wrote to the Philippians, "Brothers, join in imitating me, and keep your eyes on those who walk according to the example you have in us" (Philippians 3:17). This is so important and practical for many of us who do not have a godly heritage in the church, who do not have living examples of fathers who have lived a consistent, godly life. The apostles, then, are examples to us of what it means to live the Christian life. This is also true of us as pastors to our people. Listen to how contemporary this ancient quotation sounds: "It is the sign of a perfect teacher when he backs up his teaching with deeds … .Even if they know that what they are being taught is obviously true, if they see that it is ignored by their teacher, it will make little impression on his hearers, because his actions speak louder than words."[6]

What is interesting to think about is why this was such an issue in Thessalonica. Apparently as we piece together what Paul says in his two letters to them, some of the Thessalonians thought one of two things:

either because the false teachers had so persuaded them that Christ had already returned or because Paul's correction of this error was so persuasive therefore some thought that because Christ was returning very soon they didn't have to worry about earthly affairs. How many of us have experienced something like this? Jesus is coming back so why waste your time in college? Jesus is coming back so why have a retirement account? Sound familiar to some of you? Sadly, I've met Christians who think this way. Thankfully some of them have been delivered for this foolishness. While Paul has taught us that Christ is coming again, what does he say we should do in the meantime? Now such persons we command and encourage in the Lord Jesus Christ to do their work quietly and to earn their own living (v. 12). This reminds of the saying supposedy uttered by Martin Luther, who when asked what should a Christian do if he or she knew Jesus was returning tomorrow, said, "Plant an apple tree."

Paul then addresses the brothers in the congregation to continue working: do not grow weary in doing good (v. 13). The good he's speaking of is work. In whatever calling and vocation God has given you, God commands you to work hard. One application of this is the fact that work is a part of the goodness of God's created order (Genesis 1:28; 2:15) despite its frustrations brought about by Adam's sin (Genesis 3:17–19). God loves work. He calls us to imitate him. We are not merely spiritual beings. In fact, as C. S. Lewis (1898–1963) said, the God who made us "uses material things like bread and wine to put the new life into us. We may think this rather crude and unspiritual. God does not: He invented eating. He likes matter. He invented it."[7] Another application of this is that when we find ourselves in a difficult economic situation it is so vital for us to be working hard at what we do, and even finding other things to do so that we imitate Paul by not being a burden to anyone (v. 8).

We are called to a life of imitation of the apostles. But more than that, we are called to a life of imitation of God himself. Recall what Paul said to the Corinthians: "Be imitators of me, as I am of Christ" (1 Corinthians 11:1). Therefore, to imitate Paul was to imitate Christ, which was to imitate God himself. Back in 1 Thessalonians, Paul told them that as Christ and the apostles suffered, so did they: "And you became imitators of us and of the Lord" (1 Thessalonians 1:6).

Working hard, then, in imitation of God, takes us back to Genesis 1 and the creation story. As children of God who reflect the image of God, we can read the story of God our Father working to make the world and then resting as an example for us to imitate. Where does the Bible say God's work and rest was an example for us to imitate? God himself says this in the fourth commandment, in Exodus 20: "Six days you shall labor, and do all your work, but the seventh day is a Sabbath to the LORD your God" (Exodus 20:9). Why should we work for six days and rest on the seventh day? "For in six days the LORD made heaven and earth, the sea, and all that is in them, and rested on the seventh day" (Exodus 20:11).

As those who are being renewed into the image of God by the work of our Lord Jesus Christ and the power of the Holy Spirit, let us strive to be like our Father in heaven. We are called to a life of imitation.

We Are Called to a Life of Distinction

Second, *we are called to a life of distinction.* Imitating God is not to imitate the world. Christians and the church of our Lord are to be distinct from the world. We are to be in the world but not of the world. And we see this in our attitude and actions of work.

For instance, Paul actually says that we are to be an example to the world in our work ethic. Notice how Paul says in our text that the Thessalonian believers were called to work quietly and earn their own living, literally, their own bread (v. 12). The question is why? Go back with me to 1 Thessalonians 4:1. Here Paul wrote to them about how "to walk and to please God" (2 Thessalonians 4:1). One of the ways they did this was in their work. Look at 1 Thessalonians 4:11–12. He called upon them "to aspire to live quietly, and to mind your own affairs, and to work with your hands" (1 Thessalonians 4:11). And here is the reason why: "so that you may walk properly before outsiders and be dependent on no one" (1 Thessalonians 4:12). Working hard as Christians in any area of life among non-Christians provides them a witness. This is true whether you are a single mother or a powerful politician. This is true whether you are a government employee or self-employed. This is true whether you are a student or a stockbroker. This provides them a witness of how the transforming power of God's grace in Jesus Christ restores us to our original purpose in the Garden. This can be so powerful in our age. Will you live this example? Will you live this distinct life?

And because we are to be distinct from the world, Paul issues two commands for those in the church who do work hard concerning the idle.

First, he says to keep away from the idle (v. 6) and have nothing to do with him (v. 14). Now, he's not saying absolutely shun the wayward who is not living in accord with the tradition that you received from us (v. 6). I say that because he calls them brother[s] (v. 6), he says they are among you (v. 11), he commands and encourages them in the Lord Jesus Christ (v. 12), and the strong in the congregation are to warn him as a brother (v. 15)—and how can you warn someone you don't talk to? We are to keep away and have nothing to do with them in the sense that we do not imitate their lifestyle; we are not walk according to the pattern of their lifestyle. Again, we are to be distinct.

Second, we are to warn (v. 15). And I want you to notice a key point here: whom is Paul addressing when he says to warn these idle brothers? He addresses this to the entire congregation. This means that church discipline, accountability, and checks and balances upon the congregation begins with each individual member of the church. Each of you are to imitate the apostles' lifestyle of hard work and each of you are to live a distinct life from the world; therefore, each of you are to be looking out for those who are not. Why? To bring God glory, to cause the congregation to grow in spiritual health, and so that unbelievers would see us striving for godliness even when we are inconsistent and even when we fail to do what we say we believe.

Conclusion

Paul concludes this epistle in his customary way (2 Thessalonians 3:16–17), but as we conclude, notice how relevant his praying for peace was to this congregation. They had been attacked from those persecuting them from the outside, by those persuading them with false doctrine on the inside, and now by those on the inside who were not practicing the Christian life. What turmoil! What chaos! What a mess! Yes, and that's life in the church until Jesus comes again. Until then, what can heal our divisions, our wounds, and our internal problems is the Lord of peace himself whom Paul says will give you peace at all times in every way (v. 16), who will be with you all (v. 16), and who will grant us his grace (v. 18). May this Lord—our Lord—reign in peace in our midst now and until he comes.

Bibliography

Alleine, Joseph. *An Alarm to the Unconverted.*

Ambrosiaster, *Commentaries on Galatians–Philemon*. Trans. and ed. Gerald R. Bray. Ancient Christian Texts. Downers Grove, Ill.: InterVarsity Press, 2009.

Ames, Williams. *The Marrow of Theology.*

Aquinas, Thomas. *Commentary on Saint Paul's First Letter to the Thessalonians and the Letter to the Philippians*. Trans. F. R. Larcher and Michael Duffy. Aquinas Scripture Series 3. Albany, N.Y.: Magi Books, 1969.

Augustine, *The City of God.*

Beeke, Joel R. *Puritan Reformed Journal* 2:2 ().

———, "The Utter Necessity of a Godly Life," in *Reforming Pastoral Ministry: Challenges for Ministry in Postmodern Times*, ed. John H. Armstrong (Wheaton, Ill.: Crossway Books, 2001).

Biesterveld, P. and H. H. Kuyper, *Ecclesiastical Manual.* Trans. Richard R. De Ridder. Richard R. De Ridder, 1982.

Book of Common Prayer

Book of Psalms for Worship.

Bounds, E. M. *Power Through Prayer*

Boys, John. *An exposition of the festiuall epistles and gospels vsed in our English liturgie together with a reason why the church did chuse the same; the first part from the feast of S. Andreuu the Apostle, to the purification of Blessed Mary the Virgin.* London: Edward Griffin for William Aspley, 1615.

Bunyan, John. "The Pilgrim's Progress," in *The Works of John Bunyan*, ed. George Offor, 3 vols. 1854, reprinted; Edinburgh, Scotland: Banner of Truth, 2009.

Brooks, Phillips. *Lectures on Preaching* (New York, NY: E.P. Dutton and Company, 1878).

Bruce, F. F. *1 & 2 Thessalonians.*

Calvin, John. *Institutes of the Christian Religion*, ed. John T. McNeill, trans. Ford Lewis Battles. The Library of Christian Classics, Vols. 20–21. Philadelphia: The Westminster Press, 1960.

———, "Summary of Doctrine Concerning the Ministry of the Word and the Sacraments," in *Calvin: Theological Treatises,* ed. J. K. S. Reid. Philadelphia: The Westminster Press, 1954.

———, *The Epistles of Paul the Apostle to the Romans and to the Thessalonians*, trans. Ross Mackenzie, eds. David W. Torrance and Thomas F. Torrance, Calvin's New Testament Commentaries, 12 vols. Grand Rapids, Mich.: Eerdmans, 1961.

———, *The Epistles of Paul the Apostle to the Galatians, Ephesians, Philippians and Colossians*, trans. T.H.L. Parker, eds. David W. Torrance and Thomas F. Torrance, Calvin's New Testament Commentaries, 12 vols. 1965; reprinted, Grand Rapids: Wm. B. Eerdmans Publishing Company, 1972.

———, *Sermons on the Epistle to the Ephesians*, trans. Arthur Golding (1577; revised and reprinted, Edinburgh: The Banner of Truth, 1987).

Chrysostom, John. "Homilies on Thessalonians" in *Nicene and Post-Nicene Fathers: First Series*. Ed. Philip Schaff, trans. John A. Broadus. 1889; reprinted, Peabody, Mass.: Hendrickson Publishers, 2004, volume 13.

Denny, James. *An Exposition of the Bible: Volume 6, Ephesians–Revelation*. Hartford, Conn.: The S. S. Scranton Co., 1903.

Donfried, Karl P. *Paul, Thessalonica, and Early Christianity*. Grand Rapids: Eerdmans, 2002.

Fergusson, James and David Dickson, *Galatians, Ephesians, Philippians, Colossians, Thessalonians & Hebrews*, Geneva Series Commentary. 1841, reprinted; Edinburgh, Scotland: Banner of Truth, 1978.

Goodwin, Thomas. *Works* 1:57–58.

———, *Works* 7:463–464.

Gurnall, William. *The Christian in Complete Armour.* 2 vols. 1864, reprinted, Edinburgh: Banner of Truth, 2004.

Klauck, Hans-Josef. *Ancient Letters and the New Testament: A Guide to Context and Exegesis*, trans. and ed. Daniel P. Bailey. Waco, Texas: Baylor University Press, 2006.

"Letter to the Alexandrians," in C. K. Barrett, *The New Testament Background: Selected Documents.* 1956; rev. ed., NY: Harper & Row, 1987.

Luther, Martin. *Freedom of a Christian.*

Manton, Thomas. "Sermons on 2 Thessalonians," in *Works* 3.

Martyr, Justin. *First Apology.*

Morris, Leon. *The First and Second Epistles to the Thessalonians*, The New International Commentary on the New Testament (1959; reprinted, Grand Rapids, MI: Wm. B. Eerdmans Publishing Co., 1984)

Newton, John. *Letters.*

Owen, John. "An Answer to a Late treatise of Mr. Cawdry About the Nature of Schism," in *The Works of John Owen.* Ed. William H. Goold, 16 vols. 1850–1853, reprinted; Edinburgh, Scotland: Banner of Truth, 1991.

———, "Meditations and Discourses on the Glory of Christ," in *The Works of John Owen.*

———, "The Glory of Christ," in *The Works of John Owen.*

———, "The Grace and Duty of Being Spiritually Minded," in *The Works of John Owen.*

———, "CHRISTOLOGIA: Or, a Declaration of the Glorious Mystery of the Person of Christ–God and Man," in *The Works of John Owen.*

Perkins, William. *The Arte of Prophesying: Or A Treatise Concerning the sacred and onely true manner and methode of Preaching*. London: Felix Kyngston, 1607.

———, *The Art of Prophesying*. 1606; reprinted, rev., Edinburgh, Scotland: Banner of Truth, 1996.

Spurgeon, Charles Haddon. *An All-Round Ministry* ().

———, *Only a Prayer–Meeting!* (Pasadena, Texas: Pilgrim Publications, 1973).

Steele, Richard. *A Remedy for Wandering Thoughts in Worship*. Harrisonburg, Virginia: Sprinkle Publications, 1988.

Stott, John R. W. *The Message of 1 & 2 Thessalonians*, The Bible Speaks Today. Downers Grove: Inter-Varsity Press, 1991.

Tertullian, *On the Resurrection of the Flesh.*

Packer, J. I. *A Quest for Godliness.*

Poole, Matthew. *A Commentary on the Holy Bible*, 3 vols. Peabody, Mass.: Hendrickson Publishers, 2008.

Psalter Hymnal. Grand Rapids: Board of Publications of the Christian Reformed Church, 1976.

Ryle, J. C. *A Call to Prayer.*

———, *Shall We Know One Another, and Other Papers.* London and New York: Cassell, Petter, and Galpin, 1871.

Ussher, James. *A Body of Divinity* (1648; reprinted, Birmingham, AL: Solid Ground Christian Books, 2007).

Vakalopoulos, Apostolos E. *A History of Thessaloniki*, trans. T. F. Carney. Thessalonike: Institute for Balkan Studies, 1963.

Watson, Thomas. *A Body of Divinity.* Edinburgh, Scotland: Banner of Truth.

———, *A Divine Cordial.* Jay P. Green, Sr., 2001.

———, *The Lord's Prayer.* 1692, reprinted, Edinburgh: Banner of Truth, 1999.

Wilkinson, Henry. "The Pope of Rome is Antichrist." *Puritan Sermons* 6:2.

Wingren, Gustav. *Luther on Vocation*. Trans. Carl C. Rasmussen. Evansville, IN: Ballast Press, reprinted 1994.

Notes

Preface

1. Stott, *1 & 2 Thessalonians*, 9.

2. Calvin, *Thessalonians*, 8:332.

Chapter 1

1. For overall introduction see Bruce, *1 & 2 Thessalonians*, xix–xlvii; D. A. Carson, Douglas J. Moo, and Leon Morris, *An Introduction to the New Testament* (Grand Rapids, MI: Zondervan Publishing House, 1992), 343–358; Morris, *1–2 Thessalonians*, 15–41.

2. On ancient Thessalonica, see Apostolos E. Vakalopoulos, *A History of Thessaloniki*, trans. T. F. Carney (Thessalonike: Institute for Balkan Studies, 1963); Karl P. Donfried, *Paul, Thessalonica, and Early Christianity* (Grand Rapids: Eerdmans, 2002). On ancient letter writing, see Hans-Josef Klauck, *Ancient Letters and the New Testament: A Guide to Context and Exegesis*, trans. and ed. Daniel P. Bailey (Waco, Texas: Baylor University Press, 2006).

3. On this term see, *Walter Bauer, A Greek-English Lexicon of the New Testament and Other Early Christian Literature*, trans. and rev. William F. Arndt, F. Wilbur Gingrich, and Frederick W. Danker (Chicago: University of Chicago Press, 1979), 686; *Dictionary of New Testament Background*, eds. Craig A. Evans & Stanley F. Porter (Downers Grove, IL: InterVarsity Press, 2000), 1233; F. F. Bruce, *New Testament History* (1969; Garden City, NY: Doubleday and Company, Inc., 1980), 308.

4. "Letter to the Alexandrians," in C. K. Barrett, *The New Testament Background: Selected Documents* (1956; revised edition, NY: Harper & Row, 1987), 49.

5. Cited in J. I. Packer, *Rediscovering Holiness* (Ann Arbor: Servant Publications, 1999), 33.

6. On this text, see Robert Traill, "By What Means May Ministers Best Win Souls?" *The Works of Robert Traill*, 4 volumes (1810; Choteau, MT: Old Paths Gospel Press, n.d.), 235–251.

7. John Bunyan, "The Pilgrim's Progress," in *The Works of John Bunyan*, ed. George Offor, 3 vols. (1854, reprinted; Edinburgh, Scotland: Banner of Truth, 2009), 3:243.

8. Calvin, *Thessalonians*, 8:333.

9. Ambrosiaster, *Commentaries on Galatians–Philemon*, trans. and ed. Gerald R. Bray, Ancient Christian Texts (Downers Grove, Ill.: InterVarsity Press, 2009), 101 col. 2.

10. Stott, *1–2 Thessalonians*, 27–28.

11. Aquinas, *Thessalonians*, 5.

12. Calvin, *Thessalonians*, 8:333; Matthew Poole, *A Commentary on the Holy Bible*, 3 vols. (Peabody, Mass.: Hendrickson Publishers, 2008), 3:731. This is in contrast to Chrysostom's interpretation that Paul spoke this way "because the men [of Thessalonica] were newly instructed." "Homilies on Thessalonians" in *Nicene and Post-Nicene Fathers: First Series*, ed. Philip Schaff, trans. John A. Broadus (1889; reprinted, Peabody, Mass.: Hendrickson Publishers, 2004) 13:323 col. 2.

13. Hence, Stott's assertion that the omission of "apostle" was because his behavior was being challenged, not his apostleship. *1–2 Thessalonians*, 25–26.

14. John Owen, "An Answer to a Late treatise of Mr. Cawdry About the Nature of Schism," in *The Works of John Owen*, ed. William H. Goold, 16 vols. (1850–1853, reprinted; Edinburgh, Scotland: Banner of Truth, 1991), 13:302.

15. Fergusson, *Thessalonians*, 382 col. 1.

16. On the issue of "multi-campus" pastors in the seventeenth-century, see John Owen, "A Brief Instruction in the Worship of God and Discipline of the Churches of the New Testament," in *Works*, 15:496–499.

17. Fergusson, *Thessalonians*, 382 col. 2.

18. John Owen, "The Grace and Duty of Being Spiritually Minded," in *Works*, 7:390.

Chapter 2

1. See William Perkins, *The Arte of Prophesying: Or A Treatise Concerning the sacred*

and onely true manner and methode of Preaching (London: Felix Kyngston, 1607); *The Art of Prophesying* (1606; reprinted, rev., Edinburgh, Scotland: Banner of Truth, 1996).

2. Cited in P. Biesterveld and H. H. Kuyper, *Ecclesiastical Manual*, trans. Richard R. De Ridder (Richard R. De Ridder, 1982), 164. For a modern use of this article, see *Church Order of the United Reformed Churches in North America*: "The duties belonging to the office of minister of the Word consist of continuing in prayer and in the ministry of the Word" (article 2). https://www.urcna.org/1651/file_retrieve/23868 (Accessed September 2, 2015).

3. "A General Thanksgiving," in the 1662 *Book of Common Prayer*. http://www.eskimo.com/~lhowell/bcp1662/daily/thanksgivings.html (Accessed September 2, 2015).

4. Calvin, *Thessalonians*, 8:335.

5. Calvin, *Thessalonians*, 8:334.

6. See Morris, *1–2 Thessalonians*, 51.

7. John Stott describes faith, hope, and love as focused outward (towards God, neighbor, and the future) as well as focused to all three tenses of our existence: faith rests on the past, love is exhibited in the present, and hope is oriented to the future. Stott, *1 & 2 Thessalonians*, 29–30.

8. Chrysostom, *Thessalonians*, 13:324 col 2.

9. Fergusson, *Thessalonians*, 384 col. 1.

10. E. M. Bounds, *Power Through Prayer* (Chicago: Moody Press, 1981), 9.

Chapter 3

1. Calvin, "Summary of Doctrine Concerning the Ministry of the Word and the Sacraments," in *Calvin: Theological Treatises*, ed. J. K. S. Reid (Philadelphia: The Westminster Press, 1954), 173.

2. On the full redemptive-historical import of Paul's related phrase, "my gospel," see Herman Ridderbos, *Paul and Jesus*, trans. David H. Freeman (Grand Rapids, MI: Baker Book House, 1958), 63–70.

3. Stott, *1–2 Thessalonians*, 33.

4. Leo F. Stelten, *Dictionary of Ecclesiastical Latin* (Peabody, MA: Hendrickson Publishers, sixth printing 2004), 245.

5. Morris, *1–2 Thessalonians*, 57.

6. Calvin, *Thessalonians*, 8:336.

7. Morris, *1–2 Thessalonians*, 57–58.

8. C. H. Spurgeon, *Only a Prayer–Meeting!* (Pasadena, Texas: Pilgrim Publications, 1973), 112.

9. C.H. Spurgeon, *Lectures to My Students* (Grand Rapids: Ministry Resources Library/Zondervan Publishing House, 1954), 26–27; D. Martyn Lloyd–Jones, *Preaching and Preachers* (Grand Rapids: Zondervan Publishing House, 1972), 105–106.

10. Fergusson, *Thessalonians*, 386 col. 1.

11. Joel R. Beeke, "The Utter Necessity of a Godly Life," in *Reforming Pastoral Ministry: Challenges for Ministry in Postmodern Times*, ed. John H. Armstrong (Wheaton, Ill.: Crossway Books, 2001), 79.

12. Morris, *1–2 Thessalonians*, 58.

13. John Owen, "Eshcol: A Cluster of the Fruit of Canaan," in *Works*, 13:57.

14. John Owen, "Of the Mortification of Sin in Believers," in *Works*, 6:56.

15. Watson, *A Body of Divinity*, 154.

16. Bruce, *1 & 2 Thessalonians*, 14.

17. Beeke, "The Utter Necessity of a Godly Life," in *Reforming Pastoral Ministry*, 59.

18. Bruce, *1 & 2 Thessalonians*, 21.

Chapter 4

1. On the length of his stay, see Carson, Moo, and Morris, *Introduction*, 344, 347; Stott, *1–2 Thessalonians*, 18.

2. Aquinas, *Thessalonians*, 8–9.

3. Chrysostom, *Thessalonians*, 13:325 col. 2.

4. Calvin, *Thessalonians*, 8:337.

5. Thomas Manton, "A Treatise of the Life of Faith," in *The Works of Thomas Manton* (Reprinted, Birmingham, AL: Solid Ground Christian Books, 2008) 15:70.

6. Martin Luther, "The Second Sermon, March 10, 1522, Monday after Invocavit," in *Luther's Works: Sermons I*, ed. and trans. John W. Doberstein, 55 vols. (Philadelphia: Fortress Press, 1959), 51:77.

Chapter 5

1. Calvin, *Thessalonians*, 8:338.
2. Calvin, *Thessalonians*, 8:338.
3. Calvin, *Thessalonians*, 8:339.
4. On this divine title for Jesus, see Bruce, *1 & 2 Thessalonians*, 19–20.
5. Owen, "Mortification," in *Works*, 6:59.
6. Calvin, *Thessalonians*, 8:340.

Chapter 6

1. Stott, *1–2 Thessalonians*, 45.
2. Calvin, *Thessalonians*, 8:341–342.
3. Calvin, *Thessalonians*, 8:342.
4. On this word, see Bruce, *1 & 2 Thessalonians*, 24.
5. Ambrosiaster, *Galatians–Philemon*, 103 col 1.
6. Calvin, *Thessalonians*, 8:342.
7. Calvin, *Thessalonians*, 8:342.
8. Martin Luther, "Ninety-Five Theses," in *Martin Luther's Basic Theological Writings*, ed. Timothy F. Lull (Minneapolis, MN: Fortress Press, 1989), 27.

Chapter 7

1. C.H. Spurgeon, *An All-Round Ministry* (1900; reprinted, Edinburgh: The Banner of Truth Trust, 1986).
2. On whether this is a mother or nurse, see Bruce, *1 & 2 Thessalonians*, 31–32.
3. Calvin, *Thessalonians*, 8:344.
4. Aquinas, *Thessalonians*, 15.

5. Lloyd–Jones, *Preaching and Preachers*, 9.

6. Spurgeon, *An All-Round Ministry*, 64.

7. See Calvin's comments in *Thessalonians*, 8:345. On pastoral visiting, see Peter Y. De Jong, *Taking Heed to the Flock: A Study of the Principles and Practice of Family Visitation* (1948; reprinted, Eugene, OR: Wipf & Stock, 2003).

8. Calvin, *Thessalonians*, 8:345.

9. Calvin, *Thessalonians*, 8:345.

10. Fergusson, *Thessalonians*, 47.

11. Chrysostom, *Thessalonians*, 13:330 col. 2.

12. Calvin, *Thessalonians*, 8:344.

13. Phillips Brooks, *Lectures on Preaching* (New York, NY: E.P. Dutton and Company, 1878), 5.

14. Calvin, *Thessalonians*, 8:346

15. See an excellent summary of this in Stott, *1–2 Thessalonians*, 68–71.

Chapter 8

1. Justin Martyr, *First Apology*, ch. 67.

2. On the difference between the two grammatically, see Morris, *1–2 Thessalonians*, 87 n41.

3. Second Helvetic Confession, ch. 1.

4. John Calvin, *The Gospel According to St. John 1–10*, trans. David W. Torrance and Thomas F. Torrance, Calvin's Commentaries, 12 volumes (Grand Rapids, MI: Wm. B. Eerdmans Publishing Company, 1959), 4:18.

5. John Calvin, *Institutes, Institutes of the Christian Religion*, ed. John T. McNeill, trans. Ford Lewis Battles. The Library of Christian Classics, Vols. 20–21 (Philadelphia: The Westminster Press, 1960), 3.2.6.

6. Calvin, *Thessalonians*, 8:347.

7. E.g., J.I. Packer, *A Quest for Godliness: The Puritan Vision of the Christian Life* (Wheaton, IL: Crossway Books, 1990), 285.

8. On this, see Richard Steele, *A Remedy for Wandering Thoughts in Worship* (Harrisonburg, Virginia: Sprinkle Publications, 1988).

9. Calvin, *Thessalonians*, 8:346.

10. Joseph Alleine, *A Sure Guide to Heaven* (London, 1689), 20.

Chapter 9

1. On *satanas*, see Bruce, *1 & 2 Thessalonians*, 55.

2. See Calvin's comments in *Thessalonians*, 8:350–351.

3. For a fuller discussion of these difficult verses, see Stott, 55–58.

4. From the hymn, "A Mighty Fortress is Our God," by Martin Luther.

5. Calvin, *Thessalonians*, 8:390.

6. Calvin, *Thessalonians*, 8:354.

7. Calvin, *Thessalonians*, 8:356.

8. Cited in Aquinas, *Thessalonians*, 3.

Chapter 10

1. John Owen, "Pneumatologia or, A Discourse Concerning the Holy Spirit," in *Works*), 3:386.

2. Calvin, *Thessalonians*, 8:358–359.

3. Chrysostom, *Thessalonians*, 13:341 col. 2.

4. Calvin, *Thessalonians*, 8:356–357.

5. Stott, *1–2 Thessalonians*, 67.

6. Cf. Chrysostom, *Thessalonians*, 13:344 col. 1.

7. On this see Calvin, *Thessalonians*, 8:358.

8. Bruce says "to walk and to please" is a hendiadys, that is, one thought communicated through two words. To walk in a godly way is to please God. *1 & 2 Thessalonians*, 79.

9. On the term "sexual immorality" (*porneia*), see Bruce, *1 & 2 Thessalonians*, 82.

10. On the exegetical issues of whether *skeuos* is our body or a wife, see Bruce, *1 & 2 Thessalonians*, 83.

11. Chrysostom, *Thessalonians*, 13:344 col. 1.

12. Bruce, *1 & 2 Thessalonians*, 87.

13. On this see Chrysostom, *Thessalonians*, 13:344 col. 2.

14. Bruce, *1 & 2 Thessalonians*, 72.

15. Cited in Gustav Wingren, *Luther on Vocation*, tr. Carl C. Rasmussen (Evansville, IN: Ballast Press, reprinted 1994), 10.

16. Ambrosiaster, *Galatians–Philemon*, 108 col. 1.

Chapter 11

1. http://www.beliefnet.com/faiths/Christianity/2005/10/Rick-Warrens-Second-Reformation.aspx (Accessed September 2, 2015).

2. "Six Megathemes Emerge from Barna Group Research in 2010." As found at http://www.barna.org/culture-articles/462-six-megathemes-emerge-from-2010 (Accessed September 2, 2015).

3. http://www.leftbehind.com (Accessed September 2, 2015).

4. On this see Calvin, *Thessalonians*, 8:363.

5. Aquinas, *Thessalonians*, 35.

6. Calvin, *Thessalonians*, 8:363.

7. "Burial of the Dead," in *The Book of Common Prayer* (The Standing Liturgical Commission of the Reformed Episcopal Church, 2003), 530.

Chapter 12

1. Fergusson, *Thessalonians*, 430 col. 1.

2. J. C. Ryle, *Shall We Know One Another, and Other Papers* (London and New York: Cassell, Petter, and Galpin, 1871), 16–18.

3. Fergusson, *Thessalonians*, 430 col. 2.

4. Aquinas picked up on this theme in *Thessalonians*, 40.

5. Aquinas, *Thessalonians*, 40.

6. John Owen, "Meditations and Discourses on the Glory of Christ," in *Works*, 1:288, 290.

7. Owen, *Meditations*, in *Works*, 1:291.

Chapter 13

1. On this "cry of command" (*keleusmati*), see Bruce, *1 & 2 Thessalonians*, 100.

2. On the use of the trumpet in the Old Testament, see Ambrosiaster, *Galatians–Philemon*, 108 col. 2–109 col. 1; Aquinas, *Thessalonians*, 38.

3. On the use of *parousia*, see Bruce, *1 & 2 Thessalonians*, 56–57.

4. Ambrosiaster, *Galatians–Philemon*, 109 col. 1.

5. On the anti-"Chiliasm" of this pericope, see Calvin, *Thessalonians*, 8:366.

6. "Celebration of the Lord's Supper: Form Number 3," in *Psalter Hymnal* (Grand Rapids: Board of Publications of the Christian Reformed Church, 1976), 157 col. 2.

Chapter 14

1. William Ames, *The Marrow of Theology*, ed. and trans. John Dykstra Eusden (1968; reprinted, Grand Rapids: Baker Books, second printing 1997), 1.1.1.

2. Bruce, *1 & 2 Thessalonians*, 109.

3. Calvin, *Thessalonians*, 8:367.

4. Calvin, *Thessalonians*, 8:367.

Chapter 15

1. John Calvin, *The Epistles of Paul the Apostle to the Galatians, Ephesians, Philippians and Colossians*, trans. T.H.L. Parker, eds. David W. Torrance and Thomas F. Torrance, Calvin's New Testament Commentaries, 12 vols. (1965; reprinted, Grand Rapids: Wm. B. Eerdmans Publishing Company, 1972), 11:217.

2. John Calvin, *Sermons on the Epistle to the Ephesians*, trans. Arthur Golding (1577; revised and reprinted, Edinburgh: The Banner of Truth, 1987) 657.

3. Chrysostom, *Thessalonians*, 13:363 col. 1.

4. James Ussher, *A Body of Divinity* (1648; reprinted, Birmingham, AL: Solid Ground Christian Books, 2007), 301.

5. Bunyan, *The Pilgrim's Progress.*

Chapter 16

1. John Newton, *Letter 13*, in *The Works of the Revelation John Newton* (London: T. Nelson and Sons, 1853), 65.

2. R. Kent Hughes, *Set Apart: Calling a Worldly Church to a Godly Life* (Wheaton, IL: Crossway Books, 2003), 128–130.

3. Chrysostom, *Thessalonians*, 13:330 col. 1.

4. These three participles are governed by one definite article. On this, see Bruce, *1 & 2 Thessalonians*, 118.

5. John Boys, *An exposition of the festiuall epistles and gospels used in our English liturgie together with a reason why the church did chuse the same; the first part from the feast of S. Andreuu the Apostle, to the purification of Blessed Mary the Virgin* (London: Edward Griffin for William Aspley, 1615), n.p.

6. Calvin, *Thessalonians*, 8:372.

Chapter 17

1. Stott, *1 & 2 Thessalonians*, 117.

2. From the hymn, "Glorious Things of Thee Are Spoken," by John Newton.

3. Fergusson, *Thessalonians*, 171.

4. Stott, *1 & 2 Thessalonians*, 122.

5. Fergusson, *Thessalonians*, 171.

6. From the hymn, "The Church's One Foundation," by Samuel J. Stone.

Chapter 18

1. *The Book of Psalms for Worship* (Pittsburgh, PA: Crown & Covenant Publications, third printing 2009), 113A.

2. Fergusson, *Thessalonians*, 175.

3. "Collect for Peace," in the 1662 *Book of Common Prayer*. http://www.eskimo.com/~lhowell/bcp1662/daily/thanksgivings.html (Accessed September 2, 2015).

4. Thomas Watson, *A divine cordial, or, the transcendent priviledge of those that love God and are savingly called* (London: Tho. Parkhurst, 1663), 171.

5. William Gurnall, *The Christian in Complete Armour*, 2 volumes in 1 (1864 edition; reprinted, Edinburgh: The Banner of Truth, 2002), 1:297 col. 1.

6. Fergusson, *Thessalonians*, 176.

7. Cited in I.D.E. Thomas, *A Puritan Golden Treasury* (1975; reprinted, Edinburgh: The Banner of Truth, 1989), 159.

Chapter 19

1. Calvin, *Thessalonians*, 8:376.

2. Aquinas has a practical discussion of this text in *Thessalonians*, 51–52. Cf. Calvin, *Thessalonians*, 8:375.

3. Aquinas, *Thessalonians*, 51.

4. J.C. Ryle, *Home Truths: Being Miscellaneous Addresses and Tracts*, 2 volumes (London: Wertheim, Macintosh, and Hunt, 1859), 2:109.

5. Thomas Watson, *The Lord's Prayer* (1692; reprinted, Edinburgh: Banner of Truth, 1999), 10.

6. Gurnall, *The Christian in Complete Armour*,, 2:294 col. 1.

7. Joel R. Beeke, "The Age of the Spirit and Revival." *Puritan Reformed Journal* 2:2 (July 2010): 39.

8. Ambrosiaster, *Galatians–Philemon*, 111 col 1–2; Aquinas, *Thessalonians*, 52.

9. http://allianceradio.org/AP/2010/AP1210.pdf

10. Fergusson, *Thessalonians*, 180.

11. Fergusson, *Thessalonians*, 180.

Chapter 20

1. Calvin, *Thessalonians*, 8:379.

2. Hence, prior to Bellarmine the Council of Trent (1545–1563) stated in response to the Protestant doctrine of justification that "no one can know with a certainty of faith … that he has obtained the grace of God" (Sixth Session, January 13, 1547). Then it made the following pronouncement of anathema (eternal condemnation):

"If any one saith, that a man, who is born again and justified, is bound of faith to believe that he is assuredly in the number of the predestinate: let him be anathema." *The Creeds of Christendom*, ed. Philip Schaff, rev. David S. Schaff, 3 vols. (1931; reprinted, Grand Rapids, MI: Baker Books, 1993), 2:99 col. 2; 113 col. 2.

3. Owen, "The Nature of Apostasy," in *Works*, 7:188.

4. Chrysostom, *Thessalonians*, 13:372 col. 1.

Chapter 21

1. See the exposition of 1 Thessalonians 1:1 above (pages 17–28).

2. Calvin, *Thessalonians*, 8:387.

3. Owen, *Works* 3:370–371.

4. Owen, *Works* 3:371.

5. On this word, see Bruce, *1 & 2 Thessalonians*, 144–145.

Chapter 22

1. From the song, "What If God Was One of Us," by Joan Osborne.

2. Calvin, *Thessalonians*, 8:391.

3. Sadly, many Christians have fallen by this rhetoric from writers such as Rob Bell, *Love Wins: A Book About Heaven, Hell, and the Fate of Every Person Who Ever Lived* (New York, NY: HarperOne, 2011).

4. David Brooks, "Creed or Chaos." (http://www.nytimes.com/2011/04/22/opinion/22brooks.html?scp=4&sq=book%20mormom&st=cse. Accessed September 2, 2015).

5. Calvin, *Thessalonians*, 8:392.

6. From "Man of Sorrows! What a Name," by Philip P. Bliss.

7. Calvin, *Thessalonians*, 8:392.

8. Chrysostom, *Thessalonians*, 13:384 col. 1–col. 2.

Chapter 23

1. On verse 9, see Bruce, *1 & 2 Thessalonians*, 152.

2. Calvin, *Thessalonians*, 8:392.

3. Cf. Calvin, *Thessalonians*, 8:392.

4. Ambrosiaster, *Galatians–Philemon*, 114 col 1.

Chapter 24

1. Calvin, *Thessalonians*, 8:392.

2. Calvin, *Thessalonians*, 8:392.

3. Calvin, *Thessalonians*, 8:394.

Chapter 25

1. Chuck Smith, *End Times* (Costa Mesa, CA: The Word for Today, 1978), 35. For more documentation from several out-of-print booklets, see http://calvarychapel.pbworks.com/w/page/13146568/1981.

2. Thomas Manton, "Eighteen Sermons on the Second Epistle of the Thessalonians," *Works* 3:15.

3. Chrysostom, *Thessalonians*, 13:355 col. 1.

4. On the interpretive difficulty of the verb *enestēken*, see Bruce, *1 & 2 Thessalonians*, 165–166.

5. See Westminster Larger Catechism, Q&A 113, which says among the sins forbidden by the third commandment are "curious prying into, and misapplying of God's decrees and providences; misinterpreting, misapplying, or any way perverting the Word, or any part of it."

6. Manton, "Second Epistle of the Thessalonians," *Works*, 3:17.

7. Henry Wilkinson, "The Pope of Rome is Antichrist," in *Puritan Sermons 1659–1689*, 6 vols. (1675; reprinted, Wheaton, IL: Richard Owen Roberts, Publishers, 1981), 6:2.

8. Cf. Chrysostom, *Thessalonians*, 13:386 col. 1.

9. Calvin, *Thessalonians*, 8:397.

10. From a versification of Psalm 46, "God Is Our Refuge and Our Strength," in *Psalter Hymnal*, 84.

Chapter 26

1. This is the hermeneutical and theological system that understands the Bible to teach a sharp distinction between God's dealings with national Israel and the Church; and an emphasis on "literal" interpretation of Old Testaments prophecies, which leads to an overly-political understanding of their fulfilment. For more, see "Dispensational Theology," in *New Dictionary of Theology*, eds. Sinclair B. Ferguson, David F. Wright, and J.I. Packer (Downers Grove, IL: InterVarsity Press, 1988), 200–201.

2. Hal Lindsey calls him "the future fuehrer" repeatedly in *The Late Great Planet Earth* (Grand Rapids, MI: Zondervan, 1970).

3. "Meditation on Human Redemption," in *The Prayers and Meditations of Saint Anselm*, trans. Sister Benedicta Ward (1973; reprinted, New York, NY: Penguin Books, 1979), 237.

4. Calvin, *Thessalonians*, 8:399.

5. Gurnall, *The Christian in Complete Armour*, 1:55 col. 2.

6. Calvin, *Thessalonians*, 8:407.

Chapter 27

1. Cited in *W. E. Vine's New Testament Word Pictures: Romans to Revelation* (1996; reprinted, Nashville, TN: Thomas Nelson, 2015), 602.

2. Calvin, *Thessalonians*, 8:399. Calvin went on to describe his view that as Islam has conquered the Eastern church, the Roman Papacy would do the same in the Western church. *Ibid.*, 399–408.

3. From the song, "The Dragon," by Michael Card.

4. Calvin, *Thessalonians*, 8:406.

5. Calvin, *Thessalonians*, 8:400.

6. Calvin, *Thessalonians*, 8:401.

7. Tertullian, *On the Resurrection of the Flesh*, 24; Chrysostom, *Thessalonians*, 13:388 col 1–389 col. 1; Ambrosiaster, *Galatians–Philemon*, 114 col 2–116 col. 1; Manton, "Second Epistle of the Thessalonians," *Works*, 3:49–50. While Calvin said this interpretation was "too stupid to need lengthy refutation," he also went on to say of Chrysostom, that he "is speaking the truth as far as history is concerned." Calvin, *Thessalonians*, 8:398–399, 403.

8. *Saint Augustine: The City of God, Books XVII–XXII*, trans. Gerald G. Walsh, S.J. and Daniel J. Honan, The Fathers of the Church (New York, NY: Fathers of the Church, Inc., 1954), 24:298.

9. Calvin's view was that the "impediment" spoken of in verse 6 ("what is restraining;" *to katechon*) was neither the Holy Spirit or the Roman Empire, but the universal preaching of the Gospel, while verse 7 ("he who restrains;" *ho katechōn*) refers to the Antichrist. *Thessalonians*, 8:403–404.

10. For the view that this means the Jewish temple, albeit in a metaphorical sense, see Bruce *1 & 2 Thessalonians*, 168–169.

11. Calvin, *Thessalonians*, 8:402.

12. Martin Luther, "The Freedom of a Christian," trans. Timothy J. Wengert in *The Annotated Luther: Volume 1, The Roots of Reform* (Minneapolis, MN: Fortress Press, 2015), 528.

13. Chrysostom, *Thessalonians*, 13:386 col. 2.

14. Ambrosiaster, *Galatians–Philemon*, 116 col 1.

15. Calvin, *Thessalonians*, 8:402.

16. From the hymn, "Safely Through Another Week."

Chapter 28

1. Owen, "CHRISTOLOGIA: Or, a Declaration of the Glorious Mystery of the Person of Christ–God and Man," in *Works*, 1:268.

2. On this doctrine, Aquinas said, "… you did not merit this election; rather you are freely chosen by God. And I know this because God granted me abundant evidence of this in preaching, that is, that those to whom I preach are chosen by God, for God gives them the grace to listen profitably to the word preached to them." *Thessalonians*, 7.

3. From the hymn, "'Tis Not That I Did Choose Thee," by Josiah Conder.

4. Owen, "CHRISTOLOGIA," in *Works*, 1:166–167.

5. Owen, "CHRISTOLOGIA," in *Works*, 1:166–167.

6. From the anonymous hymn, "I Sought the Lord, and Afterward I Knew."

7. Among modern commentators there is disagreement concerning the correct reading of the Greek manuscripts. F. F. Bruce favors *aparchēn*: *1 & 2 Thessalonians*,

190. In favor of *ap' archēs,* see Leon Morris, *1–2 Thessalonians*, 237–238, n48; William Hendrickson, *I and II Thessalonians* (Grand Rapids, MI: Baker Books, 1955), 187–188.

8. E.g., firstfruits *of the Spirit* (Romans 8:23), firstfruits *of Asia* (Romans 16:5), firstfruits *of those who have fallen asleep* (1 Corinthians 15:20), firstfruits *of Achaia* (1 Corinthians 16:15), and firstfruits *of his creatures* (James 1:18).

9. James Denny, in *An Exposition of the Bible: Volume 6, Ephesians–Revelation* (Hartford, Conn.: The S. S. Scranton Co., 1903), 372 col. 2.

10. Calvin, *Thessalonians*, 8:409.

11. Fergusson, *Thessalonians*, 484, col. 2.

12. Calvin, *Thessalonians*, 8:409; Fergusson, *Thessalonians*, 485, col. 1.

13. Calvin, *Thessalonians*, 8:409; cf. *ibid.*, 8:410.

Chapter 29

1. Owen, "The Glory of Christ," in *Works*, 1:316.

2. Thomas Goodwin, "An Exposition of the First Chapter of the Epistle to the Ephesians," in *The Works of Thomas Goodwin*, 12 vols. (1861–1866; reprinted, Eureka, CA: Tanski Publications, 1996), 1:57–58.

3. Goodwin, "Exposition of Various Portions of the Epistle to the Ephesians," in *Works* 2:411.

4. "Turn Your Eyes Upon Jesus," by Helen Howarth Lemmel.

5. Owen, "The Glory of Christ," in *Works*, 1:286.

6. Owen, "CHRISTOLOGIA," in *Works* 1:66.

7. Goodwin, "Of the Blessed State of Glory which the Saints Posses After Death," in *Works* 7:463–464.

8. Owen, "The Glory of Christ," in *Works*, 1:330.

Chapter 30

1. From the hymn, "How Firm a Foundation," by John Rippon.

2. See Chrysostom, *Thessalonians*, 13:390 col. 1–2.

3. F. F. Bruce says there are three components of the apostolic tradition: 1) a summary of the gospel story, 2) a rehearsal of the deeds and words of Christ, and 3) ethical guidelines for Christian living. Bruce, *1 & 2 Thessalonians*, 78–79.

4. Calvin, *Thessalonians*, 8:412.

5. From the hymn, "When I Survey the Wondrous Cross," by Isaac Watts.

Chapter 31

1. Owen, "A Discourse of the Work of the Holy Spirit in Prayer," in *Works* 4:237.

2. Calvin, *Thessalonians*, 8:413.

3. Calvin, *Institutes* 3.20.3.

4. Calvin, *Thessalonians*, 8:413.

5. Bruce, *1 & 2 Thessalonians*, 202.

6. Ambrosiaster, *Galatians–Philemon*, 118 col 1–2; cf. Calvin, *Thessalonians*, 8:417.

7. C.S. Lewis, *Mere Christianity* (1952; reprinted, San Francisco, CA: Harper Collins, 2001), 63–64.